OP 10

H

D1274437

PSYCHOLOGY IN LEGAL CONTEXTS

OXFORD SOCIO-LEGAL STUDIES

General Editors: J. MAXWELL ATKINSON, DONALD R. HARRIS, R. M. HARTWELL

Oxford Socio-Legal Studies is a series of books and conference proceedings published by the Centre for Socio-Legal Studies, Wolfson College, Oxford (a research unit of the Social Science Research Council). The series is concerned generally with the relationship between law and society, and is designed to reflect the increasing interest in this field among lawyers, social scientists and historians.

Published previously
J. Maxwell Atkinson and Paul Drew: ORDER IN COURT: THE ORGANIZATION OF VERBAL INTERACTION IN JUDICIAL SETTINGS
David P. Farrington, Keith Hawkins and Sally M. Lloyd-Bostock (*editors*): PSYCHOLOGY, LAW AND LEGAL PROCESSES
Ross Cranston: REGULATING BUSINESS: LAW AND CONSUMER AGENCIES
Mavis Maclean and Hazel Genn: METHODOLOGICAL ISSUES IN SOCIAL SURVEYS

Forthcoming titles
Donald R. Harris, Mavis Maclean and Hazel Genn: COMPENSATION AND SUPPORT FOR ILLNESS AND INJURY
Doreen J. McBarnet: CONVICTION: THE LAW, THE STATE AND THE CONSTRUCTION OF JUSTICE
Alan Paterson: THE LAW LORDS

PSYCHOLOGY IN LEGAL CONTEXTS

Applications and Limitations

Edited by

Sally M. A. Lloyd-Bostock

First published 1981 by
THE MACMILLAN PRESS LTD
London and Basingstoke
Companies and representatives
throughout the world

Printed in Hong Kong

British Library Cataloguing in Publication Data

Psychology in legal contexts – (Oxford
    socio-legal studies)
    I. Law – Psychology – Congresses
    I. Lloyd-Bostock, Sally M.   II. Series
    340.I'9   K487.P75

ISBN 0 – 333 – 27275 – 7

Contents

The Contributors

Ivan D. Brown is Assistant Director of the Medical Research Council's Applied Psychology Unit at Cambridge

Ray Bull is Senior Lecturer in the Psychology Department at North East London Polytechnic

Brian Clapham is a Circuit Judge on the South Eastern Circuit

Brian Clifford is a Senior Lecturer in the Psychology Department at North East London Polytechnic

Michael Freeman is a Reader in Laws at University College London

Lionel Haward is Professor of Clinical Psychology at the University of Surrey

Linden Hilgendorf is Joint Research Director of the Legal Studies Group at the Tavistock Institute of Human Relations, London

Marquita Inman is a Lecturer in Law at Leicester University

Barrie Irving is Joint Research Director of the Legal Studies Group at the Tavistock Institute of Human Relations, London

Michael King is a Lecturer at the School of Law, University of Warwick

Sally M. Lloyd-Bostock is Senior Research Officer at the SSRC Centre for Socio-Legal Studies, Wolfson College, Oxford

Albert McKew is currently serving with the Metropolitan Police

David Miers is a Senior Lecturer in Law at University College, Cardiff

Patrick Rabbitt is a University Lecturer in Psychology and a Fellow of Queen's College, Oxford

A. Philip Sealy is a Lecturer in Social Psychology at the London School of Economics

Donald West is Professor in Clinical Criminology and Fellow of Darwin College, Cambridge

Patricia Wright is a member of the scientific staff at the Medical Research Council's Applied Psychology Unit at Cambridge

Preface

The scope of the psychology and law field has widened considerably beyond its origins in questions about testimony and other courtroom procedures. Current developments in Britain discussed in this book cover several areas of substantive law, and aspects of legal procedure outside as well as within the courts. Some of the contributions are in comparatively new areas – for example, voice identification, police interrogation, and legal communication – while others are now quite well established – for example, eyewitness research.

This range is an encouraging indication of a growing interest in psychology and law, but the volume of such work in Britain remains small, and it is still not widely known among lawyers. A primary aim of this book is therefore to stimulate more interest and further, improved research. The book as a whole provides an introduction to present work and thinking in the psychology and law field in Britain, and suggests realistic future possibilities. In addition, several of the contributions will have particular interest for more specialist audiences already acquainted with specific topics. An important consideration throughout has been to ensure comprehensibility both to non-lawyers and to non-psychologists.

The chapters originated as papers given at a three-day conference on Law and Psychology, held in Oxford in September, 1978. This was the first meeting of the SSRC Law and Psychology Seminar Group, which was established to provide an opportunity for psychologists and lawyers to meet regularly to discuss subjects of mutual interest, especially research findings and ideas for future research. Lawyers as well as psychologists presented papers, practising as well as academic. The proposal to start a group of this kind followed the 1977 Law and Psychology Conference, held in Oxford by the Centre for Socio-Legal Studies, which highlighted the demand, and need, for closer contact and communication between lawyers and psychologists.

The seminar group is funded by the Social Science Research

ix

Council, and the Centre for Socio-Legal Studies provides an institutional base and further support. As well as acknowledging this support, I would particularly like to thank Keith Hawkins, Donald Harris and Geoffrey Stephenson for their help in organising the conference which gave rise to this book, and for their advice and comments as the editing of the book proceeded; John Boal for his help with the final editing; Linda Cleland, Ginny Rosamond and Angela Palmer, who between them carried out the excellent typing; and Robert Irvine who compiled the index.

June 1979   S. L-B.

Introduction: Does Psychology have a Practical Contribution to make to Law?

Sally Lloyd-Bostock

The field of psychology and law is generally conceived of as an applied one. Other models of psychology and law research are certainly possible. The study of behaviour in legal contexts can, of course, be of interest in itself to psychologists, without the need to seek practical applications; the legal literature on a topic such as responsibility, or intention, can provide a conceptual clarity often lacking in psychological theory; and so on. But there can be little doubt that at present most lawyers, and probably also most psychologists, see the psychology and law field as one which aims eventually to offer practical help or advice in the various tasks of formulating and applying the law – or, more grandly, to promote justice.

Yet a recurring theme at the conference which gave rise to this book, both in the papers and in discussions, was an apparent ambivalence about whether psychology in fact has a practical contribution to offer. On the one hand, it seems clear that the justice, efficiency and fairness of law and legal procedures raise questions and problems which fall within the province of psychology. On the other hand, psychologists repeatedly stress the limitations on practical conclusions to be drawn from their work, and are often worried about the ethics of involvement in legal matters. This is, of course, the dilemma which faces, or should face, all social scientists acting as specialists but which is not always given the careful consideration it deserves. Writing in the US in 1961 about the area of psychology and the courtroom, Toch warned:

> Szasz (1957) has suggested that psychiatry may have been 'oversold'. This possibility presents itself in the case of psychology with equal force. In their zeal to obtain entry into the court-room as experts, psychologists may make promises which they are in no position to redeem (p. 19).

Rather than persuading lawyers prematurely to take more notice of psychology, several contributors to the present volume are anxious to resist or forestall overenthusiastic incorporation and use of psychology in legal contexts. Indeed, three of the chapters (by Patrick Rabbitt, Brian Clifford and Michael King) are largely about when and why the findings of psychology should _not_ be 'used'. Clifford and King in particular are highly critical of what they regard as unjustified claims made in the past for psychology.

This apparently rather negative emphasis on caution does not imply a negative view of the future for psychology and law. On the contrary, the contributions are all forward-looking, suggesting directions for further and improved research, ways of improving understanding between lawyers and psychologists and ways of avoiding past mistakes. In several areas an important practical contribution is already being made (see for example, Lionel Haward's Chapter 8); or clearly already could be made (see for example, Patricia Wright's Chapter 9). But where the present state of research evidence places limitations on its usefulness, these limitations must obviously be understood if serious mistakes are to be avoided, and if progress is to be made. Lawyers, no less than psychologists, need to have a clear idea of what can and cannot be expected from psychology. Both also need to consider ethical and pragmatic questions about the place of psychologists in the legal system, and about research with social policy implications, questions which arise as soon as psychologists begin to become involved in work in the legal field, and assume increasing importance as their work is put to practical use.

Questions of an ethical kind are returned to below. More prominent at the conference was the question of extrapolation from research findings in psychology to 'real-life' applications. It is important to make a distinction between applications in particular cases, and more general contributions to policy formation, because the kind of research evidence needed in the two kinds of circumstances will be different. Examples in the first category would be the suggestions made by Patrick Rabbitt for assessing the accuracy of a witness report of an event (Chapter 1); or the possibilities raised by the development of voice-matching techniques discussed by Ray Bull (Chapter 3). Examples of the second would be the five chapters in areas of substantive law (Part V), which suggest that the law can be useless, or worse than useless, if it is based on a misunderstanding of the causes of the behaviour which it seeks to control, whether it be gambling, traffic offences, deviant sexual behaviour or child abuse. This distinction is important because it is easy to fall into the trap of unjustified application of a general principle to an individual case, which may not be typical or average. Thus, Brian Clifford argues in Chapter 2 that certain current lines of research may be of policy relevance, but can never produce results which can justifiably be applied to evaluate eye-witness testimony in particular cases. Similar arguments could be made in other areas of research.

As Brian Clapham discusses in Chapter 7, the psychological evidence which an expert witness wishes to put before the court often relates not to the individual case as such (as would, for example, the outcome of forensic hypnosis) but may be based on the psychologist's knowledge of the results of studies and experiments, the views of other 'experts', and so on. For instance, Brian Clapham mentions the expert who gave what he, as judge in the case concerned, recognised as a neat précis of John Bowlby's *Child Care and the Growth of Love* (Bowlby, 1968). The use of evidence of this kind in individual cases can raise more acute problems of extrapolation than would the application of research findings in policy making. For quite different reasons, it may fall foul of the hearsay rule: perhaps the law should not be in too much of a hurry to relax the rules and make it easier to put any evidence of a psychological kind before the courts.

Application of research findings and theories to individual cases is especially hazardous, but problems of extrapolation from one setting – often a laboratory – to another arise in any applied work, including research aimed at a more general policy level. Several contributors emphasise that their conclusions must be regarded as tentative or speculative because they are based on results which may be of limited application. The sample as well as the task used in an experiment limits the generalisability of results (see Philip Sealy's discussion in Chapter 6). Patrick Rabbitt (Chapter 1) in particular makes very clear, not only just how tempting it is to draw a mistaken conclusion from experimental results, but also how the kinds of questions which experimental psychologists are trying to answer and the methods they therefore use, strictly limit the conclusions which legitimately *can* be drawn from experiments.

It can also be tempting to draw on theoretical interpretations of apparently relevant research findings because these interpretations are plausible or intriguing, or even simply because they appear authoritative since they come from psychology. However, psychological theory has a particular role to play within research. Theories frequently conflict, and it is recognised – indeed expected – that they will be revised in the light of subsequent research. Psychological theory is often based on or supported by a particular, limited type of experimental finding, which may not in fact provide an appropriate parallel. Moreover, as Crowle (1976) convincingly demonstrates, several interpretations of the same experiment are often possible, making it essential to look carefully at the experiment itself and the data obtained.

Marquita Inman's Chapter 4 illustrates some of the problems involved in drawing on psychological theory. For example, she discusses why suspects appear sometimes to believe their own false confessions. Several alternative theoretical interpretations can be derived from the psychological literature, all of which might account for this type of phenomenon, but none of which is entirely convincing if examined closely, because it draws its support from findings obtained in quite different (and sometimes rather bizarre) experimental situations which were designed not to find out something about *confessions* but to test a theory, often against another theory. Similarly, Patrick Rabbitt emphasises that *theory* in the area of recognition research, as well as the bulk of the research evidence, is based on laboratory experiments using tasks quite unlike that facing a witness to a 'real-life' event.

These kinds of difficulties lead to the conclusion that, in order to tell us anything definite of relevance to legal questions, research must be specifically designed for the purpose. In the confessions area, for example, Linden Hilgendorf and Barrie Irving (Chapter 5) conclude that what is needed is multi-dimensional research examining interactions amongst a range of variables, specifically in the interrogation setting. Most experimental psychology adopts the reverse strategy of reducing sources of variance to a bare minimum, for reasons set out in Chapter 1 by Patrick Rabbitt. A similar call for realism has been made frequently in the area of identification research, where the large gap between settings in which most of the research evidence has been gathered and settings with which the law is concerned, has the alarming consequence that research results may in fact lead to conclusions about eye-witness testimony which are the reverse of the truth (see for example, Clifford and Bull, 1978).

The doubts mentioned so far about applying psychological findings have arisen primarily from the dangers of going too far on the basis of too little evidence, or inappropriate evidence. They are in a sense the anxieties of psychologists as scientists. The remedies suggested are along the lines of more research, or different, more appropriate kinds of research, and careful, limited application of research findings. However, just as important may be doubts over the ethics of work in the legal field. The most vehement views in the present collection are probably those of Michael King (Chapter 10), whose reservations go beyond the question of the generalisability of research findings, and who raises fundamental questions about the whole enterprise of psychology and law as an applied subject. His chapter shows clearly that psychologists engaged in attempting to 'improve' the law venture into the sphere of societal values, and that involvement in law, whether in the role of expert or in policy formation, brings very serious responsibilities. In the instance of the law relating to children, he suggests that at worst the application of research findings from psychology becomes a means for lawyers, when faced with impossible decisions, to pass the buck to the 'expert'. Psychologists may be only too willing to hold themselves out as experts, and lawyers only too happy to be relieved of their especially difficult responsibilities.

The illustrations from family law which Michael King and Michael Freeman provide in Chapters 10 and 11, should not be taken as typical of the way the application of psychology to law has developed and the rôles which psychologists have adopted, but the patchy experience in this area holds lessons for other areas. Psychologists have a responsibility to control and, where appropriate, to limit the extent to which, and the ways in which their skills, research findings and theories are used.

Tapp and Levine (1977) quote Bazelon's telling warning that hiring 1000 psychologists is cheap compared with introducing the smallest change in the social and economic structure. Lionel Haward in Chapter 8 raises rather different but related ethical issues in relation to the use of forensic hypnosis which clearly can be of unique and often astonishing practical value in legal procedures. It is also open to the most serious abuse. Lionel Haward again highlights the responsibility of the psychologist to safeguard the interests of his patients, possibly at the expense of 'justice' in the form of a conviction, and to ensure that professional standards are adhered to by those who practise hypnosis.

Further dilemmas and opportunities for bias in applying psychology to legal questions arise from the fact that psychologists, like lawyers, differ amongst themselves. This is clearly illustrated in the differing theoretical perspectives on the etiology of child abuse which are discussed by Michael Freeman (Chapter 11). Similarly, David Miers shows in Chapter 12 how different psychological theories may be drawn on to support quite different approaches to the legal control of gambling. Differences of opinion of course assume enormous importance when it comes to the evidence of experts in individual cases. As Brian Clapham points out, under our adversarial legal system, each 'side' is bound to seek an expert whose evidence will be favourable, and it will be the duty of the 'other side' to demolish this evidence. This situation provides incentives to the psychologist to adopt a particular position. Among many other problems arising from this system is the reluctance of psychologists to appear in court to be attacked in cross examination. However, Brian Clapham's suggestion that the way out of many of these problems lies in the appointment of a 'court expert' who is supposedly on neither side, met with less than enthusiasm from the audience at the conference. A system which encourages opposing evidence to be presented and attacked was seen to have its advantages, given that it is very often possible to find experts whose views are opposed, and usually impossible to find one whose views can be said to represent 'psychology'. Indeed, one member of the group felt that the purpose of appearing as an expert could be to show that experts disagree rather than to persuade a court or jury of his own, perhaps minority, view. The rôle of the expert seems likely to provoke controversy amongst psychologists for a considerable time yet.

The current climate of increasing interest amongst lawyers in applying the social sciences raises dangers as well as possibilities. Premature, uncritical, unskilled or unreflective use of psychology in legal contexts must obviously be guarded against or it will produce worse problems than those it is intended to solve. Given the awareness of limitations which have been discussed, more emphasis is now being placed on psychology as offering ways of approaching questions and problems rather than as offering their final solution. For example, Chapters 5 and 13, by Linden Hilgendorf and Barrie Irving, and by Ivan Brown, show how the use of a decision-making model can bridge conceptual gaps between law and psychology, and offer a systematic way of analysing and diagnosing problems in applying the law by offering an understanding of the behaviour of individuals placed in a particular setting. The result is a new perspective rather than a ready solution to a problem. Psychology, despite its internal differences and controversies, and the provisional nature of many of its theories and findings, does have distinctive ways of approaching the explanation of human behaviour, and a vast body of research literature which if used carefully can bring important insights, throw doubt on established beliefs, or clarify the dimensions of a problem, without necessarily prescribing a particular consequence. It is also important to realise that psychology may be able to make a valuable and valid contribution to the formulation of law and legal policy, while not claiming to be able to provide answers in individual cases. Informing Royal Commissions is one way in which this kind of contribution is increasingly being made by psychologists in a variety of areas, from the law on gambling to interrogation procedures.

If these kinds of contribution are to be successful, both the lawyer and the psychologist need to extend their horizons and increase their acquaintanceship with the other's field. If lawyers sit back and wait to be offered solutions, they will continue to be disappointed and frustrated by psychology. And psychologists can all too easily make naive assumptions about the law and its functions and practicalities, and about their own discipline's contribution. Obviously specialisation within law and within psychology is such that no-one can claim expertise in more than a small area, and some areas, such as hypnosis, should clearly be left in the hands of the professional clinician. But it should be possible for psychologists to learn much more about the law, and for legal education to familiarise lawyers with the concerns and methods of psychology, the essential nature of psychological research, and with what psychology is and is not likely to be able to offer, now or in the foreseeable future.

This introduction has concentrated on questions which arise when practical implications for law are sought from psychology. It should not be assumed that a straightforward applied rôle is the only possibility or even the obvious one. In contrast to most psychologists working on legal topics, many sociologists of law have strongly resisted the rôle of applied social scientist, which they see as subservient – 'on tap but not on top' – atheoretical and politically biassed or naive because it involves working for legally defined ends. They argue that sociology *of* law should treat law as subject matter, as a social institution (see Campbell and Wiles, 1976). It is not easy to see an approach within psychology which would parallel this: whole social systems such as law are not the subject matter of psychology. Perhaps the work being carried out on legal socialisation (e.g. Tapp and Levine, 1974) comes the closest at present to a psychology *of* law. But many alternatives to the overtly applied approach exist and need to be explored more fully. In particular the possibility that law has something more than subject matter to offer psychology has scarcely been considered, yet lawyers have written extensively on the nature of rules and other topics of central importance in some branches of psychology. Nonetheless, whether or not a researcher intends his work to be applied, it will not be possible to escape the fact that psychological research on legal topics and behaviour is especially likely eventually to have, or appear to have, practical implications.

The reservations outlined above may give the misleading impression that the prospects for psychology and law are bleak. On the contrary, recent developments are extremely promising. Though the volume of work is still small in this country, progress is rapidly being made, new approaches are being explored, and new areas are being opened up. Tapp and Levine (1977) are probably right to see this kind of sobering of psychologists' (and lawyers') expectations as one healthy sign of a much closer rapprochement between law and psychology. On that, and the real possibilities for a contribution from psychology to legal concerns, I leave the contributions to this volume to speak for themselves.

REFERENCES

J. Bowlby, *Child Care and the Growth of Love* (London: Penguin, 1968).
C. Campbell and P. Wiles, 'The study of law in society in Britain', *Law and Society Review*, *10* (1976) 547–78.
B. R. Clifford and R. Bull, *The Psychology of Person Identification* (London: Routledge and Kegan Paul, 1978).

A. J. Crowle, 'The deceptive language of the laboratory', in R. Harré (ed.), *Life Sentences* (London: Wiley, 1976).

J. S. Szasz, 'Psychiatric expert testimony: Its court meaning and social function', *Psychiatry*, *20* (1957) 313–16.

J. L. Tapp and F. J. Levine, 'Legal socialisation: Strategies for an ethical legality', *Stanford Law Review*, *27* (1974) 1–72.

J. L. Tapp and F. J. Levine, 'Reflections and redirections', in J. L. Tapp and F. J. Levine (eds.), *Law, Justice and the Individual in Society* (New York: Holt, Rinehart and Winston, 1977).

H. Toch, *Legal and Criminal Psychology* (New York: Holt, Rinehart and Winston, 1961).

PART I

THE RELIABILITY OF WITNESS EVIDENCE

1: Applying Human Experimental Psychology to Legal Questions about Evidence[1]

Patrick Rabbitt

It is said that when Gertrude Stein lay dying her sometimes overbearing[2] lifelong companion[3] and superb cook[4] Alice B. Toklas hovered at the bedside, desperate to interrogate at the exact moment of transition:

'Gertrude, Gertrude! What is the answer?!'

To which the exact Miss Stein snapped with her dying breath:

'What is the question?'

Without the implication that psychology is either moribund or exact this anecdote seems to capture the current dialogue between lawyers and psychologists. Psychologists grow impatient because lawyers ask them questions which they cannot answer, and appear not to be impressed by the theoretical reasons why such questions are currently unanswerable. Lawyers faced with clumsy re-definitions of things that they know already, with accounts of 'research' done and described with obvious political bias, and with experiments which seem perversely to evade interesting testable points of fact, must conclude with Yeats that

The best lack all conviction while the worst
Are filled with passionate intensity.

Nevertheless I think that lawyers and psychologists have much to learn from each other if they could better understand each other's points of view. In this chapter I shall try to explain one branch of psychology, human experimental psychology, to lawyers. I shall try to suggest, both to lawyers and psychologists, why human experimental psychology has proved largely unsuccessful in answering practical questions posed by lawyers and policemen. I shall then suggest some new approaches which may help to overcome these difficulties in particular areas.

HUMAN EXPERIMENTAL PSYCHOLOGISTS AND THEIR PREOCCUPATIONS

Human experimental psychology may be said to have begun when physiologists such as Helmholtz, Donders and Wundt recognised that behavioural observations could provide valuable information about the central nervous system which could not be more directly obtained by neurophysiological techniques. Human experimental psychologists still retain an interest in the neurophysiological basis of behaviour, and many of them co-operate with physiologists in studying the sense-organs and the ways in which sensory information is represented in the brain. However most of the processes they study, such as memory, language, selective attention or problem solving, are so complex that it is unlikely that their physiological basis will be understood for some time. Human experimental psychologists who study such questions sometimes call themselves 'cognitive psychologists' and typically turn to cybernetics or engineering for models to describe their observations.

Given their interests in such processes as memory and perception one might expect cognitive psychologists to be able to offer lawyers useful advice on such questions as the reliability of identification and the reliability of testimony. Recent attempts to do this have only been partially successful. (See Clifford and Bull, 1978 for a useful survey). Why is this so?

Human experimental psychology has been applied with considerable success to many problems in industry, defence and aviation. Indeed a strong claim can be made that without the stimulus of such applications (Broadbent, 1973), few advances in the science would have occurred. The problem is not that this branch of psychology *cannot* be an applied science. It rather stems from the fact that nearly all human experimental psychologists earn their livings as teaching academics and do pure research in their spare time. I shall suggest that the experimental techniques they use are not designed to answer applied questions, and worse, that their experimental results can prove very misleading when generalisations for common practice are based on them.

METHODOLOGICAL IDIOSYNCRACIES WHICH LIMIT APPLICABILITY OF EXPERIMENTS

1. *Tight control of variables*

Since the beginnings of the subject experimental psychologists have been impressed by the enormous complexities of the systems of relationships which they wish to study. For example, simple reaction-time experiments, such as those made by Wundt in 1879 may involve timing minute finger flexions in response to single signals. This may seem as elementary (if not as trivial) a piece of human behaviour as could possibly be investigated. However, 100 years later the literature on this topic still expands and is still full of surprises and contradictions. Any one of a dozen or more variables (e.g. nature of signal to respond, intensity of signal, presence or absence of a warning signal, nature of warning signal, interval between warning and response signal, and so on) have very marked *systematic* effects on the reaction times recorded. Further, some of these variables will affect reaction times *independently* of each other, and some only *in combination* with others. Some affect only variation in reaction time from trial to trial, some only affect average reaction times and some both.

Faced with similar complexities in all the experimental tasks which they use, psychologists have adopted the standard scientific strategy of exploring the effects of changes in only one variable at a time, holding all others constant, proceeding eventually to test the effects of joint changes in two or more variables. This style of experimentation has the immediate effect that when psychologists are asked about performance on simple tasks they become evasive and when asked about complex tasks they fall silent. The natural reaction of competent academic psychologists faced with a complex applied problem is to look for ways of restricting the focus of the investigation.

This is not necessarily a bad initial approach but it restricts the application of the data they obtain. In most real-life situations, particularly in the complex situations with which lawyers must deal, we really want to know the effects of a number of simultaneous changes in many variables. In such cases investigations of effects of changes in isolated variables can tell us little and will only be counter-productive if they distract us from the real problem. It is only recently that the use of control systems analysis has begun to give us mathematical models which we can use to describe such complex systems of relationships in ways which do not oblige us to depend on earlier styles of experimentation (Broadbent, 1977; Hamilton, Hockey and Rejman, 1977; Macfarland, 1971; Rabbitt, 1979a; b; Toates, 1975).

2. *Data gathered on one laboratory task may not generalise to another.*
Experimental psychologists tend to re-use familiar laboratory tasks rather than design new ones. I found it striking that when I ran through all issues of six journals published over the period 1950 to 1978, over eighty per cent of all investigations *did not use an original experimental paradigm*. Furthermore very few paradigms were in general use at any one time and it was hard to account for their selection in other terms than arbitrary fashion.

An elegant experimental paradigm may be useful because it taps one process rather than another. But psychologists can make at least two different kinds of mistake when they do not carefully consider the paradigms they use. First a paradigm may provide data which are specific to one particular process and which do not reflect other, apparently very similar, processes. Second we may assume that a paradigm is specific to a particular process when in fact it reflects quite another. My own experiments, unfortunately, can be used to illustrate both kinds of mistake.

I made an experiment to compare memory efficiency in young and elderly people, borrowing a clever paradigm (as I said most of my colleagues do) invented by Shepherd and Teightsoonian (1961). Subjects were shown 300 words, one at a time. As each word was presented they had to say whether or not it was one they had seen before in the list (i.e. whether it was 'old' or 'new'). My purpose was to compare both the number and the types of errors made by the two groups. Two kinds of error can occur in this task – failure to recognise an 'old' word, or false identification of a word which is in fact 'new'.

As I expected the elderly made more errors than the young, but it was striking that they made almost no false identifications. Fortunately I did not commit myself in public to the claim that elderly people are *less* likely to confabulate than their juniors when they fail to recall a particular event. The experiment I have described required people to *recognise* words which they may or may not have seen during a task. I next required subjects to *recall* lists of words. My older subjects recalled fewer words than their juniors but also, unlike their juniors, 'recalled' many words which I had *not* presented to them. I had found an interesting difference between the relative efficiency of recall and recognition in old and young people, which raises various theoretical questions. But any general-isation as to whether old people are more or less prone to confabulate on points of evidence would clearly have been unreliable. I had found a difference between *paradigms*: a difference between *processes* or *people* still had to be sought.

Had I generalised from these experimental results to the sweeping statement that old people confabulate in recall but not in recognition I should have made another mistake. This difference also seems to be specific to the material and the tasks which I used. Experiments with material more complex than lists of unrelated words fail to reveal these differences, but produce others. Again the limitations of the paradigms which I used make general statements unreliable.

A second kind of mistake is to assume that a tried and tested laboratory task is sufficiently tight to explore only one variable at a time, and that we can be certain what that variable is. Another example will show that this is not the case.

Conrad (1964, 1967) showed that people recall strings of printed letters of the alphabet better if they have names which sound different (e.g. A, S, D) than if they have names which sound similar (e.g. A and K; X and S; P and D). This is good evidence that even when letters are visually presented they are habitually re-encoded and stored as auditory traces, so that confusions in recall represent confusions between similar auditory traces rather than between similar visual traces (such as might occur, for example, between visual representations of C, O, Q and G). I wished to discover whether elderly people were more prone to make such errors than the young. I showed young and old subjects strings of between four and seven random letters which might, or might not be acoustically confusible. Elderly subjects remembered fewer letters and were particularly error-prone when letter strings contained confusible elements. I concluded that the old do, indeed, suffer more than the young from the effects of acoustic confusibility.

I was quite wrong. Alan Baddeley told me that he had made a similar experiment and found that his old and young subjects suffered from confusibility to about the same extent. Baddeley had exposed his sequences one letter at a time whereas I had exposed each sequence simultaneously as a letter string. I repeated the experiment using both techniques and replicated both results. The difference seemed to be due to the fact that when young subjects see a letter string which they have to remember they try to encode it as an approximation to a familiar word (e.g. HSEBXS might be remembered using the mnemonic 'horseboxes'). If they can do this, acoustic confusibility of individual letters does not matter. But old people are not good at mnemonic tricks of this kind. They therefore perform relatively poorly, and also show the full effects of letter confusibility which the young evade by their mnemonics. When one letter is presented at a time neither young nor old can easily make up mnemonics. The old then show no more effect of item confusibility than do the young.

Thus though both experiments had been competently carried out, and both were replicable, any general conclusion about age-differences based on either alone would have been misleading. Even in such very simple tasks human performance may be more complex and more strategic than we suppose, and our hope that we have tight control over a single variable we wish to study (in this case confusibility) may turn out to be illusory.

3. *Laboratory tasks are often tenuous abstractions of 'real-life' situations.*
Over ninety per cent of the studies quoted in standard textbooks on the psychology of memory (e.g. Baddeley, 1976; Crowder, 1976; Murdock, 1974) only test recognition or recall of words or nonsense trigrams. Even experiments on recall of sentences are quite rare. Experiments on accuracy of recall of pictures, photographs or faces or filmed episodes are often quoted in reviews of the literature directed at lawyers (see Clifford and Bull, 1978) but actually comprise only a small fraction of the data on which theories of memory are based. It must be emphasised that laboratory psychologists owe more allegiance to theories based on recall of very simple materials than they may admit in public discussions of practical applications. Very few studies cited in Clifford and Bull's complete review of work on person identification escape criticism on these grounds.

4. *The 'significance' of results from laboratory experiments is usually evaluated in terms of the presence rather than the size of effects*
When a psychologist claims that his results are 'significant at the

$p < 0.001$ level' a semantic trap must be recognised. 'Significant' here does not mean 'important'. It simply means that it is very unlikely that the effect came about by chance.

My own line of work illustrates this. I am concerned with effects which produce differences in mean reaction times of nine to twenty *milliseconds* against a background of trial-to-trial variability in human choice reaction time which may be 100 milliseconds or more. I am primarily concerned to discover whether these tiny effects exist at all. If the probability that a particular effect has appeared in my data by chance is less than one in a thousand, I have a very definite result indeed.

It is usually of no theoretical interest to me to ask the further question 'How large ("significant" in a quite different sense) is this effect compared with all the others which contribute to variance in reaction time?' In fact, it turns out that the effects I examine account for less than 0.8 per cent of the trial-to-trial variability in human choice reaction time. In short, although I had to go to a great deal of trouble to record them, although I can be sure they are there, and although I find them theoretically fascinating, they are totally insignificant for any practical purpose.

The first statistician to emphasise for behavioural scientists the difference between these two criteria for estimating the 'significance' of effects was Jacob Cohen (1975, 1977). Lawyers should be aware that most psychological data on human performance, including data on the reliability of testimony, has not been analysed by the power statistics recommended by Cohen and others, which would tell us not merely whether an effect is *present*, but whether it is *large enough* to matter for practical purposes, and how it *compares* with many other effects in the data.

5. *Experimental comparisons are based on group means and may not represent the performance of any individual person*

Psychologists investigating performance typically test a large group of people on each of the tasks which they wish to compare. They tabulate the *arithmetic means* (averages) of performance scores on each task, and present the results of statistical tests designed to assess whether or not differences in these *means* might have come about by chance. Summary statements of the type '42.8 per cent of errors occurred in recall' thus usually mask the fact that some subjects recalled everything perfectly while others may have remembered nothing at all.

As with all other difficulties I have discussed, this does not happen because experimental psychologists wish to deceive their readers or to be evasive. Rather, psychologists who wish to compare one *task* with another have regarded differences between the performance of *individuals* simply as an annoying source of random variation which blurs the precision with which they can detect small effects. They take elaborate care to minimise effects of individual differences both by deliberately selecting tasks which are known to reduce variability and by adopting experimental designs which are balanced so that the effects of individual differences can cancel each other out. Naturally the existence of these techniques implies that we also know how to look for individual differences if we wish. But theoretical models to account for such differences hardly exist so that experimental psychologists tend to ignore them and to miss their implications when they try to provide answers to practical questions.

6. *Experiments on human performance are designed to reveal and to stress performance limitations. They tend to neglect successful performance.*
To see why this is the case let us consider the behavioural psychology of archangels. St Thomas Aquinas defined an archangel as an entity which 'responds perfectly to all commands of the creator'. This means that there is no way in which experimental psychologists could construct useful models of the functional processes underlying the performance of archangels. They would always have a reaction time of zero to all stimuli, would never make errors of perception or memory and would perfectly control their infinitely fast responses. Fortunately human beings are imperfect, and out of their delays and errors, and on *no other evidence*, the entire science of experimental psychology is constructed.

This biasses techniques in experimental psychology towards the discovery of subtle limitations. No experiments are designed to discover whether all subjects tested can perform perfectly. I think that training in such techniques may be one of the chief reasons why many academic psychologists find applied work difficult. They have been chiefly concerned to establish the limitations of human performance on cognitive tasks, and are not used to thinking in a more positive way how some of these limitations can be mitigated. I believe that this accounts for the unhelpful tone of much of the discussion of problems of accuracy of identification and reliability of testimony which psychologists offer lawyers. It is certainly of great social importance to stress that eye-witness accounts may be very unreliable indeed. Of course practising lawyers have always realised this, but even they may have been surprised by the large numbers of carefully conducted studies which have shown just *how* poor some people can be at remembering what has happened in their vicinity. However these studies do not discuss how it is that most subjects, although they may make individual errors on critical details of testimony (which are rather arbitrarily chosen details in most studies), can nevertheless perceive and remember most details of complex events quite accurately.

I believe that it is time that experimental psychologists began to take a more positive point of view. If we must start from the premise that most witnesses are to some extent unreliable, can we nevertheless distinguish those parts of a man's testimony which are most likely to be accurate from those which probably are not? Can we develop techniques to elicit more accurate information from uncertain witnesses, or to facilitate recall of complex events? Can we advise lawyers how to tell whether some witnesses are likely to be more reliable than others? Finally, can we help evaluate artificial aids to identification (e.g. Identikit pictures, computer graphic feature assembling systems, voice prints etc.)?

On the basis of some very preliminary experiments of my own I shall speculate on some ways in which experimental psychologists may begin to apply some of the techniques which they have developed for laboratory investigations along these positive lines.

POSSIBLE CONSTRUCTIVE APPROACHES TO PROBLEMS OF IDENTIFICATION AND COMPARATIVE RELIABILITY OF TESTIMONY

Some human beings, at least, are marvellously accurate observers and reporters. Luria's (1968) subject S could easily recall, in any order, lists of 128 random digits. He could retain them indefinitely, apparently without using mnemonic systems. His ability to remember the precise physical characteristics of voices seems to have been inconveniently exact. He reported that he never forgot voices, but sometimes failed to recognise them because of very slight changes in timbre or intonation due to respiratory ailments or a change in acoustic environment! Such remarkable performance is uncommon but there is evidence that memory skills can be developed by training and that comparable levels of attainment are not as rare as we once supposed (Bower, 1973).

Bearing such evidence in mind let us take as a working hypothesis the idea that human beings owe their evolutionary success and daily survival to their ability to observe and recall accurately most details of most events in which they participate. Can we then capitalise on this potential efficiency to obtain more accurate information from witnesses of uncertain events?

Cued recall and elicitation of information from memory
All memory theorists agree that people retain in their memories far more information than they recall on particular occasions. Some suggest that 'forgetting' should be regarded as a temporary or permanent failure to retrieve stored information (Tulving, 1972). It is natural, then, to ask how we can best help people to remember information which has been stored, but which they might otherwise not be able to retrieve.

Much good recent work reflects a natural concern that attempts to cue recall can elicit false testimony. Experimental psychologists might relax if they were to consider more neutral situations – say, evidence about alleged UFO sightings – where we may start with the assumption that all parties honestly collaborate in an attempt to obtain an accurate picture of an event. The police and others have developed pragmatic techniques for eliciting as much accurate detail as possible from uncertain witnesses. These involve patience in allowing a man to pursue his own patterns of associations, prompts, sketch maps or photographs, views of the scene of an event or staged reconstructions. There is no question that such techniques can be misused to bias recollection, but this should not prevent research being done to discover how people can be cued to recall accurately.

In the jargon used by experimental psychologists this is related to the problem of eliciting evidence of 'incidental learning'. People concentrating diligently on one aspect of a laboratory task may also subsequently remember details quite irrelevant to those which engrossed them. We know very little about incidental learning. In particular we cannot say how much incidental information is typically stored and recalled in this way, how reliable recall of such information can be, or much about the best way to help a man to retrieve such information from memory.

Experimental psychologists have neglected to investigate the relative efficiency of aids to recollection which have been in common use for some time, or which are now feasible. Examples of such aids to recollection are: getting the witness to amplify his verbal statements by making simple plans or sketch maps from visual memory (visual memory appears more accurate than verbal memory); allowing him to play back tape-recordings of his earlier spoken recollections both to cue himself to further recollections and to edit his earlier statements for relative accuracy and reliability; showing him accurate maps or photographs; physically visiting scenes of incidents with him or staging re-enactments of events with him. The lack of formal work on these kinds of simple practical aids is emphasised by the striking fact that we cannot even say for sure whether people's accuracy of recall improves or deteriorates as successive attempts are made to elicit details from them. We also cannot yet guess over what periods of time such repeated attempts may continue to be useful, or when they should be abandoned as being likely to add false rather than accurate detail.

Reliability of 'group' testimony of complex events
Perhaps psychologists acquire a negative approach to human memory because nearly every one of them has been exposed, while a student, to one particular laboratory demonstration. Technicians or other 'stooges' stage an 'incident' in a lecture room. Written accounts of this incident are then collected from (hopefully) unsuspecting undergraduates and are compared, with much hilarity at wild discrepancies and omissions. The lecturer then usually makes two simple points. First, eye-witness accounts are (evidently) fallible. Second, distortions in recollection are systematic rather than random.

This is a very salutary and enjoyable exercise but I grew tired of it, and became interested in another question. Granted that *individual* witnesses are unreliable, is there any way in which one may extract from the reports of a *group* of witnesses the most probable version of a complex 'happening'?

I staged the usual 'incident' in my classes but then gave my students check-lists on which they had to answer 68 to 150 specific questions on points of detail.

The first point to emerge was that the amount and accuracy of information obtained from each *individual* by this procedure was much greater than when they were asked to make a 'statement in their own words'. This is an expected result since the superiority of cued over uncued recall is very well known (see Baddeley, 1976; Brown, 1976; Crowder, 1976; Murdock, 1974 and Tulving, 1972). However, I was surprised at how large the differences were. Both the quantity and the accuracy of details reported increased by a factor of three.

The more important point was that the technique allowed the 'testimony' of all witnesses to be collated and compared on each point of detail. By taking the 'majority vote' on each point of detail, it was possible to compare the accuracy of the group acting as a 'committee' with the accuracy of each of its members. I was again surprised. Committee majority reports were much more complete and accurate than the report given by any individual. The application of simple Bayesian statistics further improved this accuracy.

There were also some elementary pragmatic techniques which seemed to work very well. For example we found that subjects who answer most questions are, on average, also more accurate on any individual question. We therefore weighted the answers given by subjects who had answered *most* questions (irrespective of accuracy) to break ties when votes were otherwise equal for conflicting recollections. The accuracy of the 'committee report' was thereby greatly improved.

These results are tentative because I have only conducted these experiments to entertain my students and to give them some practice in simple statistical techniques. They, and I, are now less impressed by the fallibility of human memory than by the comprehensiveness and accuracy of the testimony which even very simple procedures can elicit. The problem of constructing weighted group reports in this way clearly deserves much more sophisticated mathematical treatment and better empirical investigation.

People accurately estimate the reliability of their own recall of particular points of detail.

It is a pity that psychologists studying human memory typically only score their subjects 'right' or 'wrong' on particular points of evidence. We have long known that people can provide good estimates of the *relative* reliability of their uncertain recollections; (see Murdock, 1974, Ch. 3). If people are allowed to use a rating scale to classify their recollections of particular points of detail from 'dubious' to 'certain' they can very usefully qualify the evidence they give. In the laboratory demonstrations described above I also asked participants to rate each of their questionnaire replies in this way. As expected, subjects were able to convey accurately extra information with this scale. They not only systematically assigned lower probability values to recollections which were, in fact, inaccurate, but also were able accurately to rank a *range* of alternatives on a multiple choice list according to relative probability. If we took into consideration the probability estimate which each individual subject assigned to each detail of his 'evidence', and used these as weightings, the reliability of 'committee reports' of incidents was greatly improved. It is possible also to use such ratings to compute an index of *bias* in each subject's recall, which suggests whether he is more concerned to avoid making errors of omission (i.e. to avoid failures to report) or is more concerned to avoid false reports on points of detail on which he feels uncertain. This allows us to compare the *relative* probability of accuracy of evidence given by different subjects on the same details.

Individual differences in reliability of testimony

In the laboratory demonstrations which I have described, individual differences in the amount and accuracy of recall were very striking indeed. No statement that 'human testimony is very unreliable' does justice to the performance of about four per cent of my subjects who gave accurate answers to at least 132 out of 150 questions on specific points of detail, nor to five subjects who were accurate on none. This raises the obvious practical question as to whether it may be possible to design tests which allow us to pick out excellent from among unreliable witnesses. There may be excellent practical and ethical reasons why we should not wish to use the results of such tests in a court of law but preliminary data suggest that we can discriminate, in a general way, between people who are relatively good and relatively poor witnesses if we wish to do so.

The results of the experiments described above indicate a number of systematic differences between individuals. Accurate reporters tended also to claim to remember many details, and they tended to give extreme ratings when asked how confident they were of particular details. In addition, analysis of these data showed that subjects were highly consistent in their level of accuracy across all the questions they attempted. The percentage accuracy of answers on a random fifty per cent of questions attempted correlated between .73 and .95 with accuracy on the other fifty per cent. Further, when split half percentage accuracies were compared by F test across all subjects there was no significant difference between sub-sets of answers. This consistency may be of practical use since it suggests that if the degree of reliability of even part of a person's account of an incident can be established we can derive a very reasonable numerical estimate of the probability of his accuracy on the remaining details he describes.

As well as recollecting staged 'incidents', the undergraduates I worked with took part in a number of other experiments involving free recall of words, rote learning, paired associate learning and so on. It was thus possible to compare their accuracy on these rather arbitrary tests with their accuracies of report on the details of a complex, unexpected event. Correlations between their scores on different tests were quite reasonable (overall 0.35 significant at $p < .01$). This simply means that subjects who perform well at laboratory experiments involving memory are also likely to perform well on recall of a single, unexpected complex event. It seems quite feasible to construct sets of 'memory tests' which will give even better correlations. I am quite aware that the possibility of calculating 'memory quotients' akin to 'intelligence quotients' may be argued to be of little practical value, and may even arouse strong emotion as being ethically undesirable. I feel personally that such tests, like IQ tests, may be useful for some practical purposes and misleading for others.

CONCLUSION

I have tried to suggest to lawyers some of the reasons why human experimental psychologists find it difficult to give useful answers to applied questions which are put to them. I have also tried to suggest to my colleagues that some of these difficulties are unnecessary, and that they partly arise out of the techniques of experimentation which experimental psychologists have developed to test their theories. In particular I have suggested that because human experimental psychologists have been chiefly concerned to establish the limitations of human performance on cognitive tasks such as memory or selective attention, they are not used to thinking in a more positive way, how some of these limitations can be mitigated. I made some suggestions for further work, arising out of preliminary, but quite reliable data, obtained in classroom experiments with groups of undergraduates.

NOTES

1. This chapter could not have been prepared without support from SSRC grant No. HR6258 for which the author is very grateful. Without tactful editing by Dr. S. Lloyd-Bostock and Dr. D. V. Bishop it would be much less comprehensible.
2. E. Hemingway, *A Moveable Feast* (Harmondsworth: Penguin, 1974).
3. G. Stein, *The Autobiography of Alice B. Toklas* (Harmondsworth: Penguin, 1976).
4. A. B. Toklas, *The Alice B. Toklas Cookbook*, (Harmondsworth: Penguin, 1966).

REFERENCES

A. D. Baddeley, *The Psychology of Memory* (New York and London: Harper and Row, Basic Books Inc., 1976).
G. H. Bower, 'Memory freaks I have known', *Psychology Today, 3* (1973) 21–32.
D. E. Broadbent, *In defence of empirical psychology* (London: Methuen, 1973).
D. E. Broadbent, 'Levels, hierarchies and the locus of control', *Quarterly Journal of Experimental Psychology, 29* (1977) 181–201.
J. Brown (ed.), *Recall and Recognition* (London and New York: Wiley, 1976).
B. R. Clifford and R. Bull, *The Psychology of Person Identification* (London: Routledge and Kegan Paul, 1978).
J. Cohen and P. Cohen, *Applied Multiple Regression/Correlation Analysis for the Behavioural Sciences* (Hillsdale, New Jersey, Lawrence Erlbaum Associates, 1975).
J. Cohen, *Statistical Power Analysis for the Behavioural Sciences* (Hillsdale, New Jersey, Lawrence Erlbaum Associates, 1977).
R. Conrad, 'Acoustic Confusions in Immediate Memory', *British Journal of Psychology, 55,* (1964) 75–84.
R. Conrad, 'Interference or decay over short retention intervals?', *Journal of Verbal Learning and Verbal Behaviour, 6,* (1967) 49–54.
R. G. Crowder, *Principles of Learning and Memory* (Hillsdale, New Jersey, Erlbaum Associates, 1976).
P. Hamilton, R. Hockey and M. Rejman, 'The place of the concept of activation in human information processing theory: An integrative approach', in S. Dornic (ed.), *Attention and Performance, VI* (Hillsdale, New Jersey, Erlbaum Associates, 1977).
A. R. Luria, *The Mind of a Mnemonist* (New York: Basic Books, 1968).
D. J. Macfarland, *Feedback Mechanisms in Animal Behaviour* (New York: Academic Press, 1971).
B. B. Murdock Jr., *Human Memory: Theory and Data* (Potomac Md: Erlbaum Associates, 1974).
P.M.A. Rabbitt, 'Some experiments and a model for changes in attentional selectivity with old age', in F. Baumeister (ed.), *Bayer Symposium No. IX on Biological Effects of Ageing* (Hamburg: Springer Verlag, 1979). (a).
P.M.A. Rabbitt, 'Information processing models for the effects of stress on human performance', in V. Hamilton and D. Warburton (eds.), *Stress and Human Efficiency* (London and New York: John Wiley, 1979). (b).
R. N. Shepherd and M. Teightsoonian, 'Retention of information under con-

ditions approaching a steady state', *Journal of Experimental Psychology*, 62 (1961) 302–309.

F. M. Toates, *Control Theory in Biology and Experimental Psychology* (London: Hutchinsons Educations Ltd., 1975).

E. Tulving, 'Episodic and semantic memory', in E. Tulving and W. Donaldson (eds.), *Organisation of Memory* (London and New York: Academic Press, 1972).

2: Towards a more Realistic Appraisal of the Psychology of Testimony

Brian R. Clifford

Psychology claims to be both a theoretical science and at the same time an applied discipline, able to serve in the practical affairs of the world. One such area in which psychologists have involved themselves, somewhat controversially, is the legal area of eye-witness evidence. In the recent past psychologists' claims to knowledge and fact finding ability were altogether too forceful, and lawyers' reluctance to use psychological evidence, insights and sophisticated techniques altogether too irrational. For a fuller reciprocity between law and psychology in this important area there must be a softening of attitudes and a fuller realisation of possibilities for cooperation. The aim of this paper is to facilitate these processes by focusing on the over-enthusiastic claims of psychology, indicating where their evidence is weak, and why, and how they are beginning to reorientate to become more acceptable and effective partners in the improvement of criminal justice.

There are three fundamental questions which the serious applied psychologist (or the lawyer) must ask before accepting the applicability of psychological findings to criminal cases. First, how trustworthy and relevant are the findings generated in the pyschologist's laboratory? Second, are there limitations on what can legitimately be done with such knowledge if it is trustworthy? And finally, how should the psychologist proceed in order to maximise the practical usefulness of his data? It is the intention of this chapter to answer these three questions.

I. HOW TRUSTWORTHY AND RELEVANT ARE THE FINDINGS GENERATED IN THE PSYCHOLOGIST'S LABORATORY?

Many researchers believe that they have amassed a body of highly relevant, integrated and appropriate findings regarding eyewitness testimony (see Table 2.1).

Now it is not what they have found, or what they have not found, but rather the legitimate use to which these findings can be put which creates controversy. The findings which have been made during the long history of eye-witness research have been employed in at least two ways: a general way and a specific way. In the general sense, psychology has benefited the legal profession by disclosing that humans are fallible and quite limited processors of information, thus dispelling the common-sense belief that testimony will be correct as long as the witness is mentally normal and has the intention of telling the truth. Psychologists have shown clearly that deviations from objective reality in testimony are due to neither intentional lying nor pathological pseudologia – but simply to the fact that man is severely limited in his ability to perceive, store and retrieve memories of what he has heard or seen.

This is an important achievement because the use and status of eye-witness testimony in court cases was developed and established long before the scientific study of perception or memory began, and tradition is much more influential than newly discovered facts generated in an unrelated discipline. This use of psychological knowledge should neither be deprecated nor denied. It is a very big plus.

But psychologists of late have attempted to go beyond this general warning and to argue either that because they have amassed a body of integrated and appropriate facts they can now state categorically that eye-witness evidence should never be admitted as evidence in a court of law, or, if such evidence is admitted, that they (psychologists) have the knowledge to ascertain the degree of accuracy or inaccuracy involved in the particular case under review. The first assertion is untenable: the second requires clear qualification.

The belief that psychological evidence clearly indicates that eye-witness evidence should never be admitted in court is untenable because the findings which are held to be applicable to issues of eye-witness evidence lack agreement, generality and comprehensiveness as a result of being generated by research which lacks an appropriate focus and which is based on the uncritical adoption of a

Table 2.1 *A taxonomic categorisation of factors known to influence eye-witness accuracy*

Social factors	Situational factors	Individual factors	Interrogational factors
Conformity Attitudes Prejudice Stereotypes (of event, of people)	Emotionality of event Duration of event Illumination of event Complexity of event	Race of criminal and of witness Sex of criminal and of witness Age of criminal and of witness Mental set Personality Cognitive style Change of appearance Training	Delay in holding ID parades or eliciting testimony. Intervening testing Medium of interrogation (verbal description, mug-shots, sketches, photo-fit) Questioning mode, styles and questioner experience. Identification parade procedures (bias, functional size) Non-verbal 'leakage'

number of simplifying assumptions and procedures. Direct applicability to legal issues is prevented by the way 'eye-witness' experiments are conceived, planned, conducted and analysed.
Laboratory research which purports to give directly relevant
evidence is characterised by methodological artificiality and procedural bias.

This comprehensive indictment of the value of research findings
is only what one would expect from a blurring of the distinction
between pure and applied research. When psychologists apply
themselves to issues of eye-witness evidence they do so largely on the
basis of pure research findings. This is unfortunate because the goals
and the means, and hence the results, of pure and applied research
are very different. While pure research is preoccupied with
considerations of formal elegance, logical rigour and theoretical
parsimony, applied research is concerned with situationally valid,
socially relevant and publicly usable knowledge. Pure research is
thus theory-driven: applied research is problem-driven. Stresses
and strains must appear when findings in one sphere are applied
wholesale to the other sphere.

Most of the supposedly applicable results in memory and
perception which psychologists quote are based on remembering
pictures of scenes or photographs of faces rather than real events or
live people. The simulated crime methodology, while being the
most mundane and experimentally real and having the greatest
ecological validity, is the least used method of research (Clifford,
1978, 1979). Most experimental situations lack both mundane and
experimental realism (Carlsmith, Ellsworth and Aronson, 1976).
That is, they are not realistic to the subject; they do not have an
impact on him; nor do they approximate real life situations. In
traditional laboratory studies the subject is passive, prepared and
non-aroused: a witness or a victim is none of these things. These are
only some of the more obvious aspects of experimental procedures
which will have to be changed if psychology is to become more
relevant to the eye-witness debate. Many other inappropriate
procedures could be described but the above should suffice to make
the point that a very large gulf exists between what the pure
psychologist knows about memory and perception and what the
applied psychologist knows about memory and perception as it
relates to eye-witnessing.

The scarcity of well-designed *applied* research means that psychologists are unable to give unambiguous answers to factual questions.

If we are asked the question, 'how good is visual memory?' the answer must be that we do not know, it all depends upon the material which has to be remembered. Face-photographs are remembered with about ninety per cent accuracy, staged live-event personnel with only thirteen to fifteen per cent accuracy. Are females better witnesses than males? We do not know. Once again it depends upon the type of material and the nature of the witnessing situation. Does delay in testing recognition adversely affect memory accuracy? Face-photograph research suggests no: event methodology suggests yes.

In terms of comprehensiveness of findings, we do not know if different crimes are differentially remembered. We do not know if some elements of a crime (e.g. physical actions) are better retained than others (e.g. physical descriptions or verbalisations). We do not know if a witness or a victim can remember three assailants as well as he can remember one. Again, we are uncertain as to what makes some faces more recognisable than others, and we do not know what overall effect disguise has on observer accuracy.

Thus, the answer to the first fundamental question we raised must be a severe scepticism concerning the trustworthiness of the 'relevant, integrated and appropriate' findings psychologists tell us they have available.

2. IF PSYCHOLOGISTS CAN OBTAIN TRUSTWORTHY FINDINGS, WHAT CAN BE DONE WITH SUCH KNOWLEDGE?

Let us assume for the sake of argument that some findings are reliable and replicable across a wide range of situations and tasks. What can the psychologist do with these when a member of the legal profession asks for advice on a specific issue of doubt concerning eye-witness evidence in a specific case? Whether the psychologist will be able, in principle, to do something or nothing will depend on the question addressed. To make this point clearer look again at Table 2.1, and ask for each entry: 'can the criminal justice system do anything about this factor, or can it not?' The answer to this question holds the key to the psychologist's potency or impotency. Factors about which the criminal system can do nothing have been termed 'estimator variables' by Wells (1978), and factors they can do something about have been termed 'system variables'. Table 2.2 shows a regrouping of the factors in Table 2.1 into this dichotomy. Now if a question is raised concerning the effect of an estimator

Table 2.2 Factors known to influence witness accuracy, divided into those the criminal justice system can do something about (system variables) and those it cannot (estimator variables).*

System variables	Estimator variables
Identification parade procedures	Attitudes
Intervening testing	Prejudice
Delay in holding I.D. parades or	Stereotyping of events and of people
eliciting testimony	Emotionality of event
Training procedures	Duration of event
Conformity-producing situations	Illumination of event
Questioning modes, styles and questioner	Complexity of event
experience	Race of criminal and of witness
Questioner status	
Photofit technique, mug-shots, sketches,	
verbal descriptions	

	Estimator variables
	Sex of criminal and of witness
	Age of criminal and of witness
	Personality
	Cognitive style
	Changes in appearance
	Description giving
	Non-verbal 'leakage'
	Artist's impressions
	Mental set

* After Wells, 1978

variable (or factor) in a specific case then the psychologist is incapacitated because, logically, there is no way he can estimate the particular effect of that particular factor on a particular witness at a particular time, nor its interaction with other important variables. Further, knowledge of, for example, a female witness's current memory ability on a specific test (which can be easily ascertained) neither predicts nor confirms her memory performance at some other time under some other circumstance with the full degree of accuracy needed in this context.

Thus the very most that a psychologist can do in such a case is offer general warnings about the unreliability of eye-witness evidence and the kinds of factors which contribute to this unreliability; he can do no more than this. This is a bitter pill for the over-enthusiastic researcher to swallow but it is the reality in this area of evidence. In answer to our second question then we must conclude that even where data are found to be reliable, if they are data of a certain type (i.e. estimator factors) then their use is severely limited.

3. HOW SHOULD PSYCHOLOGISTS NOW PROCEED TO MAXIMISE THEIR IMPACT IN SPECIFIC CASES?

Since 'estimator variable' research is of limited application, is it possible that more can be done with those factors labelled 'system variables'? Specifically, can 'system variable' research enable the psychologist to provide unequivocal estimates of inaccuracy in particular cases, and particular aspects of cases, without resorting to extrapolation from known general tendencies to unknown particular instances? Or can he at least point out where practices and procedures could be improved to reduce the possibility of error? The answer is yes. Inaccuracy can enter eye-witness evidence through the criminal justice procedures used to elicit evidence, and psychological techniques exist to detect the operation of these system variables. By concentrating on system variable research rather than attempting to substantiate repetitively the theoretically well motivated findings that man is a limited-capacity processor of information, and by default, supporting the dubious corollary that therefore eye-witness testimony and identification should never be admitted as evidence, psychologists would become more effective in, and accepted by, the legal profession. By this change in focus psychology could provide scientific evidence on criminal justice procedures which would allow some degree of objectivity into the court's evaluation of eye-witness testimony.

A change of focus however must not lead to a rejection of all that has gone before. Psychologists already have the insights to suggest where errors could be creeping into police methods and court procedures, and they have the methodological and statistical sophistication to investigate these potential areas of danger objectively and scientifically.

Let us take identification parades as one example from the system variables listed in Table 2.2. Psychologists could be usefully employed in the generation, conducting and evaluation of such techniques of evidence elicitation to the mutual benefit of suspects, police and courts. The legal profession has been having a bad press for the last few years over the fact that identifications have been made at parades which ultimately were shown to be in error. Such incorrect identification can result from a parade being 'unfair', 'biased' or 'suggestive', where these terms refer to the fact that one individual stands out from the rest in such a way that anyone, furnished with the witness's original verbal description, could pick him out, whether they were present at the crime or not. Psychological investigation can detect this at its inception and thus prevent poor case-building by police or a possible miscarriage of justice. This detection is essentially very simple, involving the dual notion of chance level and bias. Theoretically the chance level of the suspect being selected by a person who did not witness the crime is arrived at by dividing one by the number of parade members, including the suspect $(1/N)$. This theoretical value works only if there is no systematic bias in the parade composition. Such bias can be detected by presenting police parade photographs to non-involved persons and asking them, on the basis of the witness's verbal description, to pick out the suspect (perpetrator). If the subjects have not seen the criminal and the parade is properly constituted then the subjects should be merely guessing and thus should select the suspect at chance level only.

A variant of this method of estimating the presence of bias has been developed by Wells *et al.* (in press) who distinguish between the functional and nominal parade size. Functional size is calculated by dividing the total number of 'mock' witnesses by the number who choose the suspect. The closer this calculation approximates to 1, the smaller the functional size of the parade irrespective of its actual nominal size, and the greater the likelihood that bias is operating in the parade.

The former type of approach to estimation in identification parades has been used in America. For example Bob Buckhout (1976) presented to the jury, in *State of Florida* v. *Richard Campbell*, scientific evidence that the 'line-up', in which Campbell was identified, was biassed. He used the $1/N$ procedure and was able to show that the defendant was selected fifty-two per cent of the time by uninvolved college students whereas chance is an unbiased parade (of six members) would have had him selected only 16.7 per cent of the time. For whatever reason, Campbell was found 'not guilty'. Given that the other factors listed under system variables in Table 2.2 are equally amenable to test and estimation this suggests that there is a whole area of criminal justice awaiting the attention of serious and committed applied psychologists.

Fruitful reciprocity will only be achieved in this area of mutual interest if psychologists are willing to accept that their case for blanket rejection of eye-witness evidence is untenable, that they are required to appreciate clearly what an applied discipline involves in the way of assumptions about man, methods of investigation and relevance of experimentation, and that there is an urgent need for a focus change – from a focus on theory-support to one on problem-understanding. All that remains now is for our legal colleagues to tell us what problems they would like addressed.

REFERENCES

R. Buckhout, 'Expert testimony by psychologists', *Social Action and the Law*, Centre for Responsive Psychology, *3* (1976) 41–53.
J. Carlsmith, P. Ellsworth and E. Aronson, *Methods of Research in Social Psychology* (California: Addison-Wesley Publishing Comp. 1976).
B. Clifford, 'A critique of eyewitness research', in M. Gruneberg, P. Morris and R. Sykes (eds.), *Practical Aspects of Memory* (London: Academic Press 1978).
B. Clifford, 'Eyewitness testimony: Bridging a credibility gap', in D. Farrington, K. Hawkins, S. Lloyd-Bostock (eds.), *Psychology, Law and Legal Processes* (London: Macmillan 1979).
G. Wells, 'Applied eyewitness-testimony research: system variables and estimator variables', *Journal of Personality and Social Psychology*, *36* (1978) 1546–57.
G. Wells, M. Lieppe, M. Baumgardner, D. Simpson, J. Lingle, R. Petty, R. Bassett and T. Ostrom, 'Guidelines for assessing the fairness of a line-up', (submitted for publication).

3: Voice Identification by Man and Machine: a Review of Research

Ray Bull

Most criminal identifications are made using visual cues, but there are some instances when both visual and verbal information is available, and others when only verbal cues exist. In obscene telephone calls, for example, often the only possible method of identifying the speaker is by his voice. Similarly, in kidnap cases information concerning the kidnapper's voice is sometimes made available by him over the telephone. In such situations, when a suspect is in the hands of the police a voice-matching exercise may be undertaken. Here a witness may be asked whether the suspect's voice resembles the criminal's voice, or a machine may be employed in an attempt to answer these questions if a record (e.g. a tape) of the original criminal voice is available. In the Psychology Department of the North East London Polytechnic, Brian Clifford and I have recently begun a programme of research (funded by the Home Office) concerning the voice identification performance of human listeners in this kind of context.

The Devlin Committee, which reported to the Home Secretary in 1976 its findings in respect of the evidence of identification in criminal cases, stated in connection with person recognition that, 'as far as we can ascertain there has been no scientific research into this question' (p. 68). We have commented elsewhere (Bull and Clifford, 1976) that this committee did not avail itself of much of the psychological information which is available on the topic of person identification, by voice or otherwise. Although considerably more attention has been given to visual recognition, there has in fact been quite a lot of research conducted on voice recognition especially in connection with the spectrographic analysis of speech. This topic will be examined below. First, however, studies of voice recognition by man rather than by machine will be described.

VOICE RECOGNITION BY MAN

As early as 1937 psychologists had begun to examine the reliability of voice identification. McGehee (1937) was concerned with attempting to answer the questions: (i) what is the influence of time-interval upon memory for voices? (ii) what is the effect of increasing the number of voices heard in a series in which occurs a voice to be subsequently recognised? (iii) to what extent is a voice recognised as having been heard previously when disguised by a change in pitch? and (iv) are there sex differences in the recognition of voices? The experimental procedure involved groups of students listening to an adult reading aloud a paragraph of fifty-six words from behind a screen. Each of the readers was unacquainted with any of the listeners and none had a noticeable dialect or speech defect. In all there were thirty-one male and eighteen female readers, and a total of 740 listeners. All the groups of listeners were tested for voice recognition after time intervals ranging from one day to five months. At the recognition stage, each of five readers successively read aloud the initial passage and the listeners were required to note down which of the five readers they had heard previously. For listeners who initially heard only one reader McGehee observed 83, 83, 81 and 81 per cent accuracy for time intervals of one, two, three and seven days respectively. After an interval of two weeks performance dropped to 69 per cent and after a further week to 51 per cent. Intervals of three and five months led to accuracy scores of 35 and 13 per cent respectively. Thus, it was concluded that with the passage of time, 'there is a general trend towards a decrease in percentage of listeners who were able to correctly recognise a voice the second time it is heard' (p. 262).

During the initial part of the experiment some listeners heard not one voice but several, and it was found that the more voices were heard initially the more difficult was it to recognise subsequently any one of them (83 per cent accuracy for the case in which only one voice was heard initially, down to 50 per cent when more than three voices were heard initially). Accuracy was also affected by changes in pitch. Thus, if only one voice was heard initially, recognition on the next day was 83 per cent accurate only when the voice demonstrated its normal pitch on both occasions. If, however, on the second day the voice was disguised by a change in pitch then only 67 per cent of the listeners recognised it.

Concerning sex differences, McGehee found men to be better voice recognisers than women (84 per cent accurate vs. 59 per cent), but that male voices were no better recognised than were female voices (72 per cent vs. 71 per cent). Significant interactions were noted in that men were very good at recognising female voices (96 per cent) but were not so good with male voices (73 per cent), whereas women were better with male voices (72 per cent) than with female voices .(47 per cent).

There have been some attempts to identify which aspects of speech provide identification cues. Scherer (1974) played to listeners twenty-second speech samples of various adult male speakers. Each listener was required to rate each voice for such things as pitch, height and range, loudness, breathiness, creak, glottal tension and nasality, on a thirty-five-item voice quality attribute rating form. The listeners consisted of the speaker himself, three of his acquaintances, six experienced phoneticians who were deemed to be expert judges, and groups of adult females who were considered to be lay judges. Scherer's experiment resulted in several findings. Of greatest interest here may be the fact that neither the acquaintances nor the speakers themselves agreed with the expert and lay judges on ratings of the loudness, pitch or resonance of their friends' voices. Scherer points out that, 'The lack of strong correspondence between self and acquaintance ratings of voice quality and expert ratings raises the interesting question of the validity of self and acquaintance ratings of voice,' (p. 295). He believes that, 'It is possible that if one has been acquainted with a person for a long period of time and has heard that person's voice in many situations, the resulting wealth of experience interferes with the accuracy of the description of the voice' (p. 295).

In an early and rather limited study Pollack *et al.* (1954) played to seven listeners, for varying durations, the voices of men that the listeners knew. As might be expected, it was found that the larger the speech sample the more accurate were the identifications. However, this effect must have been due to the greater speech repertoire in the longer samples and not simply to the length of time the voice was heard, since repetition of short samples did not increase the number of correct identifications. Whispered speech, which contains little pitch inflection, and which is of similar pitch for various speakers, led to some correct identifications but far fewer than normal speech. Bricker and Pruzansky (1966) also examined the effect of the duration and content of speech samples upon identification of the speaker. For the voices of people who worked together they found 98 per cent correct identifications when spoken sentences were provided, 84 per cent for syllables and 56 per cent for vowel excerpts. When the accuracy scores were plotted either against the number of different phonemes (distinct sounds) contained in the speech sample or against its duration, the former was found to provide a better picture of the relationships than was the latter. Bricker and Pruzansky concluded that the improvement in identification with sample duration is due to an increased sample of the talker's repertoire being provided.

Murray and Cort (1971) also investigated the ability to identify speakers on the basis of the duration and repertoire of the speech sample. Twenty boys and girls aged eleven years from the same school class each provided speech samples which were to act as stimuli for the others. The samples consisted of a paragraph, a sentence or a sustained vowel. For the paragraph the children read aloud for twenty seconds, the sentence took five seconds to utter and the sustained vowel was obtained by asking each child to sustain the vowel 'a', as in the word 'farmer', for five seconds. One week after these recordings were made the children were divided into two groups. One group heard each of the recordings played once only and for each voice had to write down the name of the speaker, whereas for the other group each recording was played three times in succession before the next sample was played. A further seven days after these sessions the tests were repeated. No significant difference was observed between the correct identification scores of the listeners who had heard each sample only once and those who had heard each three times.

Since the identification scores for the group which had heard each sample only once were very high for the sentence and paragraph speech samples (the mean for the sentence being 95 per cent and that for the paragraph being a few per cent higher), repetition of the samples for the other group of listeners could not be expected to boost the scores due to a 'ceiling' effect. However, this argument does not apply to the sustained vowel speech samples which led to only 48 per cent accuracy scores for the non-repetition group. Here there was room for improvement but two further repetitions of these speech samples did not improve the identification score of the group which received them. In the second (follow-up) test the identification scores were very similar for each group except for the group which heard each speech sample once. Here the accuracy of performance based on the vowel speech sample dropped from 48 to 32 per cent. This follow-up test is not a test of delayed recall since during the two weeks of the experiment the children continued to interact in class. It merely serves as a replication of the first testing session, and it strengthens the conclusions of Murray and Cort that mere repetition of the same speech sample does not lead to any increase in identification accuracy scores whereas increasing the speech repertoire provided does so.

Murray and Cort conclude that the repertoire available in a speech sample of a sentence in length is sufficient for identification performance to reach an asymptote, and that for these children a fifteen-syllable sentence provided sufficient cues for voice identification. However, in this experiment the children had been together in the same class for at least several months. The conclusions which can be drawn for situations where recognition is required of a stranger who provided only one speech sample are tentative, but the adage of 'keep him talking' seems to have validity.

A further set of factors which must be taken into account in a consideration of voice identification arises from the fact that the voice, like the face, conveys information about the speaker. Kramer (1963) examined the judgments of personal characteristics and emotions based on speech. He provides a review of the studies which have investigated the existence of vocal stereotypes and it does seem that people reliably agree (sometimes with accuracy) upon such things as the personality, profession and physical appearance that they expect certain speakers to have. Thus, if such stereotypes exist they may introduce into the voice identification situation those factors encountered when examining the effects of stereotypes on visual identification (see Bull, 1979; Clifford and Bull, 1978). Kramer also cites a number of studies which suggest that an individual's emotional state can often be judged from his speech and it is important for any system of person identification based on voice that those aspects of speech which vary within an individual as a function of his mood be omitted from the recognition system.

VOICE IDENTIFICATION BY MACHINE

Though the police and judicial procedures for the recognition of persons by the way they speak are not as firmly laid down as they are for visual identification, the topic of identification by voice is one which has received quite a lot of attention from those wishing to develop electrical hardware to this end. Some success has been claimed for identification by spectrographic analysis and given the possibility that the number of meaningful ways in which voices may differ may be less than the number of ways in which faces differ then such advances are not surprising. Whereas at the moment mechanised person recognition using visual cues is still in its infancy, recognition by voice appears to have advanced a little further and may act as a guide for the development of visual systems and for their possible acceptance in legal settings.

Recognition by spectrographic voice analysis is based upon an electronic scan of a speech sample which produces a visible amplitude/frequency/time display. This spectrogram can then be compared with other spectrograms to see if a match can be made. This matching is usually done not by the spectrographic machinery but by means of visual comparison of the spectrograms by a human, though mechanised systems of matching are being developed. The validity of this technique as a means of identification rests on the assumption that the sound patterns produced in speech are unique to the individual and that the spectrogram accurately and sufficiently displays this uniqueness. Further, a speaker recognition system should focus on those speech characteristics which cannot be modified or disguised by the speaker and which do not vary with health or mood.

Kersta (1962) was one of the first advocates of spectrographic voice analysis, claiming that voiceprint identification is closely analogous to fingerprint identification and that it is a more reliable method than handwriting comparisons. Fingerprint identification is widely accepted in the judicial setting, but fingerprints are far less prone than are voiceprints to the within-individual variations to which Wolff (1972) draws attention. In 1969 the Technical Committee on Speech Communication of the Acoustical Society of America asked some of its members to examine scientifically speaker identification by speech spectrograms. Their report concluded that the differences between identification by voice spectrograms and identification by fingerprints seemed to exceed the similarities and it was stated that, 'we doubt that the reliability of voice identification can ever match that of fingerprint identification' (Bolt *et al.*, 1969, p. 600). Hall (1974), compares the reliability of fingerprints and voiceprints and concludes that, 'it is not valid to compare fingerprints with voiceprints' (p. 157).

Kersta formulated the theory of invariant speech which holds that the spectral patterns of the same words spoken by two different people are more dissimilar than two such patterns resulting from the same person. He provided evidence that, at least to some extent, this theory is supportable. Trained spectrogram examiners were able, with minimal error, to select from a small set of spectrograms those two which were most alike, knowing that a match existed somewhere in the set.

Kersta's early experiments were criticised on the grounds that the number of spectrograms provided to the examiners for their search for a match was small and that the examiners were told that a match did exist. In a later experiment Kersta enlarged the samples and he also developed an automated system of voice identification (see Hennessy and Romig, 1971). This automated system counted the amplitude levels portrayed by the contour spectrogram at ten different locations on the spectrogram and a numerical code was devised for each voice sample. Fairly low error rates in identification were produced by this system if it was provided with speech samples five words in length or longer. These errors were due to (i) the same word from the same speaker not always giving rise to the same code, and (ii) the same code resulting from two different people uttering the same word. For shorter speech samples the number of mismatches increased and this is in line with the studies cited earlier which suggested that a speech sample of about a sentence in length is the minimum required for attempts at identification. Recognition based on samples of isolated words is not so good and, as Young and Campbell (1967) have shown, the lexical context of words is an important factor in spectrographic voice analysis. These researchers found that the identification error rate was far greater when the trained spectrogram examiners were provided with the spectrograms of the same words uttered in different sentences than when the same words were uttered individually and not in the context of a sentence.

One of the questions that has only infrequently been asked of spectrographic voice identification is whether it is any better than simple identification by the human ear. It would seem rather a waste of time and money if this were not the case. Stevens *et al.* (1968) found error rates of over 20 per cent for speaker identification employing spectrograms, but the persons who matched the spectrograms in this study were not as extensively trained in the art as Kersta claims they should be. (It was noted that as the study proceeded the examiners' efficiency increased). These examiners were required both to identify speakers by visually comparing spectrograms and also to identify speakers by simply listening to the tape recordings on which the spectrograms were made. It was found that the identification performance accuracy from aural comparisons was far higher than that resulting from the visual comparison of spectrograms (94 vs. 79 per cent at the end of the study), and that the time taken to arrive at the identifications was less for the aural input. Overall, not only did the aural tests lead to better performance at the beginning of the study, they also were the ones which derived the greatest improvement with practice. Further, for the aural information the length of utterance required for identification was shorter than that required by the spectrographic comparisons. Stevens concluded that, 'authentication of voices is much poorer on a visual basis than on an aural basis' (p. 1607). This suggests that spectrographic voice analysis may certainly be no better than comparing the same voices by ear. Hecker (1971) stated that, 'whether future visual tests will provide lower error scores than future aural tests is debatable. . . . The question about the perceptual bases of speaker recognition and their acoustical correlates remains largely unsolved' (p. 73).

Many people have been sceptical about the claims made by the proponents of the accuracy of spectrographic voice identification and until a few years ago evidence based on such procedures was ascribed little status. However, as Cutler *et al.* (1972) reported, a study by Tosi does lend some support to Kersta's view. Not only were Tosi's results similar to those of Kersta for the matching-in-sample test, they also tested the accuracy and reliability of experiments employing a more realistic identification format. Cutler *et al.* point out that the original matching-in-sample tests are not true 'identification' tests but involve simple 'similarity' judgements. In matching-in-sample tests all the examiner is required to do is find the sample in the set which best matches the spectrograph in hand, whereas in identification the examiner has to be sure that two spectrographs are not only somewhat similar but are similar enough to have definitely come from the same speaker even when he has no prior knowledge of whether or not a true match exists in the sample provided.

Tosi *et al.* (1972) employed both matching-in-sample and realistic identification tests. The speech samples contained fewer than ten words. A number of samples were obtained from each speaker and for some speakers a considerable time elapsed between the providing of the speech samples. Further, not all samples included the vocalisation of identical sentences, though the sentences did have some words in common. Realism was added to the study by recording the voices in three different ways. These were either directly into a tape recorder in a quiet setting, or via a telephone in a quiet or noisy situation. A speaker population of 250 students was employed, selected so as to have no speech defects nor strong regional dialects. Each of the twenty-nine examiners was given considerable training in the interpretation and matching of speech spectrograms.

Tosi *et al.* found that the matching-in-sample tests resulted in over 95 per cent accuracy and an average of 83 per cent accuracy was obtained for the trials wherein the examiner was not told whether a true match existed in the sample or not. The error rate of 17 per cent combines an 11 per cent false elimination rate (i.e. a match was in fact present but the examiner failed to make it) with a 6 per cent false identification (i.e. a match was present but the examiner made the wrong one, or a match was not in reality present but the examiner made one). Stevens *et al.* (1968) also found that matching-in-sample tests lead to much higher accuracy than 'open' tests.

Prior to the appearance of these results a number of courts in the USA had held spectrographic voice identification evidence to be inadmissible because it was believed that the technique's reliability had not been sufficiently demonstrated. Subsequent to the appearance of Tosi's results the technique was deemed admissible by several courts but not without some discussion of the weaknesses of Tosi's study. Though Tosi *et al.* had employed a larger sample of speakers than had previous investigations, doubts were raised concerning whether this data contained as much inter-speaker and intra-speaker variability as any other possible group of speakers. It was believed that although the study appeared to be methodologically sound it just did not go far enough. Further, since the matching of the spectrograms was performed by eye it was held to be a purely subjective comparison which involved less scientific quantification than the polygraphic 'lie-detector' tests. The admissibility of the latter is still being debated (see Lykken, 1974), and there are a number of parallels between the judicial status of these two techniques.

Further problems for spectrographic voice analysis are the facts that no two examples of phonetically identical utterances from the same speaker are ever exactly alike and that different speakers can produce very similar spectrograms (Ladgefoged and Vanderslice, 1967). Thus any match between two voice spectrograms can never be exact but can only involve a probability of having come from the same speaker and thus error is introduced. The question of probability is one which has always been a problem in legal settings, but all evidence contains a degree of probability or error. A person's face seen twice never provides the same visual input to the observer. No two fingerprints are ever the same. Even your house has changed shape since you last saw it. Over and above these changes in the stimuli being perceived are the changes in physical viewing position of the observer, his mood and expectancies. The important question is whether the error inherent in any recognition technique is acceptable or not. A further criticism of Tosi's study was that none of his spectrograms came from subjects under psychological stress. Such stress may well be present in a criminal investigation and Cutler *et al.* suggest that it may have a significant effect upon speech production. Further, Hargreaves and Starkweather (1963) found that more identification errors were made when an individual's to-be-compared utterances were recorded on different days.

Edwards (1973) points out that the earlier judicial situations in which voiceprint evidence was admitted were those involving (i) the determination of 'probable cause', – a point in criminal proceedings where 'incompetent' evidence can traditionally be used (e.g. the issuing of an arrest warrant) or (ii) the use of voiceprint information in a secondary role in the process of proof. Greene (1975) draws attention to the fact that in Tosi's study the greatest type of error involved the spectrogram examiners failing to make a match when in fact one existed. He takes this to mean that the use of spetrograms will more often result in the guilty going free than in an innocent person being accused, and he points out that, 'this technique has resulted in the elimination of far more criminal suspects than have been positively identified'. He concludes that,

Criticisms of the Tosi study are grounded largely upon misunderstandings about the sophistication and knowledgeability with which juries arrive at verdicts, the difference between the admissibility of evidence and the weight to be given evidence by factfinders in our legal system, the similarities and differences between voiceprint identification and other forensic disciplines such as fingerprint and handwriting identification, and the proper application of legal standards to the admissibility of scientific evidence. Thus it is not surprising that the overwhelming number of jurists at both trial and appellate level who have considered the issue have concluded that voiceprint identification has reached the standard of scientific acceptance and reliability necessary for its admissibility into evidence (p. 200).

Block (1975) provides interesting anecdotal accounts of many legal trials in which the admissibility of voiceprint evidence played a part and in which scientists from various backgrounds argued either for or against its validity. Whether such evidence was finally admitted was a function of many factors including the nature of any other evidence, the type of crime, the expert witnesses and the US state in which the court was located. At the present time such evidence is still not widely accepted and the current status was well summed up by one Judge McGuire who concluded that, 'the voiceprint process requires substantial additional research before it is accepted by the scientific community, let alone admissible by the legal community' (Block, 1975, p. 67).

To sum up, spectrographic voice analysis, just like any other sort of evidence, can never conclusively prove guilt. However, it can be used sometimes to establish a high likelihood of guilt. Such an act requires not merely that two spectrograms (the perpetrator's and the suspect's) be deemed to have come from the same person when only these (or a few more others) are compared by an expert. What needs to be established is that one, or preferably more than one, expert can reliably pick out, from a large number (say in excess of thirty) of spectrograms from different but similarly spoken people, the one which best matches the sample provided by the perpetrator.

At present it seems that not all courts agree on the admissibility of spectrographic voice identification evidence. Some deem it inadmissible whereas others view its shortcomings as insufficient to warrant ignoring it. Most seem to accept it in a way similar to their acceptance of visual identification evidence in that it is left to the court to note the possible weaknesses and unresolved questions that surround this technique. Both spetrographic voice analysis and polygraphic lie-detection can be used not only by the prosecution but also by the defence. The use of these techniques to exclude persons from suspicion receives less criticism than does their use positively to identify an individual. It is rather rare for criminal guilt to be assigned solely on the basis of such techniques and at the moment they are employed mostly during the investigation stage of enquiries, proof of guilt requiring other sorts of evidence.

Mechanised speech recognisers have had some success with a limited number of inputs from a small group of persons. If, for example, it was required that a door should open in the presence of a few specified persons then modern automated speech recognition systems are available which will respond to certain specified words spoken by these people if they have on previous occasions provided the machine with similar inputs for it to use in its matching task. It will respond to these people if they say the specified words in their usual manner. Martin (1974) presents evidence that in such situations 99 per cent accuracy of response can be achieved but he is quick to point out that this kind of situation is far removed from one wherein a machine can respond to (or match) any words spoken by any person. In 1974 he stated that 'no universal systems have been developed up to now that can perform for most users with an accuracy sufficient to be useful' (p. 121). Thus, though voice recognition can be achieved by some machines for a very restricted sample, if a large sample of different voices were presented then today's machines would most certainly be confused by them. Consequently, given the present level of development of voice recognition (or matching) machines there is little evidence that they could be of much use in person identification, especially since recognition is a different task from identification. However, since a substantial amount of research is taking place on this topic there may be some major developments in the next ten years. Any such developments will need to realise that a human identifies speech not only by the acoustic information upon which today's machines rely but also by the grammatical and contextual cues that are available. Denes (1974) believes that 'the [human] listener relies on contextual cues for satisfactory perception. Most automatic recognition devices of the past utilise acoustic cues only and they are therefore at a strong disadvantage compared to the human listener' (p. 204).

One further problem facing the acceptance of identification by voice is the possibility that, as Bolt *et al.* (1969) noted, voices can be mimicked. Many professional entertainers are able to speak in a way which to our ears sounds very similar to the speech of the person they are impersonating and it should be remembered that it has not been shown that the human ear is any less sensitive than a spectrograph. It is not unreasonable to suppose that an innocent individual could be wrongly convicted or 'framed' by his voice being mimicked. Hollein and McGlone (1976) report details of an experiment which examined the sensitivity of the voiceprint method to the effects of speakers purposely disguising their voices. Each of twenty-five speakers read aloud a passage first in their normal voice and then they were instructed to do the same again, this time 'disguising their voices in any way they chose except by whispering or using a foreign dialect' (p. 41). Thus two speech samples similar in lexical content were provided by each speaker. The spectrogram examiners were 'familiar with the voiceprint method of speaker identification' (p. 41). Each examiner was required to match in turn each of the twenty-five exemplars with one of the 'normal voice' spectrograms. It was observed that, 'even skilled auditors such as these were unable to match correctly the disguised speech to the reference samples as much as 25 per cent of the time' (p. 42), and that,

> many of the subjects presented configurations for the disguise condition in which so many features were varied (relative to their normal production) that the two passages did not bear as much resemblance to each other as they did to productions by other subjects. Thus, except for the very small percentage of talkers who were relatively unsuccessful in disguising their voices (even they were misidentified nearly one-half of the time), these groups were able to disguise their voices, in such manners, that their identification by the voiceprint technique became little more than a matter of chance (p. 42).

Hecker (1971) concluded his literature survey by pointing out that, 'in speculating on possible reasons for the superiority of listeners over machines in recognising speakers, it is well to remember that even the most naive listener has lived in a speech environment for a considerably longer period of time than any machine. The experience he has thus acquired cannot be readily defined or analogised' (p. 97).

Thus, to conclude, there is evidence that the performance of electro-mechanical spectrographic voice identification systems is no more accurate than that of human listeners. This being the case it is important at the moment that courts, and especially jurors, are not led to believe that apparently sophisticated electrical hardware and apparent experts are infallible. In some cases both human listener and machine voice identification could be employed but this would not necessarily improve performance. The conducting of research on the topic of person identification poses a problem in this context in that if the research reduces bias, error and so on, then the jury may be led to believe that, with improved techniques, identification evidence is always infallible. This latter, in fact, is most unlikely to be the case.

REFERENCES

E. Block, *Voiceprinting* (New York: McKay, 1975).

R. Bolt, F. Cooper, E. David, P. Denes, J. Pickett and K. Stevens, 'Speaker identification by speech spectrograms: A scientist's view of its reliability for legal purposes', *Journal of the Acoustical Soceity of America*, *47* (1969) 597–612.

P. Bricker and S. Pruzansky, 'Effects of stimulus content and duration on talker identification', *Journal of the Acoustical Society of America*, *40* (1966) 1441–9.

R. Bull, 'The influence of stereotypes on person identification', in D. P. Farrington, K. Hawkins and S. M. Lloyd-Bostock (eds.), *Psychology, Law and Legal Processes* (London: Macmillan, 1979).

R. Bull and B. Clifford, 'Identification: the Devlin Report', *New Scientist*, *70* (1976) 307–8.

B. Clifford and R. Bull, *The Psychology of Person Identification* (London: Routledge and Kegan Paul, 1978).

P. Cutler, C.Thigpen, T. Young and E. Mueller, 'The evidentiary value of spectrographic voice identification', *Journal of Criminal Law, Criminology and Police Science*, *63* (1972) 343–55.

P. Denes, 'Speech recognition: old and new ideas', in D. Reddy (ed.), *Speech Recognition* (New York and London: Academic Press, 1974).

Devlin Report, *Report to the Secretary of State for the Home Department of the Departmental Committee on Evidence of Identification in Criminal Cases* (London: HMSO, 1976).

J. Edwards, 'The status of voiceprints as admissible evidence', *Syracuse Law Review*, *24* (1973) 1261–78.

H. Greene, 'Voiceprint identification: the case in favour of admissibility', *American Criminal Law Review*, *13* (1975) 171–200.

M. Hall, 'The current status of speaker identification by use of speech spectrograms', *Canadian Journal of Forensic Science*, *7* (1974) 152–76.

W. Hargreaves and J. Starkweather, 'Recognition of speaker identity', *Language and Speech*, *6* (1963) 63–7.

M. Hecker, 'Speaker recognition', *American Speech and Hearing Association monograph no. 16* (1971).

J. Hennessy and C. Romig, 'A review of the experiments involving voiceprint identification', *Journal of Forensic Science, 16* (1971) 183–98.

H. Hollein and R. McGlone, 'An evaluation of the voiceprint technique of speaker identification', Proceedings of the *Garnahan Crime Countermeasures Conference* (1976) 39–45.

L. Kersta, 'Voiceprint identification', *Nature, 196* (1962) 1253–7.

E. Kramer, 'Judgement of personal characteristics and emotions from nonverbal properties of speech', *Psychological Bulletin, 6* (1963) 408–20.

P. Ladgefoged and R. Vanderslice, 'The voiceprint mystique', *Working Papers in Phonetics, 7* (1967) University of California.

D. Lykken, 'Psychology and the lie detector industry', *American Psychologist, 29* (1974) 725–39.

F. McGehee, 'The reliability of the identification of the human voice', *Journal of General Psychology, 17* (1937) 249–71.

T. Martin, 'Application of limited vocabulary recognition systems', in D. Reddy (ed.), *Speech Recognition* (New York and London: Academic Press, 1974).

T. Murray and S. Cort, 'Aural identification of children's voices', *Journal of Auditory Research, 11* (1971) 260–2.

I. Pollack, J. Pickett and W. Sumby, 'On the identification of speakers by voice', *Journal of the Acoustical Society of America, 26* (1954) 403–6.

K. Scherer, 'Voice quality analysis of American and German speakers', *Journal of Psycholinguistic Research, 3* (1974) 281–98.

K. Stevens, C. Williams, J. Carbonnel and B. Woods, 'Speaker authentication and identification: A Comparison of spectrographic and auditory presentation of speech material', *Journal of the Acoustical Society of America, 44* (1968). 1596–1607.

O. Tosi, W. Oyer, C. Lashbrook, J. Pedrey and E. Nash, 'Experiment on voice identification', *Journal of the Acoustical Society of America, 51* (1972) 2030–43.

J. Wolff, 'Efficient acoustic parameters for speaker recognition', *Journal of the Acoustical Society of America, 51* (1972) 2044–56.

M. Young and R. Campbell, 'Effects of content on talker identification', *Journal of the Acoustical Society of America, 42* (1967) 1250–4.

PART II

INTERROGATION AND CONFESSION

4: Police Interrogation and Confessions

Marquita Inman

Although many Continental jurists regard a confession of criminal guilt as an inherently unreliable form of evidence, courts and juries in England generally consider such statements to have high probative value. Although mediaeval judicial procedures designed to extract confessions from accused persons have long been discarded, special weight is still attached to such evidence, rendering it admissible on the basis of presumed reliability, notwithstanding its hearsay quality. Conviction for even the most serious offences can be based upon a totally uncorroborated confession.

Following an outline of the procedural significance of interrogation, this chapter seeks to demonstrate the complexity of confessions as social and psychological phenomena, and hence to question certain *a priori* assumptions reflected in current legal rules and debates on reform of this area of the law.[1]

THE PROCEDURAL SIGNIFICANCE OF INTERROGATION

The process of police interrogation forms an integral part of the framework of criminal procedure. The outcome of such interrogation will affect the destiny of an accused person at each subsequent stage in the proceedings. Any confession made will be difficult to retract, and the perceived futility of subsequent assertions of innocence may lead to strong or overwhelming pressures to plead guilty, emanating not only from the police and legal advisers, but also from the accused's family and friends

(Baldwin and Bottomley, 1978; Bottoms and McClean, 1976; Brandon and Davies, 1973; Heberling, 1978).

It has been estimated that confessions result from seven out of ten interrogations (see e.g. Deeley, 1971, p. 139; note also the empirical findings of Zander, 1979), and that only four per cent of persons charged with an indictable offence are in fact given a jury trial (Baldwin and McConville, 1978). The confessions and guilty pleas made by the overwhelming majority of accused persons expedite criminal process in a way claimed to be indispensable to a tolerable level of efficiency in crime control. Such claims are seldom accompanied by a definition of the term 'efficiency', and the danger of inefficiency arising from convictions based upon confessions by the innocent is seldom expressly recognised.

The utility of confessions, especially if followed by guilty pleas, cannot be denied. Confessions can result in appreciable savings in police man-hours at the investigatory stage, and a guilty plea entered at the trial generally ensures that occurrences during the pre-trial stages will not be called into question in a judicial setting. This compounds difficulties attributable to the low visibility of the largely unregulated mechanisms of interrogation, treatment of suspects, bail bargaining and plea bargaining, which render covert justice the rule and contested trials the exception (Baldwin and Bottomley, 1978). Whilst this does not necessarily lead to injustice, strong pressures to make crucial decisions and statements during interrogation may create risks of wrongful conviction (Dell, 1978; Justice, 1970, Royal Commission on the Police, 1962, para. 369), and even where overt pressures are absent, the perceived power differential between the police and the individuals with whom they deal, may introduce implicit elements of threat, bargaining and coercion (Morris, 1978; Radzinowicz and King, 1979). The total number of wrongful convictions attributable to such causes is impossible to quantify, but it may be noted that confessions and statements made by accused persons ranked second only to mistaken identification as a cause of wrongful conviction amongst cases referred to the Court of Appeal by the Home Secretary, or in respect of which free pardons were granted between 1950 and 1970 (Brandon and Davies, 1973).

In the atypical cases where a confessor is tried and enters a plea of 'not guilty', his confession is *prima facie* admissible in evidence. The uniquely damaging effect of a revealed confession at trial can seldom be offset by factors such as the weakness or contradictory nature of other evidence in the case.[2] The defence must therefore seek to invoke legal rules to prevent the prosecution from adducing evidence of the confession. In cases tried on indictment, the arguments are presented at a *voire dire* in the absence of the jury.

There are only three possible grounds upon which a confession might be excluded. Exclusion on the first two grounds is at the discretion of the judge, in cases where non-compliance with the Judges' Rules (Home Office, 1978a) can be established, or where the judge is satisfied that the prejudicial effect of the confession outweighs its probative value. The admissibility of a confession is seldom affected in practice by breaches of the Judges' Rules,[3] notwithstanding the common legal assumption that the risk of false confessions is diminished or even eliminated by adherence to procedural safeguards of the type embodied in the Rules (e.g. Fisher, 1977, para. 12.130). Accused persons with a record may in any event be deterred from alleging breaches of the Rules since by doing so they risk the disclosure of their past convictions for the purpose of impeaching their credit. The few reported instances of exclusion on the ground of insufficient probative value are cases where the confessor's mental condition was severely abnormal or subnormal.[4] However, precise guidelines regarding the full scope and exercise of this exclusionary discretion have not been promulgated.

The third ground of exclusion leads to automatic, as opposed to discretionary rejection of a confession, in cases where it can be shown to be 'involuntary', in that is was obtained 'by fear of prejudice or hope of advantage, exercised or held out by a person in authority, or by oppression'.[5]

The last three words of this formula were omitted from the rule in its original form, and the precise meaning of 'oppression' awaits definitive judicial interpretation. It is clear, however, that the legal notion of voluntariness does not import the usual connotation of conscious volition or free will, since the rule stresses a narrow range of objective and externalised criteria. This reflects a pervasive rationalist legal assumption that the supposed capacity of individuals to exercise free will merely necessitates protection against forms of overt force or coercion.

Courts and law reform bodies in England, the Commonwealth and the United States have articulated a variety of rationales of the voluntariness principle. The most significant of these for present purposes is the assertion that the rule ensures that only reliable confessions will be adduced in evidence.[6] However, the restricted scope of the legal test precludes consideration of many factors which may affect confession reliability, not least psychological factors. Moreover, the Criminal Law Revision Committee (1972) has advocated an admissibility test, which would direct enquiry at whether alleged threats or inducements would be likely to render unreliable not the actual confession of the accused, but any (hypothetical) confession which someone in that situation *might* have made. The objective character of the suggested test is emphasised by the Committee's observation that when determining admissibility: '. . . the *judge* should imagine that *he* was present at the interrogation and heard the threat or inducement' (para. 65; italics supplied).

Although modern police interrogation practice is based in the main upon subtle psychological techniques rather than physical or overt coercion, the implications of the methods employed have yet to be fully acknowledged by courts, commentators and reform bodies. The legal determination of confession reliability fails to recognise the accused's subjective experience as a factor significant in its own right, whilst the police may be largely unaware that methods designed to elicit compliance by guilty suspects may also operate unselectively upon the innocent. Debates on reform have been characterised by vague allusions to 'law and order' and 'civil liberty', whilst systematic delineation and analysis of some of the most crucial issues has yet to be undertaken.

CONFESSIONS AS SOCIAL AND PSYCHOLOGICAL PHENOMENA

THE MENTAL STATE OF THE SUSPECT

In an early psychological approach to criminal confessions, Münsterberg (1909) criticised what he described as the 'crudest standards of easy-going psychology' applied in legal proceedings, which considers individual mental life as typical and unaltered as long as a man is neither insane nor intoxicated. Münsterberg and others (e.g. Bem, 1966 and 1967; Lifton, 1961) have observed that innocent persons may confess to crimes and may even come to believe the truth of their utterances. Experience of political and wartime interrogations and subsequent experiments further support the conclusion that under appropriate conditions most persons can be made to act in ways quite alien to their normal behaviour (see e.g. Schein, 1956; Sterling, 1965; Watson, 1978). However, English courts have yet to recognise that the line between mental normality and abnormality is not clear cut, so that the susceptibility to confess falsely in the absence of overt pressures or conscious ulterior motive is not confined to pathologically abnormal or subnormal suspects. Moreover, conditions of interrogation, the mode of questioning and attendant pressures and circumstances can lead to states of *temporary* abnormality, such as hysteria, in otherwise normal persons. Furthermore, as Brown (1963) observes, inconsistent or unusual behaviour is not always attributable to changes in the *external* environment, but rather to the changed way in which a person *perceives* his environment and himself.

In some cases, false confessions may result from pathological tendencies towards self-accusation (Burtt, 1931; Healy, 1969; Larson, 1932; Münsterberg, 1909). But even psychologically normal persons might be affected by a state of 'guilt anxiety' during interrogation. Psychoanalysts have postulated the existence of unconscious feelings of unfocussed guilt which, together with unconscious inner rebellion, lack of love and the need for punishment, have been hypostatised as key factors motivating the 'compulsion to confess' identified by Reik (1959), Lifton (1961) and others. This compulsion may be reinforced by adherence to certain religious doctrines, notably Roman Catholicism (Eliasberg, 1946; Hepworth and Turner, 1974), and may possibly precipitate false confessions if external criminal accusations become merged with subjective feelings of guilt or sinfulness during a guilt-orientated interrogation. On a theoretical level, Freudian analysis has been applied to criminal confessions (e.g. Lowen, 1974) and psychoanalytic theories from the basis of exploitive interrogatory techniques advocated in some police interrogation manuals (e.g. Royal and Schutt, 1976).

Whether or not psychoanalytic interpretations are accepted, it is apparent that feelings of guilt and anxiety may contribute to the spontaneous loquacity of many suspects even if informed of their rights (Leigh, 1978). Deeley (1971) cites the view of a Chief Superintendent at New Scotland Yard which identifies tendencies averred to in the psychological literature:

. . . we are all anxious to talk to somebody about our guilt feelings it's just that most of us never find the right vehicle. And that vehicle can be the psychiatrist or the policeman. It happens from the smallest crime to the biggest – 'everything will be alright if you tell me the truth' . . . he feels at the moment 'that these people are going to like me a little more if I say something they want to hear', (p. 159).

And as another officer observes 'get them to make the first admission, no matter how small: "Yes, I drink a lot." You've immediately got them going' (p. 159).

Whilst psychological factors may vitiate the voluntariness and reliability of a confession made by mentally normal persons, they are still largely overlooked by English rules of evidence and procedure. A recent modification of the guidelines attached to the Judges' Rules reflects continued application of 'easy-going psychology' by confining the requirement of independent observers to interrogations of mentally handicapped suspects (Home Office, 1978(a), Appendix B, para. 4A). This followed a debate in Parliament on a proposed Bill, the terms of which were also confined to securing increased protection for the mentally *abnormal* during police questioning.[7] Moreover, in *R. v. Isequilla*, the Court of Appeal rejected the argument that a confession made by a suspect in a state of temporary hysteria should be ruled involuntary and inadmissible. Lord Widgery C. J. further opined that in what he described as *extreme* cases of mental defect, a confession *might* be excluded, but only as a matter of discretion on the ground of insufficient probative value.[8]

PHYSIOLOGICAL EFFECTS OF INTERROGATION

In some cases, interrogation or its connected circumstances, such as custody, may cause brain syndromes attributable to deleterious changes in temperature, oxygen and carbohydrate levels, fatigue, sleep deprivation, hunger, isolation and sensory deprivation. Hinkle (1961) observes that such factors may induce memory defects, compensatory tendencies to confabulate and increased suggestibility. Anxiety caused by a perceived threat might also disorganise brain function, leading to similar results. The threat need not be explicit. Indeed, there is some evidence that *vague* threats or mere uncertainty can create a much greater degree of fear and psychological discomfort than explicit threats (Watson, 1978).

Notwithstanding psychological evidence, the courts discount such effects in determining confession admissibility. In *R*. v. *Isequilla*, Lord Widgery C. J. declared that '. . . such considerations as fatigue, lack of sleep or emotional strain cannot be efficacious to deprive a confession of its quality of voluntariness . . .'.[9] In *R*. v. *Elliot*[10] the confession of an accused who had only slept for two out of the thirty-six hours preceding the statement was held to be admissible, even though he had also been denied access to a solicitor in contravention of the Judges' Rules. Furthermore, in *R*. v. *Houghton and Franciosy*[11] the isolation of a suspect in a small police cell for five days during a summer heatwave was held not to affect the voluntariness of his ensuing confession. Yet, Hinkle (1961) observes that isolation *per se* is capable of producing effects similar to those occurring when a person is beaten or starved.

Of course, most police interrogations and their attendant circumstances will be unlikely to produce such severe physiological effects, and account must always be taken of variations in personality, attitudes and perception of the situation. However, some policemen are evidently prepared to undertake lengthy and intensive questioning in order to achieve the desired goals of interrogation by deliberately and gradually wearing down suspects in order to render them pliable (Deeley, 1971; Firth, 1975). The practice of midnight or week-end arrests for the purpose of 'softening up' suspects during incommunicado detention has been referred to in the parliamentary debates on the Confait case,[12] and elsewhere (Deeley, 1971). Furthermore, in evidence submitted to the Royal Commission on Criminal Procedure, the Metropolitan Police Commissioner, Sir David McNee, has urged that legal power should be given to the police to detain suspects for up to seventy-two hours before charge, and longer with magisterial authorisation (McNee, 1978). This recommendation has been fully supported by the Police Federation in its own evidence to the Commission.

In the light of such practices and recommendations, it is regrettable that English courts continue to reject the approach to confession admissibility adopted in some Australasian decisions. These cases have declared that the test of legal voluntariness must involve an investigation into all aspects of the motivation of the accused, to determine whether his judgement was clouded at the time he confessed, even in the absence of overt coercion or promises.[13]

INTERROGATION TECHNIQUES AND SOCIAL PSYCHOLOGICAL
THEORY

The secrecy which characterises police interrogation precludes
positive assertions regarding the precise frequency of specific
patterns of interviewing. However, conversations with policemen
and published advice on interrogation (e.g. Inbau and Reid, 1967:
Royal and Schutt, 1976; Wicks, 1974)[14] reveal a fairly standardised
repertoire of techniques. Some of these techniques are reminiscent
of practices developed by wartime and political interrogators,[15] and
the fact that in most cases they have doubtless been moulded by long
experience rather than by systematic application of research
evidence does not detract from their psychological sophistication.

The psychological advantage of interrogation away from familiar
and supportive surroundings is universally emphasised, (e.g. by
Crowley, 1973; Deeley, 1971; Firth, 1975; Watson, 1978) and in
practice many suspects who mistakenly believe that they are not
free to leave the police station are seldom disabused of that
impression. Attention is also often devoted to ecological detail, and
stark interview rooms which eliminate tension-relieving distraction
and comfort have, in some cases, been incorporated into the
architectural design of police stations. Such surroundings certainly
fail to offset the inherent pressures of interrogation, although the
extent to which they might increase suggestibility as a result of
sensory deprivation is debatable (see Kubzansky, 1961; Watson,
1978).

Special arrangements of furniture, close proximity of the interrogator to the suspect, and emphasis on inequalities in status,
authority, power, competence, knowledge and ability to take the
initiative are all recommended ingredients of effective interrogatory
strategy. Much published advice on interrogation recognises that
express threats or open hostility may be counter-productive,
resulting in, or increasing recalcitrance and reluctance to co-
operate with the interrogator (e.g. Goodsall, 1974; Inbau and Reid,
1967). Advice often stresses that, instead, rapport should be
established with a suspect by such devices as feigned sympathy and
concern for his welfare (note Home Office, 1978b, para. 12). Such
manipulation of the interrogation environment and of the social
psychological situation, together with bluff or deception regarding
the state of the evidence – a technique regarded as legitimate by
many policemen (Royal Commission on Police Powers and

Procedure, 1929 pp. 100–3) – can adversely affect innocent as well as guilty suspects.

Whilst many policemen recognise the effectiveness of such techniques, it is probably fair to say that relatively little thought has been devoted to the theoretical basis of their superiority over overt coercion. Some psychological explanations of these or analogous effects have, however, been attempted. Many pressures on suspects undergoing police interrogation are likely to far exceed those exerted on subjects in the experiments upon which present social psychological theories and notions are based. For this and other reasons, extrapolation from some of this research must be circumspect, and explanations tentative. However, the psychological literature does offer some suggestive data and theory which might explain such phenomena as the power of relatively subtle interrogation techniques, and suspects' expressions of belief in their false confessions.

At one level of interpretation, analogies have been suggested between the progressive mental deterioration observed in Pavlovian conditioned reflex experiments and the psychological effects of a guilt-orientated interrogation (Meerloo, 1954; Sargant, 1957). The adequacy of so simplistic a model in explaining the complex behaviour patterns produced by interrogation has been seriously disputed by other theorists (e.g. Bauer, 1957; Brown, 1963; Farber *et al.*, 1957). Some social psychologists have placed emphasis upon aspects of rôle-playing, rôle definition and self-image projection which are often present in a conventionally structured interrogation. Such ploys as avoiding severity at the start of interrogation, employing euphemistic descriptions of the crime, and creating an illusion of empathy are viewed not merely as ways of deflecting recalcitrance, but as offering a supposedly guilty suspect a rôle in which his confession to a criminal act is compatible with the presentation of a relatively favourable self-image, which is seen as a pre-requisite to elicitation of a confession (Biderman, 1960; Danziger, 1976; Zimbardo *et al.*, 1977).

Social psychological literature regarding the relative persuasiveness of different types of communicator indicates that displays of sympathy or liking and apparent interest in the welfare of subjects may increase their vulnerability to persuasion. Perception of the communicator will also be influenced by verbal cues such as voice quality and non-verbal cues such as status, (Blake and Mouton, 1961; Goffman, 1961; Mehrabian, 1973; Trankell, 1972), or age

(Blake and Mouton, 1961). However, credibility must be maintained, and will be undermined by any perceived suspect motive. Police interrogators have recognised that the projection of both authority and empathy by a single interrogator can impair his credibility, and have developed an interrogation technique whereby two officers may assume respectively friendly and authoritarian attitudes towards the suspect. This device is evidently most effective in obtaining confessions and co-operation via exploitation of affiliation towards the 'friendly' officer (Deeley, 1971).

The act of confessing during interrogation may be principally an act of compliance. Experiments and observations in the field of experimental and social psychology indicate that appropriate manipulation and influence can produce seemingly non-obvious effects of compliance and conformity (e.g. Asch, 1952). Moreover, where compliant behaviour runs counter to the individual's previous attitudes or beliefs, it may be accompanied by an apparent change in those beliefs or attitudes. There is, however, some dispute over the causal basis of the observed phenomena. For example, from a group dynamics perspective, key factors in attitude change are improvisation and counter-attitudinal rôle-playing (Janis and King, 1954; King and Janis, 1956). According to cognitive dissonance theory on the other hand, it is the *absence* of any obvious justification or reason for the behaviour, such as material gain; which results in attitude changes (Festinger, 1957; Rosnow and Robinson, 1967). Applied to a false confession not elicited by overt coercion, the theory might explain any subsequent statements of belief in the truth of the statement as a mechanism whereby the confessor reduces dissonance engendered by the fact that he has made a statement very damaging to himself in the absence of any perceived compulsion in the form of force, threats or promises.

Bem's self-perception theory, however, postulates that it is behaviour which influences the development of attitudes and other internal states, so that an individual infers his beliefs from his most recent actions (Bem, 1972). Bem has applied this theory to police confessions, arguing that the very act of uttering the admission leads the confessor to infer its truth – *especially* if overt threats are absent and cautions reminding him of his rights have been administered (Bem, 1966; 1967).

Other writers have also noted that cautioning suspects that they need not speak may reinforce an illusion of voluntary co-operation, and may even help to establish rapport with the interrogator (e.g. Zimbardo, 1967). Even where this is not their effect, cautions regarding silence and other 'rights' may be delivered in a manner which minimises their impact – especially if suspects are ill-educated or overwrought (Deeley, 1971; Lewis and Allen, 1977; Zimbardo, 1967). In cases where the right to silence is understood, continuous questioning, structured interrogatory pressures and the social situation may preclude its invocation (Biderman, 1960; Driver, 1970). Police interrogators are aware of the embarrassment caused by silence in the face of continuous questioning (e.g. Firth, 1975), and that this may be intensified by the physical proximity of the interrogator or by other manipulations which may preclude rôle enabling spatial adjustments (Gross and Stone, 1973; Kinzel, 1970). Embarrassment and disorientation may also be caused or increased by arrest, detention and associated procedures (Driver, 1970), which, according to some sociologists, bear the hallmarks of a degradation ceremony (McBarnet, 1976).

The investigatory bias affecting some interrogations may have psychological implications. Advice is often given to form hypotheses in advance of interrogation (e.g. Wicks, 1974). Such hypotheses tend to be formulated around a presumption of guilt, since, as was confirmed by police evidence during the Fisher enquiry (Fisher, 1977, para. 23.13), once a suspect has become the focus of suspicion, investigative endeavours tend to shift toward proving *his* guilt, rather than continuing to explore alternative possibilities. This may influence the emphasis of interrogation. As one policeman uncompromisingly advises: 'You, the interrogator, know he's done it. He knows you know and he'll tell you. It's up to you to encourage him to tell the truth' (Firth, 1975).

The danger inherent in such an approach is that questions are posed in order to confirm the hypothesis and the suspect's responses may be selectively perceived and remembered. There is thus a risk that the hypothesis is falsely confirmed (Mullaney, 1977; Trankell, 1972). This danger may be increased by the influence of the form and sequence of the questions used (Greer, 1971; Muscio, 1916; Rosnow and Robinson, 1967), as well as by their constant repetition. If, in addition, actual or fabricated circumstantial evidence is over-emphasised, and natural manifestations of anxiety are constantly declared to indicate guilt (Danziger, 1976; Deeley, 1971), truth and falsehood may become hopelessly confused in the mind of the interrogator as well as the suspect (see for example the discussion of the interrogation of Timothy Evans by Sargant, 1957).

If an innocent person is also held incommunicado, he will be cut off from any objective frame of reference against which to weigh and assess suggestions posited by the police. Although in 1929, a Royal Commission on Police Powers and Procedure recognised that some police practices reflected a tendency to press interrogation too hard against persons *believed* to be guilty (see also Devlin, 1960), the implications of this tendency have yet to be fully explored in arguments concerning reform of the relevant rules of procedure and evidence.

However, the interrogation practices sometimes adopted will not always yield optimum results. For example, *negatively* perceived communicators may in some cases produce more profound attitude change effects than those who are positively perceived (Rosnow and Robinson, 1967). Moreover, in some instances, the presentation of alternative viewpoints may be a more effective means of persuasion than one-sided communications (Lumsdaine and Janis, 1953).

INDIVIDUAL SUSCEPTIBILITY TO PERSUASION

There is presently no clear indication that particular sorts of person will be more likely than others to yield to persuasion to confess to crimes (Morris, 1978). Some empirical evidence suggests that prior experience of police interrogation tends in some cases to strengthen the capacity to resist plea bargaining pressures (e.g. Dell, 1978). During interrogation, however, this factor may be offset by a tendency toward greater persistence and rigour in questioning suspects with previous convictions (Firth, 1975).

Psychological researchers have made a number of attempts to establish personality profiles of persons most susceptible to persuasion by identification of such factors as submissiveness, cognitive need, authoritarianism and ego defensiveness (Blake and Mouton, 1961; Reich and Adcock, 1976). Other psychologists have argued that for predictive purposes, it is unsatisfactory to confine analysis to personality correlates of persuasibility, and have emphasised such factors as the type of change occurring (e.g. Kelman and Cohler, 1967), and interactions amongst several personality dimensions (McGuire, 1968).

Findings regarding sex differences are inconclusive (Blake and Mouton, 1961; Rosnow and Robinson, 1967). Some psychologists, however, have attached significance to the possible influence during police interrogation of a feminine desire to please (e.g. Bem, 1967).

In contrast, some policemen evidently feel that women make astute liars, and should be subjected to rigorous interrogation (Firth, 1975).

The literature supports a null, a positive and a negative relationship between intelligence and persuasibility (Rosnow and Robinson, 1967). It is thus interesting that in *R.* v. *Houghton and Franciosy*, the Court of Appeal regarded the high intelligence of a confessor as strongly indicative of the voluntariness and reliability of his confession.[16]

Whilst much social psychological research illustrates the limitations of the rationalist legal model of human behaviour, its extrapolatory utility is presently limited by excessive concentration upon unidirectional influence. Police interrogation may bear more resemblance to linear experimental situations than some other non-laboratory encounters, yet a suspect, unlike a laboratory subject, has the ability to influence the interrogator, and hence affect the outcome of the interrogation. Moreover, several key elements of social interaction present during interrogation are left out of account in many experimental designs. These include kinesics (Birdwhistell, 1972; Polhemus, 1978), proxemics (Danziger, 1976), paralinguistics (Danziger, 1976) and the dynamics of reciprocal feedback in dyadic and group interaction. In police interrogation, as in other types of encounter, such elements may be as significant as verbal and unidirectional influences (Argyle, 1969; Mehrabian, 1973).

IMPLICATIONS OF PSYCHOLOGICAL RESEARCH AND THEORY

Despite its present limitations, the psychological literature highlights the need to challenge certain current legal assumptions. Lawyers have still to recognise that any comprehensive determination of reliability must survey *all* factors which may affect the probative validity of a confession. It is as unsatisfactory to assume that all non-coerced confessions are reliable as it is to assume that all coerced confessions are unreliable – yet present legal rules urge these very conclusions. Moreover, whilst procedural safeguards may serve to offset some of the inherent psychological disadvantages of interrogation, it is inadequate to argue that arbitrary procedural rules or verbatim records necessarily provide foolproof precautions against false confessions. Failure to appreciate that a legally unobjectionable interrogation may still subject innocent persons to psychological coercion and possible verbal entrapment has prompted much misplaced fervour in reform debates, where many real issues have so often been obscured by a fog of sterile rhetoric.

TECHNIQUES OF ASSESSING CONFESSION RELIABILITY

It is desirable that any issue of confession reliability should be raised and dealt with by the judge before a jury is empanelled to try the case. This would save much time and expense in cases where the prosecution cannot continue if the confession is held inadmissible, and would avoid possible prejudice or suspicion engendered by exclusion of the jury from the courtroom when the trial is already in progress (Inman, 1977).

Certain psychological forensic techniques have already been developed which may aid expert witnesses in forming opinions on the reliability of confessions or statements retracting admissions made to the police. The acceptability of such evidence has yet to be determined by English courts, though many of the relevant technical issues have been considered by courts in North America, where a variety of conclusions have been reached (Inman, 1977). In some Commonwealth cases, psychiatric opinion evidence has been tendered and admitted on the question of confession voluntari-ness.[17] Even if English courts were prepared similarly to admit such evidence notwithstanding technical objections, its utility is confined to cases concerning pathological or temporary abnormality. Some forensic psychologists would stress the need to view individual psychological data in conjunction with social and situational variables. Thus, in Trankell's method of statement evaluation, exclusive concentration on the trustworthiness of a suspect or witness is replaced by a complex analysis of the etiological development of his crucial statements (Trankell, 1972).

The application of psycholinguistic analysis to written con-fessions has been advocated by Arens and Meadow (1956) who claim that it is possible by this technique to detect whether a confession is the product of emotional instability, physical or emotional exhaustion or suggestive questioning as well as fabri-cation or alteration. It is interesting to note that Svartvik's linguistic analysis of the confessions made by Timothy Evans, although based on limited documentary material, lends support to Evans's contentions at his trial that some of his statements were the product of fear and distress rather than true acknowledgements of actual culpability (Svartvik, 1968). During the Confait enquiry, arguments based on discrepancies between the language in alleged confessions and the general linguistic capacity of the accused were presented, although not accepted on the particular facts (Fisher, 1977 paras. 12.67–12.72).

The study of any available tape-recordings of interrogations may facilitate the elimination of artificial products of the interrogator's technique. It has also been suggested that results in the field of paralinguistic research could be applied to the study of deceitful communication (Mehrabian, 1973). Videotapes, which have proved to be a valuable evidential aid in the United States, would also facilitate forensic application of the work of Ekman and Friesen (1969), who suggest that clues from non-verbal 'leakage' such as body movement and facial expression might be utilised to develop lie detection procedures. It must be remembered, however, that most verbatim records will relate to only part of the accused's period of contact with the police, so that evidence of vital psychological significance may be absent. Although for this and other reasons, it is highly desirable that the full period of contact between the police and suspects is recorded, strong opposition to such a precaution has been expressed in police evidence to the Royal Commission on Criminal Procedure (e.g. McNee, 1978). The arguments upon which such opposition rests have been criticised in a number of quarters (e.g. Williams, 1979), and two law reform bodies have expressed the view that the use of pocket tape-recorders by the police when making enquiries or effecting arrests would not create insuperable practical or financial difficulties (Justice, 1979, para. 37; Law Reform Commission of Australia, 1975, paras. 156–8).

The polygraph technique, which involves recording and interpreting autonomic physiological changes in persons undergoing questioning, is claimed to detect mendacity with a level of accuracy at least as high as that of scientific evidence readily admitted by the courts and higher than that of psychiatric diagnosis (McCormick, 1972; Reid and Inbau, 1977). Similar claims have been made for the Dektor Psychological Stress Evaluator, which measures stress-related voice components of persons undergoing questioning. Such methods as well as more traditional techniques of hypnosis might be utilised during interrogation itself as well as to test post-confession retractions. At most, however, these techniques can only indicate whether the subject undergoing the test believes the truth of his responses. In cases where that belief is mistaken, that fact will not be revealed by these methods.

Most of the forensic techniques outlined are time-consuming, and their optimum utility in relation to issues of confession reliability would necessitate significant changes in rules of pre-trial disclosure and other aspects of procedure and evidence. The case for the introduction of such changes and the reception of such evidence may be thought to be weakened by the absence of agreement in general psychological circles on the validity or accuracy of the techniques. This has enabled Ziskin (1970), to support a sustained attack on the use of psychiatric and psychological evidence in the legal process with criticisms emanating from within the psychological profession itself. Such approaches, however, overlook the fact that absence of consensus at the theoretical level does not necessarily detract from the actuality of empirically observed phenomena, and that in any event, techniques would be better judged by the standard of agreement amongst those working within each specialty rather than amongst the psychological profession as a whole. Forensic techniques are no more infallible in ascertaining truth than the legal process itself. However, the recognition of possible sources of error has prompted continuing research and refinement of techniques, and competent experts would not seek to mislead the court when presenting their data and conclusions. The process of legal fact finding can never be foolproof. However, in a modern age a court or jury aided by expert opinion evidence on psychological matters may, in many cases, reach a more informed conclusion than one which relies exclusively upon conjecture, 'common sense' or atavistic legal assumptions.

CONCLUSION

In one of the most recent contributions to the debate on the right to silence, the editor of *Police* magazine made the following observation: 'By definition, innocent people cannot incriminate themselves if they have committed no crime' (Judge, 1978). The continued reiteration of this common misapprehension emphasises the need for a psychological dimension in discussions on procedural reform. Much is already known in general terms, but there is an urgent need for situation-specific research in the field of police interrogation. The necessary theoretical integration of the multi-dimensional components of interaction and their effects on statement reliability may in turn lead to new or revised forensic techniques.

In the absence of immediate opportunities for empirical observation of actual interrogations, simulated interrogations might be conducted, possibly after subjects have engaged in a period of role-playing. It is important that lawyers and psychologists work together on future experimental designs so that results of direct legal relevance may be produced. Research might also take the form of systematic psycho-legal analysis of authenticated cases of wrongful conviction of innocent confessors. A body of useful information may thus be collected which could contribute as much to the development of a pathology of the criminal justice system as to the further elucidation of the myriad psychological facets of police interrogation. The use of such knowledge in the formulation of enlightened policy decisions and improved standards of accuracy in processing criminal cases, would prove as great a benefit to society, and to the police as its agents, as to suspects themselves.

NOTES

1. The legal argument in this chapter reflects the law as it stood as 1st March 1979.
2. The trial of *R. v. Lattimore, Salih and Leighton* (1976) 62 Cr. App. R. 53 provides a notable illustration of such difficulties. See further the Fisher Report (1977) and Price and Caplan, *The Confait Confessions* (1977).
3. A rare case is *R. v. Allen*, [1977] Crim. L.R. 163. Note also *R. v. Westlake*, [1979] Crim. L.R. 652. cf. *R. v. Elliot*, [1977] Crim. L.R. 551; *R. v. Prager*, [1972] 1 W.L.R. 260; *R. v. Williams* (1977) 67 Cr. App. R. 10; and *R. v. King* [1978] Crim. L.R. 632.
4. *R. v. Stewart*, (1972) 56 Cr. App. R. 272; *R. v. Kilner* [1976] Crim. L. R. 740.
5. Judges' Rules, 1978, Introduction, Principle (e), based on *Ibrahim* v. *R.*, [1914] A.C. 599, at 609 *per* Lord Sumner (omitting the reference to 'oppression'), approved by Lord Reid in *Commrs. for Customs and Excise* v. *Harz and Power*, [1967] 1 A.C. 760, at 818, and Lord Hailsham in *D.P.P.* v. *Ping Lin*, [1976] A.C. 574, 597–8 (substituting 'excited' for 'exercised').
6. *R. v. Warwickshall*, (1783) 1 Leach 263, at 263–4, *per* Nares J. and Eyre B., *R. v. Isequilla*, [1975] 1 W.L.R. 716, at 719, *per* Lord Widgery C. J., Criminal Law Revision Committee 11th Report, Evidence: (General) (1972; Cmnd. 4991) para. 56.
7. Protection of Mentally Retarded Persons (Evidence) Bill (No. 101, 1975). For

debate, see 887 H.C. Deb., cols. 1486–1488 (5th March 1975).
 8. *R.* v. *Isequilla*, [1975] 1 W.L.R. 716, at 723.
 9. [1975] 1 W.L.R. 716 at 720.
 10. [1977] Crim. L.R. 551.
 11. (1978) 68 Cr. App. R. 197.
 12. 935 H.C. Deb., col. 506 (13th July 1977).
 13. *R.* v. *Williams*, [1959] N.Z.L.R. 502, at 505–6, *per* Hardie Boys J.; *R.* v. *Johnston*, (1864) 15 I.C.L.R. 60, at 83, *per* Hayes J., *R.* v. *Phillips* [1949] N.Z.L.R. 316, at 356. This approach is favoured by the Law Reform Commission of New South Wales Working Paper on the Rule Against Hearsay, (1976), but was rejected by the English Court of Appeal (Criminal Division) in *R.* v. *Isequilla*, (*supra*, note 8).
 14. Most published interrogation texts have been produced in the United States. In *Miranda* v. *Arizona*, (1966) 384 US at 450, the US Supreme Court noted that whilst such texts have not been designated as official manuals by police departments, their circulation figures exceed 44,000. In the United States, some police officers undergo training in interrogation by means of formal instruction and simulated interview exercises (see Mullaney, 1977). English police, in contrast, acquire interrogation skills largely by experience. However, most of the techniques advocated in the American manuals appear to be employed by English police.
 15. In 1972, an Inspector in the Durham Constabulary, writing in the Journal of the Police Federation, advocated methods of interrogation and detention based on experience in a German wartime prison camp interrogation centre, which were designed to maximise psychological pressure to confess. The Chief Constable of Durham subsequently sought to disown these views – see *The Guardian*, 13th January, 1972.
 16. *Supra* note 11, Appeal transcript p. 204.
 17. E.g. *R.* v. *Jackson* (1962) 108 C.L.R. 591; *R.* v. *Dietrich* [1971] 1 C.C.C. (2d) 49 (Ontario Court of Appeal). Compare the somewhat inconclusive decision in *R.* v. *Rosik* [1970] 2 C.C.C. (2d) 351.

REFERENCES

R. Arens and A. Meadow, 'Psycholinguistics and the confession dilemma', *Columbia Law Review, 56* (1956) 19–46.
M. Argyle, *Social Interaction* (London: Tavistock, 1969).
S. Asch, *Social Psychology* (Englewood Cliffs, New Jersey: Prentice Hall, 1952).
J. Baldwin and A. K. Bottomley (eds.), *Criminal Justice: Selected Readings* (London: Martin Robertson, 1978).
J. Baldwin and M. J. McConville, 'The influence of the sentencing discount in inducing guilty pleas', in J. Baldwin and A. K. Bottomley (eds.), *Criminal Justice: Selected Readings* (London: Martin Robertson, 1978).
R. A. Bauer, 'Brainwashing: Psychology or demonology', *Journal of Social Issues, 13* (1957) 41–7.
D. J. Bem, 'Inducing belief in false confessions', *Journal of Personality and Social Psychology, 3* (1966) 707–10.

D. J. Bem, 'When saying is believing', *Psychology Today*, (June, 1967) 22–4.

D. J. Bem, 'Self perception theory', in L. Berkowitz (ed.), *Advances in Experimental Social Psychology* vol. VI (New York: Academic Press, 1972).

A. D. Biderman, 'Social psychological needs and "involuntary" behaviour as illustrated by compliance in interrogation', *Sociometry*, *23* (1960) 120–47.

E. Birdwhistell, 'Kinesics', in D. Sills (ed.), *International Encyclopedia of Social Sciences* (London: Collier-Macmillan, 1972).

R. R. Blake and J. S. Mouton, 'The experimental investigation of interpersonal influence', in A. D. Biderman and H. Zimmer (eds.), *The Manipulation of Human Behaviour* (New York: Wiley, 1961).

A. E. Bottoms and J. D. McClean, *Defendants In the Criminal Process* (London: Routledge and Kegan Paul, 1976).

R. Brandon and C. Davies, *Wrongful Imprisonment* (London: George Allen and Unwin, 1973).

J. A. C. Brown, *Techniques of Persuasion* (Harmondsworth: Pelican, 1963).

H. E. Burtt, *Legal Psychology* (New York: Prentice Hall, 1931).

Criminal Law Revision Committee, *11th Report (Evidence: General)*, (London: HMSO Cmnd 4991, 1972).

W. D. Crowley, 'The interrogation of suspects', *International Crime and Police Review*, *28* (1973) 203–10.

K. Danziger, *Interpersonal Communication* (Oxford: Pergamon Press, 1976).

C. Davies, 'The innocent who plead guilty', *Law Guardian* (March 1970) 9–15.

P. Deeley, *Beyond Breaking Point: A Study of Techniques of Interrogation* (London: Arthur Barker, 1971).

S. Dell, 'Inconsistent pleaders', in J. Baldwin and A. L. Bottomley (eds.), *Criminal Justice: Selected Readings* (London: Martin Robertson, 1978).

P. Devlin, *The Criminal Prosecution in England* (London: Oxford University Press, 1960).

E. Driver, 'Confessions and the social psychology of coercion', in M. R. Summers and T. E. Barth (eds.), *Law and Order in a Democratic Society* (Columbus, Ohio: Charles E. Merrill, 1970).

P. Ekman and W. V. Friesen, 'Non-verbal leakage and clues to deception', *Psychiatry*, *32* (1969) 88–105.

W. Eliasberg, 'Forensic psychology', *Southern California Law Review*, *19* (1946) 349–409.

I. E. Farber, H. F. Harlow and L. J. West, 'Brainwashing, conditioning and DDD', *Sociometry*, *20* (1957) 271–85.

L. Festinger, *A Theory of Cognitive Dissonance* (Evanston, Illinois: Row Peterson, 1957).

A. Firth, 'Interrogation', *Police Review*, (28th November, 1975) 1507.

H. Fisher, *Report of an Inquiry by the Hon. Sir Henry Fisher into the Circumstances Leading to the Trial of Three Persons on Charges Arising out of the Death of Maxwell Confait and the Fire at 27 Doggett Road, London S.E.6.* (London: HMSO, 13th December, 1977).

E. Goffman, *Encounters: Two Studies in the Sociology of Interaction* (New York: Bobbs-Merrill, 1961).

J. E. Goodsall, 'The professional interviewer', *Police Review* (26th April, 1974) 525.

D. S. Greer, 'Anything but the truth? The reliability of evidence in criminal trials', *British Journal of Criminology*, *11* (1971) 131–54.

E. Gross and G. P. Stone, 'Embarrassment and the analysis of role requirements', in M. Argyle (ed.), *Social Encounters* (Harmondsworth: Penguin, 1973).

W. Hawkins, *A Treatise of the Pleas of the Crown* (8th ed. by J. Curwood) (London: S. Sweet, 1824).

W. Healy, *Pathological Lying, Accusation and Swindling* (Montclair, New Jersey: Patterson Smith, 1969 [Reprint]).

J. L. Heberling 'Plea negotiation in England', in J. Baldwin and A. K. Bottomley (eds.), *Criminal Justice: Selected Readings* (London: Martin Robertson, 1978).

M. Hepworth and B. S. Turner, 'Confessing to murder: Critical notes on the sociology of motivation', *British Journal of Law and Society*, *1* (1974) 31–49.

L. E. Hinkle, 'The physiological state of the interrogation subject as it affects brain function', in A. D. Biderman and H. Zimmer (eds.), *The Manipulation of Human Behaviour* (New York: Wiley, 1961).

Home Office, *Circular No. 89/1978* (London HMSO, 1978) (a).

Home Office, Evidence to the Royal Commission on Criminal Procedure, *Memorandum V: The Law and Procedures Relating to the Questioning of Persons in the Investigation of Crime* (London: 1978) (b).

M. W. Horowitz, 'The psychology of confession', *Journal of Criminal Law, Criminology and Police Science*, *47* (1956) 197–204.

F. E. Inbau and J. E. Reid, *Criminal Interrogation and Confessions* 2nd ed. (Baltimore: Williams and Wilkins, 1967).

M. Inman, 'Convicting the innocent confessor: The problem and its avoidance', Paper presented at the Annual Conference of The Society of Public Teachers of Law, September 1977.

I. L. Janis and B. T. King, 'The influence of role playing on opinion change', *Journal of Abnormal and Social Psychology*, *49* (1954) 211–18.

A. Judge, 'Why the police must be given more powers', *The Times* (London) 17th August, 1978.

Justice, *The Prosecution Process in England and Wales* (London: Justice, 1970).

Justice, *Pre-Trial Criminal Procedure: Police Powers and the Prosecution Process* (London: Justice, 1979).

H. C. Kelman and J. Cohler, 'Personality factors in reaction to persuasion', in R. L. Rosnow and E. J. Robinson (eds.), *Experiments in Persuasion* (New York: Academic Press, 1967).

B. T. King and I. L. Janis, 'Comparison of the effectiveness of improvised versus non-improvised role playing in producing opinion change', *Human Relations*, *9* (1956) 177–86.

A. F. Kinzel, 'Body buffer zones in violent criminals', *American Journal of Psychiatry*, *127* (1970) 54–64.

P. E. Kubzansky, 'The effects of reduced environmental stimulation on human behaviour: A review', in A. D. Biderman and H. Zimmer (eds.), *The Manipulation of Human Behaviour* (New York: Wiley, 1961).

J. A. Larson, *Lying and its Detection* (Chicago, Illinois: University of Chicago Press, 1932).

Law Reform Commission of Australia, *Report No. 2 (Interim): Criminal Investigation* (Canberra: Australian Government Publishing Service, 1975).

L. H. Leigh, 'The protection of the rights of the accused in pre-trial procedure: England and Wales', Paper presented at the Annual Conference of The Society of Public Teachers of Law, September 1978.

P. W. Lewis and H. E. Allen, ' "Participating Miranda", an attempt to subvert certain constitutional standards', *Crime and Delinquency*, *23* (1977) 75-80.

R. J. Lifton, *Thought Reform and the Psychology of Totalism* (London: Victor Gollancz, 1961).

R. G. Lowen, 'Confessions by the accused – Does *Miranda* relate to reality?' *Kentucky Law Journal* (1974) 794-823.

A Lumsdaine and I. L. Janis, 'Resistance to "Counter-propaganda" produced by one-sided and two-sided presentations', *Public Opinion Quarterly*, *XVII* (1953) 311-18.

D. J. McBarnet, 'Pre-trial procedures and the construction of conviction', in P. Carlen (ed.), *The Sociology of Law* (University of Keele Press, 1976).

C. T. McCormick, *Evidence*, (2nd ed. by E. W. Cleary), (St Paul, Minn.: West Publishing Co., 1972).

W. J. McGuire, 'Personality and susceptibility to social influence', in E. F. Borgatta and W. W. Lambert (eds.), *Handbook of Personality Theory and Research*, (Chicago: Rand-McNally, 1968).

Sir David McNee, *Part 1 of Written Evidence to the Royal Commission on Criminal Procedure* (1978).

J. A. M. Meerloo, 'Pavlovian Strategy as a Weapon of Menticide', *American Journal of Psychiatry*, *110* (1954) 173-96.

A. Mehrabian, 'Influence of attitudes from the posture, orientation and distance of a communicator', in M. Argyle (ed.), *Social Encounters* (Harmondsworth: Penguin, 1973).

P. Morris, *Police Interrogation in England and Wales: A Critical Review of the Literature Prepared for the Royal Commission on Criminal Procedure* (1978).

R. C. Mullaney, 'Wanted! Performance standards for interrogation and interview', *Police Chief*, *44* (1977) 77-80.

H. Münsterberg, *On the Witness Stand* (London: T. Fisher Unwin, 1909).

B. Muscio, 'The influence of the form of a question', *British Journal of Psychology*, *8* (1916) 351-70.

T. Polhemus (ed.), *Social Aspects of the Human Body: A Reader of Key Texts* (Harmondsworth: Penguin, 1978).

C. Price and J. Caplan, *The Confait Confessions* (London: Marion Boyars, 1977).

L. Radzinowicz and J. King, *The Growth of Crime: The International Experience* (Harmondsworth: Penguin, 1979).

B. Reich and C. Adcock, *Values, Attitudes and Opinion Change* (London: Methuen, 1976).

J. E. Reid and F. E. Inbau, *Truth and Deception: The Polygraph ("Lie Detector")* *Technique* 2nd ed. (Baltimore: Williams and Wilkins, 1977).

T. Reik, *The Compulsion to Confess: On the Psychoanalysis of Crime and Punishment* (New York: Farrar, Straus and Cudahy, 1959).

R. L. Rosnow and E. J. Robinson (eds.), *Experiments in Persuasion* (New York: Academic Press, 1967).

Royal Commission on Police Powers and Procedure (London: HMSO Cmd 3297 1929).

Royal Commission on The Police: Final Report (London: HMSO, Cmnd 1728 1962).

R. F. Royal and S. R. Schutt, *The Gentle Art of Interviewing and Interrogation* (Englewood Cliffs, New Jersey: Prentice Hall, 1976).

W. Sargant, *Battle for the Mind* (London: Heinemann, 1957).

E. H. Schein, 'The Chinese Indoctrination Program for Prisoners of War: A Study of Attempted Brainwashing', *Psychiatry*, *19* (1956) 149–72.

D. L. Sterling, 'Police interrogation and the psychology of confession', *Journal of Public Law*, *14* (1965) 25–65.

J. Svartvik, *The Evans Statements: A Case for Forensic Linguistics* (Göteborg, Sweden: Göteborgs Universitet, 1968).

A. Trankell, *The Reliability of Evidence: Methods for Analysing and Assessing Witness Statements* (Stockholm: Beckmans, 1972).

P. Watson, *War on the Mind*, (London: Hutchinson, 1978).

R. J. Wicks, *Applied Psychology for Law Enforcement and Correction Officers* (New York: McGraw-Hill, 1974).

G. Williams, 'The authentication of statements to the police', *Criminal Law Review* (1979) 6–23.

M. Zander, 'The Investigation of Crime: A Study of Cases Tried at the Old Bailey', *Criminal Law Review*, (1979) 203–19.

P. G. Zimbardo, 'The psychology of police confessions', *Psychology Today* (June 1967) 17–27.

P. G. Zimbardo, E. B. Ebbeson and C. Maslach, *Influencing Attitudes and Changing Behaviour* 2nd ed. (Reading, Massachusetts: Addison-Wesley, 1977).

J. Ziskin, *Coping with Psychiatric and Psychological Testimony* (Beverly Hills, California: Law and Psychology Press, 1970).

5: A Decision-Making Model of Confessions

E. Linden Hilgendorf and Barrie Irving

Confession, particularly false confession, is so self-evidently interesting to the psychologist that it might seem unnecessary to begin by defining where our interest in the topic lies. Nevertheless we wish to draw a distinction between confession as an interesting phenomenon to be studied for what it can tell us about human motivation and so on, and confession as a taxing practical problem for the legal profession. As applied psychologists our central concern is with the problem rather than the phenomenon itself.

The Legal Studies Group at the Tavistock Institute was formed to respond to requests for help from the legal profession. Such requests to psychologists can come from barristers or solicitors dealing with individual cases or from government agencies who have responsibility for particular aspects of the judicial system. The topics involved are varied – identification, confessions, pleas of diminished responsibility, the mentally subnormal defendant – but all have a common factor: they all involve some aspect of human behaviour, motivation or skill which cannot readily be understood or effectively dealt with in our courts by the application of 'common sense' or logical analysis. We have no illusions about these requests: they do not as yet derive from any belief in legal circles that we know the answers, but there is at least the feeling that when it comes to the queer, the odd and the unexpected, psychologists might have something useful to add even if it has ultimately to be rejected as unreliable or as yet too unorthodox to assimilate into the body of judicially accepted wisdom.

The problem with confessions made to the police is that they are frequently retracted with the same spontaneity and conviction with which they were first uttered, leaving the prosecution and defence all too often with two conflicting statements and no corroborative evidence to back either of them. The law approaches this problem by dealing with the question of the admissibility of the first incriminating statement. The vital questions in the legal view of the matter are: was the confession obtained voluntarily or not?, and if not, were the circumstances of the confession such as to render it unreliable, or were they so oppressive that as a matter of principle the statement ought to be ruled inadmissible? In practice, however, there is often no obvious pressure on the suspect, and counsel and judge may be left pondering the question of whether or not it is credible that an uncoerced suspect would provide the police with a detailed confession if it were not true.

This raises basic psychological questions: what leads a man to confess? Under what circumstances other than the legally recognised threats, inducements and oppression will a man confess falsely? It is while wrestling with these questions that lawyers have approached us on the topic of confessions. They have done so because they believe, quite rightly in our view, that the common sense conception of the problem is misleading and over-simplified, yet at the same time compelling to both judge and jury. Their concern is to see whether we can supply an alternative perspective.

The first such approach to the Institute was in relation to the departmental inquiry into the Maxwell Confait case headed by Sir Henry Fisher (Fisher, 1977). In this case and subsequently in relation to other cases involving retracted confessions, we have found that the contribution of the applied psychologist has been restricted.

1. Adequate and reliable information about the circumstances in which the confession was obtained is usually either unavailable or a matter of dispute. (The account of the circumstances is normally provided by the police officers involved and the accuracy or completeness of that evidence is often challenged by the defence.)

2. Where reliable information about the circumstances or the state of the suspect is available, the state of psychological knowledge about the relative power of the relevant variables and their possible interactions is insufficient because interrogation *per se* has not been extensively studied.

3. Even where information is available and the state of knowledge is sufficient (for example, with respect to sleep de-

privation), the ensuing expert opinion must still fit within a pre-existing legal conceptual framework. When the psychological and legal models of man are too divergent the psychological evidence may be unusable in practice.

This chapter is principally concerned with this third point, although we also touch upon the problems created by the state of knowledge about interactions between key variables. We shall try to tackle the issue of the relationship between what the psychologist might be able to say about confessions and how the lawyer conceives of the problem, by employing a simple heuristic device. We express legal thinking, as evidenced by judicial pronouncements on confessions as to their admissibility, as a special case of what psychologists will recognise as a behavioural model of human decision-making. Lawyers do not consciously use such a model. They may not recognise the logical implications of how they argue. Nevertheless some model of this kind is strongly suggested by the way legal authorities construct general principles relating to the admissibility of confessions and how they apply these principles in individual cases.

THE SUSPECT AS A DECISION-MAKER

Let us look at the situation of a person who is suspected by the police of committing or having been implicated in a crime and who is being questioned by a policeman at a police station. That person has to make a choice – possibly many choices: whether to confess or not; whether to tell the truth or part of the truth or to lie; how to answer the questions put to him; what stance to adopt towards the police. A decision-making model of the type employed by such writers as Edwards and Tversky (1967) and Luce (1967) can be applied to this situation. Such a model proposes that a decision-maker seeks to make the best possible choice among the courses of action available to him by choosing that course for which the product of 1) the probability of occurrence and 2) the value to him (or utility) of the consequences, is largest. (This model is usually referred to as the 'subjectively expected utility maximisation model'.) The action open to a suspect will have consequences: charges may be made; he may be detained at the police station; information provided may be checked. There is little doubt that such consequences are potentially significant to the suspect. He or she will, therefore, probably try to evaluate the probabilities of their occurrence, and his decision how to act will be a result of some balancing of the likelihood of various consequences in relation to their utilities for him.

The notion of the person as a decision-maker in this situation is implicit in the legal concern that any statement he makes should be 'voluntary'. Decision-making concepts are more explicit in the legal criteria for defining those situations which are thought to render a confession involuntary, namely that there existed external temporal forces which led the person to make a statement when otherwise he would have remained silent, or to make a statement which was untrue. These criteria clearly envisage that more than one course of action is open to the person and that he must choose between them.

The relatively recent introduction into legal thinking of the concept of oppression as a ground for the inadmissibility of confessions suggests that, in addition to probabilities and utilities, a further element needs to be added to the decision-making model when applied to confessions. That is, we must recognise that there are circumstances in which the capacity to decide efficiently or the will to decide at all becomes severely impaired. In the Court of Appeal decision in *Prager* (1971)[1] Sachs L. J. is quoted as defining oppression as something 'which tends to sap and has sapped free will' and Lord MacDermott has defined oppressive questioning as questioning which 'so affects the mind of the suspect that his will crumbles and he speaks when otherwise he would have stayed silent' (Criminal Law Revision Committee, 1972, p. 41). Although there is very little case law to indicate the way the law will develop operational definitions of external conditions or treatment which constitute oppression, the *Prager* decision suggests a range of possible considerations including the fact of custody, the time or periods of questioning, the nature of the questioning, proper refreshment and the possibility that some groups, notably children, old people and the inexperienced, will be more vulnerable.

In psychological terms, legal thinking about confessions can be seen as involving a decision-making model made up of a system of contingent environmental and interactional variables which when set at certain values can result in the impairment of the decision-making process. Psychology can probably contribute most to the understanding of confessions by specifying these contigencies and their effects. But before considering these we should briefly review the implications for legal thinking of adopting a decision-making model according to which a suspect's decision to confess is based on his perception of the likely consequences.

INFORMATION ABOUT CONSEQUENCES

Some of the consequences with which the suspect is concerned may be predicted from earlier events with a high degree of certainty. However, others depend on more complex decisions by other people (for example, police decisions about charging), and most people in the position of a suspect will have very inadequate information available to them about what is likely to happen. The interrogator on the other hand is in possession of a great deal of information and may supply it or withhold it. Certain types of information about consequences have been treated by the law as likely to influence a suspect's decision, namely threats and inducements, and these have constituted grounds for inadmissibility.

To a psychologist it is clear that the decision-making process is governed not by the objective probabilities of occurrence of given consequences, but by subjective probabilities of perceived consequences. Some lawyers accept this view. For example, Winn L. J. in the Court of Appeal decision in Northam (1967)[2] said, 'It is what the average, normal, probably unreasonable person in the position of the appellant at the time might have thought likely to be to his advantage' (p. 104). But many do not accept this. It is common, for instance, to encounter views which assume a fairly sophisticated knowledge of the functioning of the legal system. The most obvious example is contained in the common legal argument that to make a confession to a crime which he did not in fact commit has such dire legal consequences that it is extremely unlikely that an individual would take such a course of action against his best interests. Lawyers assume that because in legal proceedings a confession may be sufficient evidence for obtaining a conviction even if subsequently retracted, this fact will have been considered in the decision to confess. It cannot be assumed that such information is readily available to the general public and such an assumption departs from Winn L. J.'s more enlightened view.

The particular concern with threats or inducements being offered by a 'person in authority' emphasises another important aspect of the situation, namely that the decision-maker must evaluate the reliability or trustworthiness of the information relevant to his decision. The power of the police in the interrogation situation over many of the relevant consequences lends considerable credibility to information offered to the suspect and justifies the view that the threat or inducement need only be slight to have potential influence on the decision made.

SOCIAL AND SELF APPROVAL

Janis (1959), in discussing the range of consequences which a person might consider in making any given decision, suggests that there are at least four general categories: utilitarian gains or losses for self; utilitarian gains or losses for others; social approval or disapproval; self approval or disapproval. Legal thinking clearly acknowledges the first type of consequence in the prohibition placed on threats or inducements of a utilitarian kind. This may also extend to utilitarian gains or losses for others. Threats made in relation to other persons such as members of the suspect's family may also render a confession inadmissible, and Cross and Wilkins (1975) conclude that there 'seems no reason why a threat to treat a total stranger with violence should not render a confession made in consequence of it inadmissible' (p. 132). However the third and fourth types of consequence which a suspect might consider are not generally acknowledged as grounds for inadmissibility.

Social and self approval utilities are frequently invoked to explain the making of confessions by psychologists with a clinical, and particularly psychoanalytic, orientation such as Reik (1959). Interrogation by the police usually concerns the commission of a socially disapproved act. In extreme cases criminal acts may be profoundly disturbing or exciting to those involved. Social and self approval or disapproval are important factors in the aftermath of criminal behaviour and may lead to rather bizarre values being placed on certain consequences. For example, punishment for a crime committed may be seen as having a positive value in alleviating guilt.

The important question is whether manipulation of these social and self approval utilities in an interrogation can so affect the suspect's decision-making as to render a confession unreliable. Laboratory studies of the effect of groups on verbal behaviour show that people are prepared to deny the evidence of their own senses, for example when judging the comparative length of a line, so as to conform with the verbal statements of other members of a group (Asch, 1951, 1956). This tendency to conform is more likely to occur when members of the group are seen as higher in status, more competent with regard to the issues at hand or more attractive. These studies would suggest that there are pressures to conform with the expectations of an interrogator rather than to incur his disapproval. At an anecdotal level Biderman (1956, 1960) reported the apparently successful techniques of eliciting information from US prisoners of war in Korea and found that the most effective strategies were not physical torture but included the manipulation of approval or disapproval from the interrogator, particularly in relation to the prisoners' feelings of competence and self esteem.

American police manuals on interrogation, such as Inbau and Reid (1967) and O'Hara (1970), suggest a range of techniques for manipulating social and self approval – for example, that the interrogator should sympathise with the subject by telling him that anyone under similar conditions or circumstances might have done the same thing; or appeal to the subject's pride by well selected flattery or by a challenge to his honour.

The difficulty with taking social and self approval manipulations into account in the rules on admissibility is that these manipulations are not disapproved of in a general way, and in relation to the interrogation of suspects may even be seen as constituting lenient treatment. Manipulations of the values can, however, if carried to an extreme, amount to a significant distortion of reality and, as Goffman (1974) points out, only the general halo of legitimacy surrounding police activity separates such distortions from those practised by 'con men' which we would condemn as fraud, trickery and deception. Deceptions of a significant kind could be excluded on disciplinary grounds if some guidelines were developed for their evaluation. However, milder forms of social manipulation may also raise doubts about the reliability of statements obtained as a result.

The effectiveness of manipulations of the social and self approval utilities can be expected to increase the longer a suspect is held by the police isolated from other reference sources of norms, and this suggests the need for more stringent controls on the time a person can be held without external contact. A more effective control would be the requirement that the interrogation be carried out in the presence of an independent third party. The studies of conformity mentioned above also show that given a single ally the likelihood of a subject conforming is significantly reduced. However, the effectiveness of a third party probably depends on his presence at a fairly early stage. The introduction of an ally once a commitment has been made to a given course of action has a very limited effect.

IMPAIRMENT OF DECISION-MAKING

In considering the conditions of an interrogation which might impair decision-making in a systematic way we suggest that there are at least two different mechanisms which may be involved. The mechanisms are related to questions about the suspect's performance:

1. Does the suspect engage with the decision-making task which confronts him? On entering a social situation a person must read certain signs and signals in order to establish the nature of the situation and what is required of him. His performance will be determined by whether or not he sees or hears these signs and signals and what construction he places on them. While in some instances it may be obvious that an interrogation is just that, and that the suspect is required to choose between various alternative strategies, this is not necessarily the case. The interrogator may be at pains to avoid signalling to the suspect that important decisions are confronting him. Alternatively, the suspect may perceive such strong signals demanding an action of a particular kind that he fails to realise that a set of alternative behaviours exists. In either case the suspect may fail to see the real nature of the decision which confronts him.

2. Is the suspect in a fit state cognitively to carry out the decision-making task? Most of us find that we perform better at tasks such as examinations if we are slightly keyed up. If however our state of excitement is too high then our performance seems to decline or, at the extreme, disintegrates altogether. Systematic investigation of this phenomenon has demonstrated that there does seem to be an optimal level of arousal for a given task, although there are considerable variations between individuals (Welford, 1968; Yerkes and Dodson, 1908). The optimal state varies according to the complexity of the task and generally speaking the more difficult the task the lower is the optimal state of arousal. The decision-making task confronting a suspect under interrogation can in some instances be a complex one and it is also unfamiliar. We would

therefore expect decision-making performance to decline even at relatively low levels of arousal.

The characteristics of the situation in which interrogation is conducted can vary widely from one instance to another and the likelihood of the suspect's decision-making being impaired will vary accordingly. Virtually all interrogation by the police will be perceived by the suspect as involving some degree of threat, even if only because interrogation implies serious suspicion and the possibility of failing to overcome that suspicion. The threat obviously increases when the suspect is implicated in an unlawful act or the police are convinced he is in some way implicated. When a suspect is questioned at a police station he is occupying a territory which is unfamiliar, not under his control and which may in some respects be unpleasant and even hostile. Furthermore he cannot leave the station at will and may be explicitly confined. The confinement may include being detained in a cell and/or interrogation room for considerable periods, isolated from normal social contacts. The suspect is also held in a relationship with persons to whom he concedes a very high level of legitimate authority. In the remainder of this chapter we shall consider from a psychological point of view the effects these situational variables may have on the behaviour of a suspect.

Threat
First, let us consider the environment of interrogation as a stressful and possibly frightening one. The conditions which prevail in the cells in which a suspect may be detained prior to questioning and the rooms in which interrogation is conducted are often unpleasant. While in no sense could they be seen as sufficiently severe to threaten the viability of the human organism, equally they are not designed for the comfort and reassurance of suspects. More importantly the environment is under the control of the police. The suspect can no longer be sure that the basic human needs for food, drink, waste elimination and sleep will be satisfied. The police could, in fact, deprive a suspect of food, sleep, etc., they could threaten to do so, or the threat may simply be perceived as inherent in the situation. In principle it seems likely that these threats will increase the arousal level of the suspect and hence potentially impair his decision-making. The crucial question is, at what level of environmental threat does decision-making become impaired either directly by

thirst, hunger, etc. or indirectly by the fear induced by losing control over the gratification of basic bodily needs?

The effect of threat on performance is rarely studied in the laboratory because of the moral and practical difficulties of creating a genuine threat to a subject. Poulton (1970), reviewing studies where threat of injury or possible death was present in a military training exercise, reports that the experimenters found it difficult to obtain impairment measures from their subjects because of the panic induced by the situation. Impairment has been recorded however, for the threat of failure in a test (a lesser degree of personal threat than that posed by interrogation). In Poulton's opinion situations which manage to combine threats of various kinds may have semi-permanent effects on performance and personality.

These are matters which are currently left to the lawyers to debate at a common-sense level, and yet they involve empirical questions to which the answers may not be immediately apparent. For example, animal studies reviewed by Gray (1971) suggest that fight/flight reactions can be induced at relatively low levels of environmental threat particularly when their onset is sudden or when the animal is low down in the pecking order. Research on these topics may be restricted by ethical considerations but nevertheless it seems preferable that the relevant critical thresholds should be established empirically as far as possible rather than wholly by legal debate.

Physical confinement

Research on the effects of being physically confined and socially isolated is more extensive than that available on personal threat. During the 1950s research in this area was stimulated by reports of brainwashing using techniques such as solitary confinement and perceptual deprivation. The effects on man of being isolated and confined have also received considerable research attention in connection with manned space flight, underwater exploration in mini-submarines and the operation of research stations in Antarctica.

Experiments conducted in laboratories or using simulators have employed a range of experimental conditions. At their most extreme, they have deprived men of all external stimulation or provided only disorganised stimuli. Solitary confinement or confinement with another person have also been investigated. The duration of confinement has also been varied from a few hours to many days. Although the most dramatic effects are obtained with the most severe conditions, effects can still be observed where the subject is only physically confined.

The major finding of these studies is that all types of confinement produce 'stress' and the stress effects increase with duration of confinement. Sells (1973), reviewing a range of subjective reports from field studies, found stress reports of restlessness, fatigue, low morale, time disorientation, frustration, anxiety, irritability and depression. In laboratory investigations by Zuckerman *et al.* (1968) where a person was confined for eight hours with another person in a sound proof room with the lights on and access to tapes and slides, subjects reported greater levels of stress than the control group (i.e. restlessness, fidgeting, worry, depression). Zubek *et al.* (1969) confined subjects to a small room for one week. They had access to TV and radio, and received regular visitors. Similar reports were obtained in this study. In Zuckerman's study, confined subjects reported a higher rate of physical complaints such as headaches, and Sells notes that an increased number of physical symptoms are usually reported in field studies (e.g. sleep disturbance, muscular soreness or weakness, headaches, dizziness and other psychosomatic reactions).

A crude indicator of the stress of the experimental situation is the number of subjects who cannot endure the conditions and give up taking part in the experiment. There are very considerable differences between individuals: some can only stand a few hours, others seem happy to continue for two weeks. Zuckeman has noted that about one third of subjects leave experiments in the first session (regardless of the duration of the session or other conditions). Physiological measurements have only occasionally been made in these studies and then only of fairly crude indicators of neurological functioning, but they support the general conclusion that there are substantial stress effects from confinement as well as from the more severe forms of deprivation.

Clearly these laboratory conditions are not the same as those which might be experienced by a suspect detained by the police. In some ways the laboratory conditions appear to entail a greater degree of confinement, but in at least one important respect they are less severe. In an experiment the subject has entered the situation voluntarily and the pressures which detain him are social ones, such as causing inconvenience to the experimenter. A suspect, however, is likely to experience confinement as something from which he is not able to escape. Reports obtained from people experiencing other real life confinement and isolation experiences (for example, explorers, victims of shipwrecks) where escape from the situation is uncertain, suggest that in these situations more extreme stress reactions are experienced, although it is difficult to know what weight to give such reports.

The second generally reported effect of confinement is that the social relationships between people subjected to isolation and confinement show different patterns from those not so subjected. There is considerable experimental support for the notion that stimulus seeking behaviour increases during isolation. The amount of stimulus-seeking behaviour observed increases with length of time in confinement (Jones, 1969). Anecdotal evidence from small groups in confinement also suggests that other members of the group become an important source of stimulation and interpersonal relationships are distorted accordingly (Smith, 1969). Being confined with another person also seems to generate strong forces toward informality and intimacy (Altman and Haythorn, 1967). The condition of being confined with another person in a very limited space is in itself stressful. Zuckerman *et al.* (1968) found that, at least for women in joint confinement, the presence of the other person seemed to make the stress reactions more severe. In more prolonged joint confinement, withdrawal from the other person and increasing acts of territorial demarcation are usually observed.

Although much of the work on confinement and isolation has been concerned with conditions of much greater deprivation than would be experienced in an interrogation situation, the research does suggest that confinement with another person for periods as short as eight hours produces marked stress reactions, and that the situation constitutes a pressure towards a changed and more intimate relationship with another person sharing that confinement.

Perceived authority of the police

The remaining aspect of the interrogation situation which we will consider is the fact that the suspect held in a police station is subject to the legitimate authority of the police officers present. Perhaps the most dramatic series of experiments on the way people behave in relation to authority figures was conducted by Milgram (1974). The situation which he created for his experiment involved two people coming to a psychological laboratory to take part in a study of learning and memory. One (a volunteer member of the general public) is designated the teacher and the other (a member of the research team although this is unknown to the teacher) the learner. The learner is to be punished with electric shocks at increasing levels of severity administered by the teacher for mistakes made in his learning task. In fact no shock is administered but the teacher uses an impressive set of machinery labelled from 15 to 450 volts and the learner responds with grunts, increasing protests, demands to be let out and screams. When the teacher hesitates to administer the shock, the experimenter tells him to continue. Milgram found that although the teacher subjects were volunteer members of the public and were paid for coming before the experiment commenced, no one ever refused to start and despite obvious stress many people continued to give shocks to the highest level no matter how much the learner pleaded or screamed. The subjects in this experiment, in going along with the expectations of the authority figures, went against their own interests in the sense that many said they subscribed to moral values which deplored such behaviour. The results of these experiments are astonishing and difficult to dismiss: Milgram has used over 1000 members of the general public in the United States and there is no evidence to suggest that his methods of obtaining volunteers attracted particularly sadistic or submissive subjects. Similar results have been obtained in other countries including Italy, Germany, South Africa and Australia.

In interpreting the results Milgram proposes that behaviour carried out in a state of obedience to authority figures is profoundly different in character from that which is spontaneous. 'The essence of obedience consists in the fact that a person comes to view himself as the instrument for carrying out another person's wishes, and he therefore no longer regards himself as responsible for his action' (p. xii). He observes that there are powerful and continuously re-warded socially learned rôles in relation to authority. When that authority is legitimate and relevant to the situation then the propensity to adopt the obedience mode of functioning is very strong and not freely reversible. The obedience mode involves the relationship to the authority figure becoming a dominant concern: there is a wish to perform well and present a good appearance to him; to accept the definition of the situation which he provides. Other pressures tend to recede, and responsibility for the consequences of actions is attributed to the authority figure. The conversion to the obedience mode is often not complete and other considerations may still intrude. Where these conflict with the obedience requirements signs of strain can be behaviourally observed, for example, verbal protest, denial, reinterpretation of information, and physical signs such as sweating and trembling.

In interrogation the authority of the interrogator is obvious both in his legitimised role and his actual power over the physical person of the suspect. Virtually all publications by or for police officers stress the need for interrogators to reinforce and maintain authority and not to undermine it with such damaging practices as over-familiarity or disagreement between interrogators. (Milgram found that obedience can completely disappear if two experimenters disagree in their instructions to the subject.) Accepting only that Milgram's findings verify the existence of powerful pressures towards obedience to authority, it can be argued that the interrogation situation contains pressures which effectively force the decision-maker to exaggerate social approval/disapproval utilities probably at the expense of utilitarian gains and losses to self. This tendency may be enhanced by the fact that many of the consequences with which the suspect is concerned are to be experienced at some more or less distant time. Milgram found that the tendency to be obedient was facilitated when the unpleasant consequences of the actions taken were at some remove in either time or space. The question of the probability of getting bail if charged with the offence would therefore be an important factor in the suspect's susceptibility to the obedience pressures. Bail would effectively distance some of the unpleasant consequences of current actions.

If this interpretation of Milgram's findings is taken to its logical conclusion we could also propose that a person who has completely switched into the obedience mode has given up some aspects of his decision-making task altogether and could no longer be said to-be operating with that degree of free will which the law requires for the person to be acting voluntarily. In order to apply this in a legal context we would need to be able to identify confidently when a suspect was operating in an obedience mode. The observations of the behaviour of the subjects in Milgram's experiments suggest that there may be behavioural patterns which are sufficiently characteristic of a person acting 'obediently' to detect them in a full transcript or video tape of a confession. This is more likely to be possible when a person is confessing falsely since in order to comply with the authority figure's demands he must obtain clues from the interrogator as to what he must say.

CONCLUSIONS

In the preceding discussion of the situation factors of integration in relation to the suspect's decision-making we have
drawn on a number of disparate fields of psychological research. For
this reason it is not surprising that there is very little to go on when
we come to consider the question of how these variables interact.
Nevertheless the following effects are at least possible. Given that
the interrogator has considerable legitimate authority, the interrogation situation contains strong pressures on the suspect to give
excessive emphasis in his decision-making to the approval or
disapproval of the interrogator, and to be extremely sensitive to all
communications both verbal and non-verbal which he receives
from the interrogator. The situation of physical confinement by the
police supports and facilitates these pressures and the effect becomes
more pronounced the longer the total period of detention in police
custody. The personal threat inherent in custodial interrogation,
confinement and subjection to other forms of potential or real
environmental stress can all conspire to raise the arousal level of the
suspect, possibly in a multiplicative rather than an additive
manner. For many suspects arousal will reach levels which are
dysfunctional for efficient performance on the complex decision-
making task confronting them. Under such conditions they may
well take actions which they would not otherwise have taken or
produce verbal statements which are unreliable. The arousing
potential of the interrogation situation is frequently such that the
interrogator runs the risk of mobilising the flight/fight reactions of
the suspect. Flight implies that the suspect will do anything to
escape from the situation; fight that he will oppose all the obedience
demands made on him by the interrogator.

In this paper we have outlined a model of confession. It is not the
only possible psychological model which could be applied to this
phenomenon, but it does have the advantage of being closely linked
to the legal concepts of voluntariness and oppression. The model
provides a framework for analysing the circumstances in which any
particular confession was made in terms of the decision-making task
of the suspect, the information with which he is provided, the social
pressures which are brought to bear on him, and the physical
character of the interrogation. A conceptual tool of this kind is of
considerable use to a psychologist who is consulted by a lawyer in a
case where confession evidence is involved.

The model places the issue of false confession in the context of all types of confession: false confession can be seen, not as an isolated phenomenon the explanation of which is entirely separate from true confessions, but as one possible outcome of the decision-making process. It follows from the possibility that a suspect may decide to confess falsely that there is a reliability risk associated with confessions as a class of evidence. Although existing psychological research cannot help in determining the exact degree of that risk, the decision-making model and related evidence suggest three possible approaches to the problem of reliability. First, we could take the view that certain circumstances of interrogation increase the reliability risk sufficiently to constitute grounds for ruling confessions so obtained inadmissible. While we can at this stage suggest which factors should be considered it would require further research to establish relatively precise criteria for determining the functional relations between these factors and risk. Second, it should be in the interests of both the police and the courts to improve the chances of the detection of a false confession at the point at which it is made. This could be tackled by the improvement of police interrogation training (for example, to reduce directive questioning and the inadvertent provision of information); the use of technical aids such as the polygraph; or by requiring a greater degree of corroborative checking of information provided. Third, we could explore the feasibility of the *post hoc* identification of false material by the analysis of the informational, linguistic and behaviour content and structure of interrogation records. The psychological evidence reviewed in this paper suggests that cues should exist in the behaviour of both the interrogator and the suspect which could be used to evaluate the potential value of the suspect's answers to questions. This approach would suggest the need to develop techniques of analysis and the training of expert analysts for the examination of confession records.

The consideration of the psychological evidence implied by the decision-making model also highlights the policy question of the proper constraints which should be placed on the police in their interrogation of suspects. Although it is outside the role of the psychologist to define what society should accept as legitimate treatment of a citizen by the police, it is his responsibility as a scientist to bring to the attention of policy-makers the way in which people might be affected by various kinds of police treatment. The presentation of a coherent model of confessions may lead to an increased awareness of the psychological issues involved in this problematic area.

NOTES

1. *R.* v. *Prager* [1971] 56 Cr. App. R. 151.
2. *R.* v. *Northam* [1967] 52 Cr. App. R. 97.

REFERENCES

I. Altman and W. W. Haythorn, 'The ecology of isolated groups', *Behavioural Science, 12* (1967) 169–82.
S. E. Asch, 'Effects of group pressure upon the modification and distortion of judgement', in H. Guetzkow (ed.), *Groups, Leadership and Men* (Pittsburgh: Carnegie Press, 1951).
S. E. Asch, 'Studies of independence and submission to group pressure 1. A minority of 1 against a unanimous majority', *Psychological Monographs, 70* (1956) No. 416.
A. D. Biderman, *Communist techniques of coercive interrogation*, AFPTRC Development Report TN-56-132 (Airforce Personnel and Training Research Centre, Lackland Airforce Base, Texas, 1956).
A. D. Biderman, 'Social psychological needs and involuntary behaviour as illustrated by compliance in interrogation', *Sociometry, 23* (1960) 120–47.
Criminal Law Revision Committee, *11th Report (Evidence: General)*, (London: HMSO Cmnd 4991, 1972).
R. Cross and N. Wilkins, *An Outline of the Law of Evidence*, 4th ed. (London: Butterworths, 1975).
W. Edwards and A. Tversky (eds.), *Decision Making* (London: Penguin, 1967).
H. Fisher, *Report of an Inquiry by the Hon. Sir Henry Fisher into the Circumstances Leading to the Trial of Three Persons on Charges Arising out of the Death of Maxwell Confait and the Fire at 27 Doggett Road, London, SE6* (London: HMSO, 1977).
E. Goffman, *Frame Analysis* (London: Harper and Row, 1974).
J. Gray, *The Psychology of Fear and Stress* (London: Weidenfeld and Nicolson, 1971).
F. E. Inbau and J. Reid, *Criminal Interrogations and Confessions*, 2nd ed. (Baltimore: Williams and Wilkins, 1967).
I. L. Janis, 'Decisional conflicts: a theoretical analysis', *Journal of Conflict Resolution, vol. 3*, (1959) 6–27.
A. Jones, 'Stimulus seeking behaviour', in J. P. Zubek (ed.), *Sensory Deprivation: Fifteen Years of Research* (New York: Appleton-Century-Crofts, 1969).
R. D. Luce, 'Psychological studies of risky decision making', in W. Edwards and A. Tversky, (eds.), *Decision Making* (London: Penguin, 1967).
S. Milgram, *Obedience to Authority: An Experimental View* (London: Tavistock Publications, 1974).

C. E. O'Hara, *Fundamentals of Criminal Investigation*, 2nd ed. (Springfield, Illinois: Charles C. Thomas, 1970).

E. C. Poulton, *Environment and Human Efficiency* (Springfield, Illinois: Charles C. Thomas, 1970).

T. Reik, *The Compulsion to Confess: On the Psychoanalysis of Crime and Punishment* (New York: Farrar, Straus and Cudahy, 1959).

S. B. Sells, ' The taxonomy of man in enclosed space', in J. Rasmussen (ed.), *Man in Isolation and Confinement* (Chicago: Aldine, 1973).

S. Smith, 'Studies of small groups in confinement', in J. P. Zubek (ed.), *Sensory Deprivation: Fifteen Years of Research* (New York: Appleton-Century-Crofts, 1969).

A. T. Welford, *Fundamentals of Skill* (London: Methuen, 1968).

R. M. Yerkes and J. D. Dodson, 'The relation of strength of stimulus to rapidity of habit formation', *Journal of Comprehensive Neurological Psychology*, *18* (1908) 459–82.

J. P. Zubek, 'Review of effects of prolonged deprivation', in J. Rasmussen (ed.), *Man in Isolation and Confinement* (Chicago: Aldine, 1973).

J. P. Zubek, L. Bayer and J. M. Shepherd, 'Relative effects of prolonged social isolation and confinement: behavioural and physiological effects', *Journal of Abnormal Psychology*, *74* (1969) 625–31.

M. Zuckerman, H. Persky, K. E. Link and G. K. Basu, 'Experimental and subject factors defining responses to sensory deprivation, social isolation and confinement', *Journal of Abnormal Psychology*, *73* (1968) 183–94.

6: The Effects of Confession and Retraction on Simulated Juries: A Pilot Study

A. Philip Sealy and Albert McKew

Most research on the behaviour of juries using simulated trials has concentrated on the effects of judges' instructions and rules of procedure (e.g. Simon, 1967; LSE Jury Project, 1973a; Sealy, 1975, Davis *et al.* 1975, Kerr *et al.* 1976). These experiments have studied the rôle of such instructions as those on the legal definition of insanity, burden of proof, corroboration and majority verdicts. The main reason for concentrating on such factors is that some *general* instructions form a part of every trial. They recur from trial to trial, and are controversial. The simulated trial can also be used to study the effects of *specific* elements of evidence in the outcome of a trial, but the results would usually be of little value, since every trial is unique and generalisation from the simulation would be very limited. However, certain *categories* of evidence frequently occur in trials by jury. One such category, which often seems to be critical to the verdict, is the confession.

This paper reports a pilot study concerned with the rôle of confession evidence in jurors' decisions–how they use such evidence and how persuasive such evidence is. It is not concerned with processes that give rise to a confession, important as the study of these processes is. The papers by Inman and by Hilgendorf and Irving in this volume are more directly concerned with this aspect of confession. The central question here is, how does confession evidence affect jurors? Does it affect them differently if it occurs in different forms? Does confession evidence become more or less damaging to the defendant if it is retracted in court? Does the reason given in court for retracting the confession alter the views jurors have of the defendant's guilt, or the way they treat other evidence? These questions clearly fall within the area of problems that can better be answered by empirical and experimental research, than by any other means. Only experimental methods allow one to compare different versions of the same trial over a number of presentations, and thereby test the direct and indirect effects of critical independent variables. However, such methods have their problems.

METHODOLOGICAL PROBLEMS IN SIMULATED JURY RESEARCH

The main problems of experimental research using simulations are, briefly, the authenticity of the material, the adequacy of its presentation in the experiment, the relevance of the material to the general issues underlying the research and finally, the representativeness of the jurors. It is worthwhile taking each of these points in turn before describing the experiment we devised and discussing the results we obtained.

1. *Authenticity of material*
In one way this is the easiest part of the experiment since all it requires is a transcript of a trial which provides a high level of mundane realism and avoids the departure into fiction that occurs in invented trials. Obviously the trial has to be chosen carefully and it has to be evenly balanced in terms of the likely verdict, so that experimental variations may sway it one way or another. It also has to be balanced in terms of the evidence that might be used to arrive at a verdict. If the case *solely* depends on the evidence that is being subjected to experimental test then there is no way of weighing the importance of such evidence against other specific types of evidence or against any other evidence. The trial also has to be brief in presentation and likely to catch the attention of experimental subjects. We tried to achieve this by selecting a trial that had produced a mistrial in its first presentation and had topical relevance, namely possession of drugs. It was brief and hinged partly on confession evidence and partly on other undisputed evidence about the behaviour of the accused (see summary in Appendix 6.1).

2. *Presentation*

The adequacy of presentation of a simulated trial requires the case to be made realistic and engaging without being melodramatic. This we attempted to achieve by tape-recording a reconstruction of the case using actors with varying but appropriate accents (e.g. in the rôles of defendant, policeman, barristers etc.). The other important aspect of the case is the way the experimental variations are presented. If the way of doing this is too emphatic and dramatic, then any conclusions to be drawn from the experiment could be attributed to experimental artifacts (Rosenthal, 1966). If they are too subtle they may pass unnoticed in the sheer diversity of information and instructions contained in the trial.

3. *The relevance of the results to other cases*

This is the most difficult part of an experimental simulation. With material that achieves satisfactory answers to the problems of authenticity and adequacy of presentation, the experimenter may find himself in situations of high internal but low external validity (Campbell and Stanley, 1963). In other words, the better the experimental simulation becomes the smaller the range of generalisations that can be made from it. This is an inevitable consequence of the method, and can be overcome only by a combination of replication and refining the experimental hypotheses which, after all, arise from theories of law as they are tested against behavioural observations.

4. *Sampling*

To whom does one play one's authentic and carefully produced trials? There are four general approaches to the problem of sampling in experiments such as this: replication, representation, diversity and ignorance. Replication requires that the experimental juries should be composed as real ones are. This is virtually impossible since no data exist on the composition of actual juries. Representation requires that each simulated jury should consist of jurors selected from the general population of potential jurors. This is a viable method of selecting jurors, as we showed in the LSE Jury Project (1973b). The only problem with this method, apart from its expense and laboriousness, is the fact that it might provide representativeness as far as individuals called to jury service are concerned, but fail to provide representativeness as far as jury composition is concerned. We would argue that representativeness of jurors as opposed to representativeness of juries is, at the present stage of research, a distinction of marginal significance, but we have no evidence to support our opinion.

The third possibility is to select juries by as diverse a means as possible, knowing that you are neither replicating real juries nor representing the population of potential jurors. Such a method is valuable as long as the problems are clearly stated and as long as one interprets the results in the way least favourable to one's initial hypotheses or assumptions. This is not just a matter of requiring higher levels of statistical significance: it is rather a matter of judging the experimental variations in terms of the whole range of behaviour observed in the experiment, albeit qualitatively. Lastly, of course, the option of ignorance is always open. This option implies that it does not matter at all who participates in the experiment, the experimental material and variations are so robust that the results would be more or less the same regardless of how sampling was conducted.

In the pilot studies reported here we choose diversity as the only method of sampling consistent with the problem and a tiny budget. Jurors (mostly students) were recruited from the LSE, Hatfield Polytechnic, Chelsea Polytechnic and North London Polytechnic. This method provided juries that neither replicated real juries in their composition nor were representative of potential jurors. It was hoped that they would be more diverse in terms of age, social background and dominant interest than say, a sample of 'jurors' taken from a single class of university undergraduates. It was an imperfect method of sampling. Thus, the results presented here are those of a careful pilot study and we hope to suggest directions in which such research should proceed.

THE EXPERIMENT

The experiment was designed to test whether confessions in different forms or confessions retracted in court for different reasons had different effects on jurors' decisions. We therefore reconstructed four versions of an actual case in which a damaging confession was made to the police, and subsequently retracted in court (see Appendix 6.1). In the different versions we varied, firstly, whether the confession was made in writing and signed, or orally and presented by the police. Secondly, we varied the reasons given by the defendant for having confessed when he retracted his confession in court. In one condition he claimed that he had confessed because of undue pressure from the police at the time of making the confession. In the other condition he claimed that he was 'personally confused and uncertain' at the time of his confession. The experiment therefore had four conditions:

(i) a spoken confession retracted on the grounds of personal confusion;
(ii) a spoken confession retracted on the grounds of police pressure;
(iii) a written confession retracted on the grounds of personal confusion;
(iv) a written confession retracted on the grounds of police pressure.

The trials were played to two juries in each of the four conditions. The experiment was designed to test the following *ad hoc* hypotheses:

(i) a written and signed confession is more damaging to a defendant's case than a spoken one;
(ii) to retract a spoken confession is more likely to be acceptable to jurors than to retract a written one;
(iii) to retract any confession on the grounds of 'undue pressure' from the police, is likely to make jurors sympathetic towards the defendant.

These hypotheses, it must be stressed, were *ad hoc* and in no way test any psychological theories.

RESULTS

The results of this pilot study failed to confirm our hypotheses. Indeed, some of the results contradicted them. The results for the first and lesser charge are set out in Table 6.1.

Several interesting findings emerge. First there is a slight, though not significant, tendency for a written confession retracted on the grounds of 'confusion' to produce most acquittals. Secondly, where the defendant claimed to be 'pressured by the police' there were significantly more convictions. However, these results concerned only the lesser of the charges brought against Mr Robinson. Table 6.2 shows our pilot results concerning the more serious charge.

Table 6.1 Percentages of jurors voting to acquit in the different experimental conditions. Charge of possessing cannabis resin

Confession	Retraction	No. of Jurors	% voting to acquit
Spoken	confused	19	68
Spoken	pressured	21	52
Written	confused	19	89
Written	pressured	21	52

Table 6.2 Percentages of jurors voting to acquit in the various experimental conditions. Charge of possessing cocaine

Confession	Retraction	No. of Jurors	% voting to acquit
Spoken	confused	19	27
Spoken	pressured	21	42
Written	confused	19	84
Written	pressured	21	52

Again, the results are surprising. A written confession is significantly *less* damaging to the defendant than spoken admissions ($p < .01$) and it was significantly *more* damaging to the defendant to retract a confession on the grounds of police pressure than to retract it on the grounds of personal confusion ($p < .02$). Thus, contrary to our expectations, the results suggest, first, that the more damaging a confession might seem superficially (a written, signed statement), the less such evidence leads jurors to wish to convict; and second, that the accusation by the defendant that police had used 'undue pressure' was, if anything, an item of evidence *unfavourable* to him.

Of course, this is only a pilot study. Further replications are in progress. One thing is clear so far: jurors, doing their best in our simulations to behave as they would do in real life, seem to be saying that they are quite capable of evaluating confessions, quite capable of evaluating reasons for their retraction and, above all, tend to spend most of their time considering the factual elements of the case. Did the defendant try to hide the cocaine? Did the defendant lie to the police to hide a co-participant in the crime? Did the defendant obscure from the police his ownership of the fateful 'bag'? These are the things jurors in our simulations argued about. They hardly mentioned the confession. In general, we can conclude from our pilot studies, that the confessions were either irrelevant, or favourable to the defendant.

If the results of further experiments bear out, even partially, the trends shown in this pilot study, then we can conclude three things: first, we must not take for granted that a confession is *ipso facto* a damaging piece of evidence; second, we must beware of making *a priori* assumptions about how reasons for the retraction of a confession will be treated by jurors; and finally, we must look more searchingly, by detailed analyses of cases, at how often a confession is in fact a critical feature of the evidence.

The next stages are clear. Further analysis must be carried out of the effects of various types of confession and retraction; of how far jurors enhance or discount the validity of confessions as a function of how they were presented in court; and of how far jurors understand the rules of evidence as far as confessions are concerned and how they interpret the Judges' Rules about the elicitation of confessions. This study was an attempt at a first step in understanding this issue. It was taken with full appreciation of the things that it was not covering, but in the hope that it would provide material to keep open a many-sided debate.

APPENDIX 6.1.

SUMMARY OF THE CASE USED IN THIS PILOT STUDY

The defendant Robinson was stopped by police for driving his motor car with a faulty exhaust. He got into the police car since it was raining. When asked for his driving documents he handed the police a document pouch which contained some letters as well as his driving documents. One of the police officers took out these items, claiming in evidence that he handled each of them individually. Whilst putting the items back into the pouch, this officer noticed a small snuff box tucked down at the bottom of the pouch, but not concealed. This was opened and found to contain a small quantity of cannabis resin; that was the subject of the first charge.

Robinson was arrested for possessing the cannabis unlawfully. Whilst being driven back to the police station in the back of the police car, it is alleged that Robinson attempted to conceal a small package by pushing it down the back seat of the car. He was caught in the act by the second police officer. The package was found to contain cocaine, the subject of the second charge.

Although at first he denied knowledge of both the cannabis and the cocaine, Robinson subsequently admitted that both were his, having been given to him by a girl whose whereabouts were no longer known to him. He was charged with 1) possessing cannabis resin; and 2) possessing cocaine.

In his defence the accused retracted his previous admission claiming that the drugs must have been left in the pouch by a girl named 'Liz' who had lived with him for about five days. He had asked her to leave his flat when he had discovered her using drugs. She had left and he could provide no information as to her present whereabouts.

REFERENCES

D. T. Campbell and J. Stanley, 'Experimental and quasi-experimental designs for research on teaching', in N. L. Gage (ed.), *Handbook of Research on Teaching* (Chicago: Rand McNally, (1963)).

J. H. Davis, N. Kerr, R. Atkin, R. Holt and D. Meek, 'The decision processes of 6- and 12-person mock juries assigned unanimous and two-thirds majority rules', *Journal of Personality and Social Psychology*, *32* (1975) 1–14.

N. Kerr, S. Atkin, G. Stasser, D. Meek, R. Holt and J. Davis, 'Guilt beyond a reasonable doubt: Effects of concept definition and assigned decision rule on the judgements of Mock Jurors', *Journal of Personality and Social Psychology*, *34* (1976) 282–94.

LSE Jury Project, 'Juries and the rules of evidence', *The Criminal Law Review* (1973) 208–23. (a)

LSE Jury Project, 'Jurors and their verdicts', *Modern Law Review*, *36* (1973) 496–508. (b)

R. Rosenthal, *Experimenter Effects in Behavioural Research* (New York: Appleton-Century-Crofts, 1966).

A. P. Sealy, 'The Jury: Decision making in a small group', in H. Brown and R. Stevens (eds.), *Social Behaviour and Experience* (London: Hodder and Stoughton, 1975)

R. J. Simon, *The Jury and the Defence of Insanity* (Boston: Little Brown, 1967).

PART III

THE PSYCHOLOGIST AS EXPERT

7: Introducing Psychological Evidence in the Courts: Impediments and Opportunities

Brian Clapham

Psychologists who believe that they could play a valuable rôle in court procedures, at times feel frustrated at the apparent indifference of lawyers and courts. This frustration, and also the unawareness amongst lawyers of the help psychologists could offer in the ascertainment of truth, and generally in the administration of justice, was brought home to me whilst attending a seminar for lawyers and psychologists in 1977, arranged by the Centre for Socio-Legal Studies in Oxford. This chapter is an attempt to remedy the situation, by examining some of the main obstacles to the introduction of psychological evidence, and pointing to possible solutions and opportunities.

ADVERSARIAL PROCEDURE AND RULES OF EVIDENCE

It is the English approach to judicial procedure – which has been followed in many other countries with Common Law systems – that to a large extent inhibits the introduction of the results of research into most legal trials. The English legal system, both civil and criminal, is based on adversarial procedure. The judge and jury (if any) are expected to listen to the evidence and to the speeches of advocates commenting on the evidence or deficiencies in the evidence, and to reach a conclusion based on the evidence. It is not considered to be part of the function of the court, nor indeed of the jury itself, to seek out the truth of the matter by any methods of its own. The court is in effect a referee, deciding which version of the evidence it prefers. This is in marked contrast to the inquisitorial procedure common on the Continent. In inquisitorial procedure, the function of the advocate is of much less importance: it is the court itself which undertakes the task of ascertaining the truth, by whatever means it considers appropriate.

Pre-trial procedure is quite different under the two systems. Thus, in France, the function of the *juge d'instruction* is to take responsibility for the collection, examination and investigation of all the evidence and to decide whether or not a case should be remitted to trial (Sheehan, 1975). He is independent and not subject to the control of the court. All the steps taken by him are recorded in a *dossier*, which becomes a vital part of the trial documentation. He has the responsibility of ascertaining the facts.

In order to perform his duties, the *juge d'instruction* is given very extensive powers, which include the right to order experts to examine the accused or the evidence. He may instruct experts to examine any aspect of the case or the accused in person and there is no limit to the type of expert that may be employed. He might well, in an appropriate case, call in the aid of a psychologist to assist him, and the report of the psychologist could well include the results and findings of research by himself or indeed by others. Experts are normally chosen from a national list. Once appointed, an expert must perform his duties to the best of his ability, failure to do so being a criminal offence! An expert will have access to the *dossier*. He may question witnesses and, with the consent of the accused, he may question the accused. He may also ask the *juge* to put particular questions to the accused, and he may make a physical examination of the accused on the instructions of the *juge*, whether or not the accused consents (see Sheehan, 1975).

If conflicting evidence is given by different witnesses, the *juge* may confront witnesses with each other in his presence. The purpose of the confrontation is to ascertain if one party is lying, forgetful or mistaken and to find out why the discrepancy in the evidence occurs. He may also order a reconstruction. That is to say, he may request the accused, or a witness, to re-enact parts of his evidence, if need be at the *locus* itself. One can envisage wonderful opportunities for the results of psychological research to be used and applied in such confrontations and reconstructions.

Under the English adversarial system, there is no preliminary investigation comparable in any way with that of the *juge d'instruction* and consequently, no corresponding opportunities for the psychologist as expert at this stage. Committal proceedings in a magistrates' court nowadays are often concluded in a matter of minutes. The court frequently does not, and is not required to, read the papers. The defence solicitor consents to this speedy procedure and the case goes for trial. In a criminal trial a witness is normally allowed to give evidence only as to what he saw and heard, and the results of research, whether carried out by himself or others will not normally be acceptable. A criminal court might well be interested in the results of such research, but it is precluded from hearing about them by the objections of 'the other side'. The opponents of the party seeking to introduce research results can and will object that they were not present when such research experiments were carried out and all the persons who took part in the research processes are not available to be cross-examined as to the part they played. In other words, the research is not evidence.

This problem is especially difficult in criminal proceedings, where the rules of evidence are much stricter than in civil proceedings. The hearsay rule applies with full rigour. (Cross (1974) gives a brief statement of the rule against hearsay as follows: 'a statement other than one made by a person while giving oral evidence in the proceedings is inadmissible *as evidence of any fact stated*' (p. 6)). The court must have the 'best' evidence. 'What the soldier said' is not evidence of the truth of what he said, unless the accused was present and in a position to hear him. In addition, there is no exchange of experts' reports, as in civil proceedings. The Crown discloses its experts' reports, usually medical ones, but the defence is not normally under any such obligation. Apart from alibi evidence, the defence is usually able to spring whatever surprises it likes. The rules are kept strict because it is believed, rightly or wrongly, that this is necessary to avoid the risk of juries attaching importance to matters of little or no evidential value. They must decide on the evidence. If Mrs A were allowed to say that she was sure that the accused is the burglar, because Mrs B told her that she saw him leaving the house on the day in question, the jury, so it is believed, might form the view that the accused was indeed the man who left the house on the day in question.

It is sometimes possible to introduce the results of scientific research into criminal procedures. The experiment may have been carried out under laboratory conditions and the expert, his assistants, and all records may be available for inspection.

However, psychological research can seldom be of this strictly scientific character – 'controls' and 'subjects', with human characteristics, are quite unlike chemicals, acids, atoms, electrons or neutrons. The scientist's elements are very different from the elements in Kelly's Personal Construct Theory (Kelly, 1955).

The position is much easier in civil proceedings. The Civil Evidence Act, 1968, provided machinery for adducing evidence of a hearsay character about facts. This meant that the written report of an expert became admissible as evidence of fact, making personal attendance in court unnecessary. Written notice of its nature must be given before the trial and, if the other side does not object and/or if the witness in question cannot be produced at the trial (for example, because he has gone abroad) it is admissible. However, the psychologist called as an expert will often wish to give evidence of opinion rather than fact. In contrast with the evidence of a medical expert concerning a particular patient, a psychologist's opinion may be required on a set of circumstances or facts, having regard to his experience and knowledge of research in relation to similar facts and circumstances under other conditions. The Civil Evidence Act, 1972, has greatly strengthened the position of the expert giving this type of evidence, by extending the provisions of the 1968 Act, to make hearsay statements of opinion admissible in evidence in civil proceedings. A written notice of intention to rely on such statements has to be served on other parties. If no counter-notice is served, or if the witness is unavailable, the evidence may be put before the court.

Other new Rules, under Order 38 of the Rules of the Supreme Court[1] (*White Book*, 1979 p. 587), have resulted in a radical departure in the law and practice relating to expert evidence. A party can now only call expert evidence subject to the agreement of the court or agreement of the parties or subject to compliance with directions of the court that he should disclose the substance of such expert evidence before the trial. This is a significant advance in the direction of a more open system of pre-trial proceedings, which should enable parties to achieve just settlements and avoid surprises at the trial. Further, such changes should shorten trials and enable experts to prepare their evidence more thoroughly and helpfully. The Rules provide for the simultaneous mutual exchange of reports. The 1972 Act and the new Rules made following the Act, should make it much easier to put psychological expert opinion, including opinion based on research, before the courts. Indeed, provided the

Rules made under the 1972 Act are complied with, it should be possible to place before the court a psychologist's written report, including his own opinions, and the opinions of other experts on the problem generally, and even the results of research experiments.

As described above, one of the difficulties of introducing novel types of evidence is our adversarial system. If such evidence is introduced, it is the duty of the other side to try to demolish it. It may be difficult to understand, which makes the task of the opposing advocate all the more difficult. As a last resort, the other side may try to ridicule it. Experts know this and are loth to have the results of serious research attacked by counsel, and on occasions by courts, in this way.

A possible way out of this difficulty, so far as civil proceedings are concerned, lies in the appointment of a court expert. In other countries, court experts are the rule rather than the exception. In Italy, for example, it is the court which appoints the expert and although the parties are at liberty to appoint their own experts, it is the court expert whose views receive the greatest attention by the court. In this country, it is comparatively rare for a court expert to be appointed, but the Rules of the Supreme Court provide for it. Order 40, *Rule 1* of the Rules of the Supreme Court provides:

> In any cause . . . in which the question for an expert witness arises, the court may, at any time, on the application of any party appoint an independent expert to inquire and report upon any question of fact or opinion . . . In this rule 'expert' in relation to any question arising in a cause . . . means any person who has knowledge or experience of or in connection with that question that his opinion on it would be admissible in evidence (*White Book*, 1979, p. 643);

Rule 2 provides for the report to be sent to the court. If not accepted by the parties, the report 'shall be treated as information to the court and be given such weight as the court thinks fit' (*White Book*, p. 643);

Rule 3 provides for the expert to carry out experiments or tests of any kind. This would presumably cover such tests as a psychologist might need to carry out to enable him to prepare a report for the court;

Rule 4 provides that a court expert may be cross-examined (*White Book*, p. 644);

Rule 5 provides for his remuneration; and

Rule 6 provides for the calling of other experts where a court expert has been appointed (*White Book*, p. 644).

COSTS

The matter of costs impedes the introduction of psychological evidence in both civil and criminal cases. Most criminal proceedings, and a large proportion of civil litigation, are legally aided, and solicitors are rightly loth to incur expenditure which may be disallowed on taxation. Taxation is a method of checking, and approving or disapproving, legal costs and disbursements, and is carried out by court officials known as 'taxing masters'. However, in legally aided civil cases this difficulty over expenditure on expert evidence can be overcome by seeking the prior approval of legal aid Area Committees. Applications to Area Committees should, wherever possible, be supported by counsel's opinion, and some general indication, preferably from the psychologist himself, as to the nature and extent of the evidence which he could adduce, if instructed. The Area Committee can authorise expenditure, usually with a ceiling, and such expenditure will be allowed on taxation.

In criminal cases, the only way that a defence solicitor can be sure of getting unusual expenditure allowed on taxation is to seek prior approval of such expenditure from the Court Administrator. As in the case of Area Committees, such applications should be supported by an 'Opinion of Counsel' and, if possible, some indication from the expert of the manner and extent to which he believes that he could assist. So far as the prosecution are concerned, their costs are also taxed and paid out of the Central Fund. Any items of disbursements not allowed on taxation have to be paid out of police funds.

COMPREHENSIBILITY TO THE JURY

In trials before a jury, courts are often reluctant to allow expert evidence which is not obviously and manifestly relevant for fear that it may cloud and confuse the issue. All criminal trials in Crown Courts are before juries; civil juries, in this country, are great rarities. Juries are now drawn from the registers of electors and all persons over eighteen years of age, who are not excused or ineligible or disqualified for jury service, are liable to serve. (Amongst such persons are solicitors, police officers, serving soldiers and doctors). A very large proportion are women, not only because of the greater proportion in the population but also because the vast majority of persons who are excused or ineligible or disqualified are men.

The great majority of jurors are in court for the first time in their lives. The whole atmosphere is to them intimidating. I think that it would not be unfair to say that many jurors have never hitherto been required to make any really momentous decisions in their lives. Now, they are being asked to decide the fate of a fellow human being, and their own personal decision may mean freedom or life imprisonment for the accused. One can sympathise with the juror who recently sought and obtained excusal from jury service in the middle of a long trial on the grounds, in effect, that the whole matter was too much for her.

The courts feel that juries must be protected from having their attention diverted from 'real' evidence by expert evidence, unless it is strictly relevant within narrow limits, for fear that they may become confused. This is particularly so if the expert uses technical jargon which they may not understand, but may not wish to say they do not understand. When expert evidence is given in my court before a jury, I always ask the jury to retire to their room before the expert leaves the box in order that they may discuss with their foreperson whether there is any aspect of the evidence which they would like clarified, or whether there are any matters which they would like to raise with the expert. Far too often juries sit completely silent throughout the trial, because no one encourages them to speak, and then when all the evidence is completed, all the speeches made and the summing-up concluded, they send messages from their room raising most important questions which cannot be answered because the evidence is concluded and no further evidence can be adduced at that stage in the trial. They feel cheated and rightly so.

ATTITUDES AND KNOWLEDGE OF THE LEGAL PROFESSION

Just as certain kinds of evidence are acceptable as 'scientific', so are some experts more acceptable than others. The medical expert, the forensic scientist, the surveyor, the engineer and the expert in foreign law are all well recognised. The psychiatrist putting forward his clinical opinion based on his observation and treatment of a particular patient deserves, and normally receives, exactly the same respect as the orthopaedic surgeon or any other specialist. But the psychiatrist, although, of course, a medical expert, has had a hard struggle to achieve proper recognition. The psychiatrist and psychologist are still both 'trick cyclists' in certain quarters of the legal profession.

By far the most serious impediment to the adducement of the results of psychological research in legal proceedings is that, to a large extent, the legal profession is not aware of the extent to which such expert evidence is available, nor of how it could help their clients. It is for psychologists, as a profession, to remedy this by informing solicitors and the Bar. Articles in legal and other journals are one obvious way of doing this, but other more official channels may be appropriate. A recent one is the Royal Commission on Criminal Procedure. If, as I understand the position, psychologists believe that they have a valuable part to play in certain criminal proceedings, both as potential defence witnesses and as Crown witnesses, then they should certainly submit written evidence and offer to give oral evidence to this Commission. The Commission will not merely be looking at present problems of long trials, long delays, allegedly unsatisfactory jury verdicts and the increase in the number of criminal trials, but will almost certainly be looking ahead to the future, even perhaps the next 100 years. They will certainly be considering the advantages and disadvantages of the French and Scottish systems of pre-trial procedures (cf. Sheehan 1975). It is possible that they may recommend a pre-trial procedure before a *juge d'instruction* in order to shorten jury trials and reduce delays and costs. If they do, then, as I have already suggested, the expert has a most important rôle to play.

OPPORTUNITIES IN CRIMINAL PROCEEDINGS

If expert evidence in a criminal trial enables the court to get at what it believes to be the truth with a greater degree of certainty, more quickly or more easily, then its reception is a matter of great importance in criminal procedure. It is for psychologists to let the legal profession, the police and prosecuting solicitors know how they believe they can help in enabling courts to ascertain the truth in criminal matters. I have already mentioned the Royal Commission but there are other obvious channels such as the professional organisations of Chief Constables and County Prosecuting

Solicitors in addition to the Law Society and the Bar. I have been referring so far to evidence prior to, or in the course of, a trial. The evidence of psychologists is often more readily received after conviction. At the stage of sentencing, rules of evidence are relaxed and the court will more readily receive expert evidence to assist it in its task. Perhaps I should say *some* courts will do so. Judges are human, and some may more readily receive such reports than others. A most interesting development has occurred in Australia, where some probation officers have included in their reports the detailed results of criminological research and this practice has been approved in the Australian High Court. Whether, as probation officers become more familiar with criminological research in England, it spreads here, we shall have to wait and see.

A most fascinating example of expert evidence, of a very unusual nature, occurred at the Old Bailey in 1975 (see Niblett and Boreham, 1976). The prosecution case depended on statements alleged to have been made by the defendant – an all-too-common occurrence, particularly in London. The defendant had, on a previous occasion, made a statement in connection with a charge of murder, of which he had been acquitted. An international authority on stylistic analyses was called as an expert and a witness was also called to present evidence on the analyses by computer of the two sets of statements. There were eleven statements allegedly made by the defendant: of these, seven were admittedly authentic and had been made in the murder trial, and four were disputed. The expert opinion was that there was a distinct and substantial difference in style between the disputed and the undisputed documents. The method of analysis involved calculating a measure of similarity of style between every possible pair of documents. These coefficients were then used to draw a dendrogram, which would reveal the pattern in which documents most similar to each other in style clustered together. I believe that this is the first occasion in which evidence of cluster analysis has been presented in an English court. The jury acquitted on all the counts in the indictment in which the prosecution relied on the disputed statements.

No one ever knows what goes on in the jury room. In this country, unlike the USA, we are inhibited from asking, so we shall never know whether the defendant owed his acquittal to the expert. Incidentally, it is interesting to ponder on the fact that the experts using the same methods were unable to distinguish between the writings of Shakespeare and Wordsworth but were able to show conclusively that Damon Runyon did not write the Collects in the Book of Common Prayer!

I have mentioned this case at some length, as an instance to show that the courts do not have a closed mind towards the reception of expert evidence of a novel or exceptional kind.

OPPORTUNITIES IN CIVIL LITIGATION

The question whether experts are to be called, or a court expert is to be appointed, in civil litigation arises at a pre-trial stage known as the 'summons for directions'. It is then for the parties to seek the directions of the court regarding experts. The wise solicitor will have obtained an 'advice on evidence' from counsel and, if experts are to be used, counsel should have dealt with this in his advice. Counsel cannot advise about psychologists if he is unaware how they can help. So we are back with the problem of how to let the lawyers know what can be done by such experts. The ball really is in the court of the psychologists. Psychologists know better than lawyers how they could assist legal procedures. The kind of litigation I have in mind, where such evidence might be valuable, is all kinds of personal injury cases, nuisance cases and in the whole field of employment law. The latter is very much a growth sector of litigation!

OPPORTUNITIES IN CASES INVOLVING CHILDREN

There are obvious opportunities for psychological research evidence in the Family Division. Here again the problems are dealt with by judges without juries. The expert should, however, tread warily if asked to prepare a report which involves his seeing a child, as presumably he would normally need to do. He should only do so if asked to by the court itself; or by someone acting on behalf of the court (for example, a welfare officer); or by *both* parents. The courts do not approve of one party getting a report from an expert, such as a psychiatrist, without the consent of the other party, or of the court. Under our adversarial system, this may result in an immediate request for facilities for another expert's report, with the result that the child is seen by two psychiatrists. Reports of the child's own general medical practitioner are, of course, in a different category. I am referring here to reports which parties seek for the purpose of litigation or in the course of litigation, such as disputes as to access or custody.

On the other hand, reports of experts who have not seen the child are often of little value. A psychologist was recently called to give expert evidence before me in a custody case. His report and his evidence seemed to me to be a neat précis of John Bowlby's findings and opinions in *Child Care and the Growth of Love* (Bowlby, 1968). When I told the expert I was quite familiar with the contents of the book, he seemed somewhat deflated!

I have written of English courts. Children's hearings in criminal matters in Scotland are dealt with in accordance with the Social Work (Scotland) Act, 1968 and psychologists are very actively involved in these (Bruce, 1975). It is the exceptional case which reaches the court. At these children's hearings, reports are commonly called for from an assessment team consisting of a psychiatrist, a psychologist and a social worker. A word of caution to experts who may be asked to prepare reports for courts in Scotland – it is, I understand, essential to include the magic phrase 'This report is given on soul and conscience'. It is probably unnecessary and has no legal significance. Nevertheless, from time-honoured tradition, the phrase survives in use (Woodside, 1976).

Attitudes are changing. I have referred to the Australian courts and to an unusual case of expert evidence at the Old Bailey. Lawyers who followed the course of litigation in the USA after a major air disaster which took place in Europe, and heard lawyers describing their work on that case (which was shown on television) were amazed at the enormous amount of expert evidence of a far-reaching nature which was effectively introduced into that litigation, particularly in the calculation of the claimed quantum of damages for the victims and their dependants. English judges frequently complain (off the Bench) that they do not have the assistance of actuarial expert evidence in personal injury cases, especially in fatal accident cases. As the years pass, I envisage that the rôle of the expert, in all forms of litigation, both civil and criminal, will increase.

At present, the chief impediments to getting evidence of a psychological nature before the courts are not rules of evidence, nor the attitude of the courts, but unawareness among the legal profession of the ways in which psychologists can assist the courts in their search for the truth and in their attempts to ensure that justice is not only done but seen to be done. It is for psychologists to remedy this.

NOTE

1. The Rules of the Supreme Court may be found in the annual publication *Supreme Court Practice (White Book)*. The Rules are made by the Rules Committee, appointed by the Lord Chancellor. When approved by the Lord Chancellor, the Rules have the force of law.

REFERENCES

J. Bowlby, *Child Care and the Growth of Love* (London: Penguin, 1968).
N. Bruce, 'Children's hearings: A retrospect', *British Journal of Criminology, 15* (1975) 333–44.
R. Cross, *Evidence*, 4th ed. (London: Butterworths, 1974).
G. A. Kelly, *The Psychology of Personal Constructs* (New York: Norton, 1955).
B. Niblett and J. Boreham, 'Cluster analysis in court', *Criminal Law Review* (1976) 175–80.
A. V. Sheehan, *Criminal Procedure in Scotland and France* (Edinburgh: HMSO, 1975).
Supreme Court Practice (White Book) (London: Sweet and Maxwell, 1979).
M. Woodside, 'Psychiatric referrals by Edinburgh Courts', *British Journal of Criminology, 6* (1976) 20–37.

8: Expert Opinion based on Evidence from Forensic Hypnosis and Lie-detection

Lionel R. C. Haward

Truth drugs, hypnosis and the polygraph are three techniques which share a common application and engender similar problems. They are used to elicit information which cannot be obtained by more orthodox means. So effective can these techniques be that they are specifically proscribed in the USA in cases where the person concerned possesses classified information (e.g. Air Force Regulations 127-4: Section C. 12A). Such techniques are viewed by some as latter-day equivalents of the rack and thumbscrew of less happier times. Others see them as civilised alternatives to the rubber truncheon and genital electrodes employed in less democratic regimes. This paper is not concerned with the moral issues raised by the use of these techniques, important though these issues are: rather, attention is drawn to the nature of the information so obtained and the way such information is used.

In this country, the chemical substances which are used as so-called 'truth drugs' are scheduled poisons. Quite properly, they are exclusively the province of the medical practitioner, and will not be considered here. The forensic psychologist, on the other hand, is particularly well qualified to use both hypnosis and lie-detection apparatus. Historically, these techniques, including the use of truth drugs, are used for one of two different purposes, namely, to elicit from the individual concerned information relevant to the case which he will not, or more usually cannot, reveal; or alternatively to determine whether or not information, however obtained, is subjectively believed to be true or false.

Looking first at the use of hypnosis, the circumstances under which it is employed will vary according to whether the individual concerned is the victim, an independent witness, or the suspect.

The victim may be asked to consent to hypnosis when it is believed that there is some important fact known to the victim but which cannot be recalled spontaneously. Usually this is because the victim has suffered an emotional shock. As Brown (1918) showed long ago, forgetting due to emotion is the easiest type of amnesia to treat by hypnosis. Rape victims, in particular, often suffer severe emotional distress and therefore rape cases represent the most frequent offence in which hypnosis serves the purpose of assisting recall in victims. All the victims referred to me by the police in the current year have been rape victims. Other forms of physical assault can also induce partial amnesia, as a constituent of a post-traumatic neurosis. Whilst the amnesia due to organic brain damage in the case of head injury is not itself amenable to hypnosis, some elements of the amnesia in a victim with head injuries may stem from a concomitant emotional disturbance produced by the attack, and so may yield to hypnotic intervention. Head injury *per se* is therefore not a contra-indication to hypnotic recall, but the probability of success in these circumstances is considerably lower than in victims without head injury. However, direct physical assault is not the only cause of emotional shock and impaired memory recall. In one case a housewife who found her home ransacked on return from holiday suffered emotional trauma which seriously limited her ability to reply to questions put by the investigating police officer, and hypnosis was successful in obtaining an accurate and complete list of the property which had been stolen.

More usually, the immediate and urgent need of the Criminal Investigation Department is for evidence by which the offender can be identified. The success of hypnosis in yielding identification material has prompted some law enforcement agencies to consider the use of hypnosis on a regular basis. In Israel, for example, selected police officers are trained in forensic hypnosis and become specialists in this art. Since by virtue of their police training and experience they are already skilled interrogators, it is argued that the acquisition of specialist skills such as hypnosis provides the best of both worlds with maximum cost effectiveness. However, in the case of victims, one is often dealing with a psycho-pathological condition brought about by emotional and/or physical shock. For such conditions clinical insight and experience is necessary, both in obtaining the information, and in dealing with the subsequent emotional reaction. Shock amnesia is, after all, a defensive device, a mental mechanism fashioned by nature to protect the victim psychologically from overwhelming cataclysmic anxiety engendered by some event. To lift the repression and restore memory, this delicate mental protection must be stripped away and the individual exposed to a re-enactment of the experience. Whether the victim is psychologically fit enough to undergo such an experience is a clinical judgement which a police officer, however well trained in hypnosis, is neither competent nor qualified to make. Moreover, the reaction to the experience during hypnosis, devoid of the necessary mental defences, often evokes a reaction of pathological intensity, with screaming, thrashing of limbs, and crying over an extended period. This *abreaction* as it is called, is a phenomenon well known to clinicians and may require considerable therapeutic skills if the victim is to be restored to tranquility. When the victim is already suffering from some degree of pre-existing psychopathology, then such an abreaction in the absence of any immediate clinical intervention could possibly precipitate the victim into a psychiatric illness.

It is in the case of victims especially that the ethics of forensic hypnosis impinge upon the legal constraints imposed by the rules of evidence. The general procedure is for the victim, having recovered the memory of the critical event, to go into the witness box and testify as to what he or she now remembers. However, in order to do this, the repressed material has to be kept conscious. Normally, in revealing by hypnosis traumatic events which have been repressed, the clinician has a responsibility to the patient to minimise the effects of the trauma. Two alternatives are open to him. Either he can use post-hypnotic amnesia to remove memory of the events from the patient's consciousness, or he can provide intensive psychotherapy and emotional support during the period following the abreaction and so enable the patient to come to terms with the experience. If the witness is to testify in court, however, post-hypnotic amnesia cannot be employed. On the other hand, the clinical facilities for intensive support are rarely available to individuals who are not psychiatrically ill in the usual sense of the word. This means that, in dealing with victims referred for forensic hypnosis, a clinical prognosis is necessary as to the likely effects of abreaction, and a decision to hypnotise and remove the repression must be based upon this clinical evaluation.

Usually a compromise is effected, in which memories obtained under hypnosis are made available to the police, but the amnesia is reinstated to give the victim the psychological protection she needs. This enables the police to use the information in their investigation but not as prosecution evidence. This is sometimes a serious limitation which can cause an ethical conflict in which the hypnotist is forced to choose between the care of one individual or the safety of many potential victims. Under the present rules of evidence, the forensic hypnotist may not give evidence himself, as to the truth of the facts so stated, of what the victim said during hypnotic recall. This would infringe the hearsay rule. However, there should be no objection to the psychologist testifying as to what the victim said under hypnosis, as a fact that the statements were made. Thus, if a victim was unable to recall in the waking state any identifying features of the assailant, but under hypnosis described a particular tattoo on the assailant's arm, and if a suspect was known to have this particular tattoo on the correct anatomical site, it could be argued that this highly relevant piece of information should be put before the court without causing additional suffering to the victim by withholding the mercy of post-hypnotic amnesia. It has been suggested that the woman police constable, who is sometimes used as chaperone in such circumstances, would be more easily admitted as witness to fact, and could give evidence of what transpired during the hypnotic session. However, the court would normally want to know details about the validity of the information itself, on which the police chaperone would be unqualified to answer.

Forensic hypnosis has been discussed at the police colleges (BAAS, 1974), but few constabularies consider hypnosis as a possible technique in their investigations. The problem of the admissibility of hypnotic evidence and the reimposition of amnesia, although serious, is only one of several problems associated with the hypnosis of victims. Not all victims are willing to be hypnotised, some because they fear hypnosis, some because they fear the revivification of their recent ordeal. Many rape victims are minors, and parents are frequently reluctant to allow their daughters to be hypnotised. Of those adults who actually consent to hypnosis some are poor hypnotic subjects who cannot reach the required depth of trance within the time available and for whom further sessions are impracticable. Even with a good hypnotic subject, age-regression may require more than two hours to complete (Wolberg, 1945). Others, although consciously agreeing to be hypnotised, may nevertheless resist the induction for a variety of reasons. There are ways of overcoming this resistance, but some are ethically dubious, and all require the investment of more time than is usually available to the busy forensic psychologist.

In the second category of hypnotic subject, that of the witness, the effects tend to be less dramatic, since difficulties in remembering are less likely to be due to emotion engendered by the crime. Frequently the inability to recall facts is due to the physical loss of the memory trace; that is, the memory of the fact no longer exists, and in this case hypnosis is powerless to obtain recall. Very often, however, facts exist as memory traces, but cannot be recalled at the time they are required. The witness may believe that the information is 'in the mind', but cannot recall it by an act of will. As Kennedy (1957) remarks, describing the use of hypnosis to recover the location of mislaid articles, in these cases 'a very complete memory can sometimes be restored'.

At other times the witness may not even be aware of facts within his or her knowledge but available to recall. These often require reactivation by outside events, as when something long since forgotten can be recognised. Age regression is customarily employed in the recovery of forgotten memories. In this technique, the person is 'taken back' gradually under hypnosis to the age and date at which the events in question occurred. He or she is then made to relive these events, during which time the buried memories may emerge with the well-remembered ones (Reiff and Scheerer, 1960). Usually this is a non-clinical situation in which the memories themselves will be emotionally neutral. Where the witness was present at the time of the offence, however, or where the evidence itself concerns facts which have emotional connotations for the witness, then the re-enactment of the event during age regression may be accompanied by an emotional reaction which requires careful handling by the hypnotist.

The hypnosis of witnesses, as of victims, is usually undertaken for evidence of identity. However, there is a wide variety of situations in which information is sought by the police – or by the defence lawyers – which is not concerned with identity. In one case a witness was present when a will had been concealed, but had forgotten where the will had been hidden. Hypnosis enabled her to recall the event and the will was recovered. In a criminal investigation, time is often an important factor, yet witnesses may have difficulty in fixing times to experiences during the critical period. Sometimes age-regression enables the witness to recall specific visual images or sounds which can be time-located, such as a calendar on the wall, or a clock striking.

Even without age-regression, the higher level of concentration which the hypnotic state produces can assist recall, but the advantage of age-regression is that it brings before the witness the entire scene of the event, making available to memory a consider-able amount of information even before it is requested. Thus, a witness who finds an unattended bag which is later discovered to contain a bomb, can under hypnosis describe the contemporary scene, including the people hurrying away. Information of this particular kind has led to no fewer than seventeen arrests (Watson, 1974). Similarly, the Identikit pictures obtained during hypnosis are generally considered to be more accurate than those obtained in the waking state, and have proved successful in tracing the person concerned.

The third class of persons to whom hypnosis can be applied is that of the suspect. Usually, but not always, the suspect who consents to undergo hypnosis is innocent of the offence and seeks a means of proving his innocence. The use of hypnosis most frequently occurs when the suspect cannot provide an alibi. In at least two cases where the circumstantial evidence was convincing, the accused was saved from execution solely by hypnotically-derived evidence. In one case, the accused had wandered the streets in the early hours of the morning, wrestling with a personal problem and unaware of his immediate surroundings. Overwhelming circumstantial evidence pointed to him and in the absence of proof of his whereabouts he was arrested. He requested hypnosis in the hope of establishing his exact whereabouts at the critical time of the offence. Under hypnosis he was able to recall passing some gas fitters checking a gas leak in a particular street shortly after midnight. The workmen were present at that place only briefly and this located him fairly precisely in place and time and excluded him as a suspect.

In the second case, the evidence was even more damning. The corpse of a woman was found in a ditch bordering some waste ground, her panties beside her, and tyre tracks over her body, death being due to crushing. The tracks led to the suspect's car, in which the deceased woman's curlers were found. The suspect admitted taking the victim out for the evening, but claimed drunken amnesia for the sequel. He was charged with murder. Reliving the events under hypnosis, he described how they both got drunk, and on the way home pulled on to the waste ground to allow his companion to urinate. She started to do so, but slipped into the ditch and subsided into drunken unconsciousness. Meanwhile the accused also passed into a drunken stupor. Many hours later he awoke, finding his acquaintance missing and assumed she had gone home. He drove off, unaware that he was reversing the car over her body. This account explained numerous otherwise inexplicable details which were consistent with his story, and the jury convicted on a charge of manslaughter (Mikesell, 1952).

Few cases where forensic hypnosis is used are as dramatic as these two, but frequently an accumulation of corroborative detail is obtained by this method which would otherwise be absent and leave the suspect's story to stand on its face value. In the preparation of the appeal by an alleged IRA bomber, the person convicted was hypnotised in prison and age-regressed to two critical phases – one where he shared a London squat with some hippies and the other when he was in Ireland. At the former stage he was able to give evidence concerning a raid on a chemist's shop which located the date precisely, and in the latter stage his description of the operation of automatic weapons indicated an unfamiliarity with firearms incompatible with IRA membership.

Apart from the modern offences of absolute or vicarious liability, other offences require proof of *mens rea* by the prosecution before a conviction can be obtained. For this purpose hypnosis is particularly useful. Indeed Gulotta (1976) maintains that it is the only method by which the true mental state of the offender at the time of the *actus reus* can be determined.

Hypnosis against a person's will is not practicable, quite apart from the moral and legal objections, but suspects who are in fact guilty are sometimes prepared to undergo hypnosis when the circumstances of the event are hidden from consciousness. This raises ethical problems, for the suspect can be led to believe that the hypnotist is an accomplice, or friend in the past, and make statements he would probably not admit to in the waking state. In two cases of murder admissions of guilt have been obtained from the accused under hypnosis (Kubis, 1957). Where does the prisoner's right to silence stand then? When the offender is not an habitual criminal, as, for example, in an isolated case of theft by a middle class clerk, he may be too ashamed to plead guilty, yet be willing to reveal his guilt under hypnosis when he no longer feels 'responsible' for his actions. This is particularly the case when the offender believes that the offence should not be a crime, but nevertheless has guilt feelings about his action which arise from early moral training. The use of cannabis by students is a common example of this attitude, and it is interesting that one of the earliest recorded uses of forensic hypnosis, by Münsterberg (1909) describes how a student who denied possessing cocaine, submitted to hypnosis and in the subsequent trance revealed the secret place where the drug was hidden.

When used on the suspect or accused, hypnosis is, in a sense, also being used as a lie-detector. It is, of course, much more than this, since it elicits additional information, but it shares at least one of the uses, and many of the problems, of lie-detection generally. Indeed, Hilgard's finding that the greater the propensity for lying, the greater the susceptibility to hypnosis (Gibson and Corcoran, 1975) has encouraged the use of forensic hypnosis in lie-detection. About the methods of lie-detection, little more need be said here, since they are already well-known. In the USA, where over 3000 polygraph operators are employed, several million lie-detection interviews take place each year, though not all for forensic purposes (Lykken, 1974). The validity of both lie-detection and hypnotic age-regression has been examined scientifically in the artificial conditions of the laboratory (Skolnick, 1961), and they have received cautious acceptance. In real life, they are considerably more potent. The detection rate for lies on the polygraph has been claimed to be as high as ninety-seven per cent, and age-regression has been repeatedly authenticated by such instances as the recovery of early childhood language in immigrants from remote parts of the globe (Ås, 1962), and by the recall of infant school classmates checked against old registers. However, lie-detection and the recovery of memories by hypnosis are not automatic procedures. They are psychological techniques relying as much on the interactive nuances between the hypnotist and his client, and the personality of each, as on the purely mechanical aspects which past validity studies have examined. This fact justifies the plea that a professional psychological training should precede the use of these techniques for legal purposes. The forensic psychologist, professionally trained and experienced in the application of his specialty to legal problems, is well qualified to undertake these techniques, and certainly satisfies the conditions laid down in *Bell* v. *Kroger* (Ungerman, 1959).

If it is accepted that the evidence obtained by these techniques is valid, that is, corresponds as much to reality as normal human memory (itself far from infallible) then the question of admissibility still has to be faced. There are long-standing precedents for the admission of hypnotic evidence in foreign law. According to Bryan (1962) a court in Verona, as long ago as 1860, agreed to the hypnosis of a witness, who then made statements in the trance state which led to the conviction of the accused. In America, Münsterberg (1909) introduced forensic hypnosis at the turn of the century. At first it was ruled that a witness could not give evidence under hypnosis, on the grounds that a person in a trance was not the same person as when awake and taking the oath. This ruling excluded the evidence of a suspect who requested the court that she might be cross-examined under hypnosis so that her innocence could be established. In contrast, by 1955 Levy was able to examine a wide variety of decisions concerning the admissibility of hypnotically derived evidence. As in other aspects of American law, there are differences between the various states with regard to admissibility, although in general it can be said that the courts are sensibly disposed to admit prosecution evidence of this kind whilst being cautious of that tendered by the defence. Situations in which the witness has given evidence under post-hypnotic suggestion may have already occurred, and this raises particularly difficult legal issues, since the authenticity of the evidence is questionable and the trial court may not even be aware that the witness is in a post-hypnotic state. Indeed, the nature of post-hypnotic suggestion is such that during the hypnotic session ostensibly to derive information, the hypnotist could implant suggestions of what the witness should recall and testify to when in the witness box, without the witness being aware of the source of this information. It would then be given in good faith under oath. The current practice of hypnotising nervous witnesses before the trial so that they can be relaxed and give their evidence effectively leaves the door open to the greatest possible abuses.

In English law, the precedent for the expert witness to give evidence on lie detection was provided in *R*. v. *Spencer* (1960)[1] when a psychiatrist administered 'truth' drugs at the request of the accused in order to ascertain facts which the latter could not recall. In admitting the evidence, the jury were told that they must not discredit it just because it was novel, which suggested that the court was prepared to afford it some weight. However, the details of the crime, which concerned theft from a corpse, were such that the jury found the accused guilty despite the expert evidence which negated *mens rea*. Whether the admissibility of evidence from methods of lie-detection other than truth drugs will follow from this precedent remains to be seen. Already in the current year I have seen five persons accused of murder for investigation by lie-detection, and in each case the evidence has been admitted as part of the prisoner's testimony rather than as expert evidence. This has had a twofold disadvantage. In the first place the accused is not able to present the evidence scientifically, to discuss its validity, and to qualify conclusions drawn from it. Secondly, because the testimony of the accused which is in his own interest is suspect, the evidence of the lie-detector test is similarly suspect. Indeed it could be deservedly so, for there is nothing but moral scruples to prevent the accused from distorting the actual findings in his favour when giving evidence. There would seem to be every reason for letting the independent expert report his own findings to the court, expressing the necessary caveats, and giving an expert opinion on the validity and meaning of the results.

If England and Wales have lagged a little way behind the United States in getting expert evidence derived from hypnosis and lie detection into court, the British forensic psychologist is perhaps in advance of his American colleagues in the facilities for obtaining the evidence provided by the Home Office and police authorities. The Supreme Court of California (1952)[2] ruled that the attorney has the right to engage a hypnotist to interview his client under hypnosis and to learn facts not recoverable by reason of amnesia, intoxication, shock, etc. for the preparation of the case, irrespective of whether the evidence so obtained is admissible. The report also states that the accused has a basic right of access to any third person who can help in this way, together with the right of privacy without the presence of a law enforcement officer. Refusal by the trial court can be·remedied by a writ of *mandamus*. At the time of writing few other states have made these rights so explicit. Within my own experience there has never been any difficulty in conducting age-regression by hypnosis in prisons, and privacy is generally provided by the prison authorities as a matter of course. The prison environment is not always conducive to facile hypnosis, but the prison authorities go out of their way to provide the best available conditions. The techniques have been validated, the Home Office and constabulary provide the facilities for them to be used, and forensic psychologists are being trained in this specialty.

While the prosecution can make effective use of information obtained from victims, witnesses and suspects even if not presented in court, the defence is severely limited in this respect and recognition of the admissibility of this evidence by the courts would help to redress the balance. Consideration of these matters by those responsible for law reform in this area has been requested. Meanwhile, forensic psychologists practising these techniques will continue to do so with the customary scientific caution, accepting fallibility, but with sufficient confidence in the validity and utility of these methods to encourage their further examination, use and development.

NOTES

1. *R.* v. *Spencer*, *The Times*, 21st January 1960.
2. Supreme Court Report: 52 Cal. 2nd Series 99. L.A. no. 25328 (1952).

REFERENCES

A. Ås, 'Recovery of forgotten language through age-regression', *American Journal of Hypnosis, 5* (1962) 24–9.
BAAS *Science and the Police* (London: British Association for the Advancement of Science, 1974).
H. Brown, *Advanced Suggestion* (London: Bailliere, Tindall and Cox, 1918).
W. J. Bryan, *Legal Aspects of Hypnosis* (Springfield, Ill.: Thomas, 1962).
H. B. Gibson and M. E. Corcoran, 'Hypnotic susceptibility in relation to personality, lying and sex', *Bulletin of the British Psychological Society, 28* (1975) 232–42.
G. Gulotta, 'Psychoanalysis and criminal responsibility', (Milan: Giuffre Editore, 1976).
A. Kennedy, 'Medical use of hypnotism', *British Medical Journal, (1)* (1957) 1317–19.
J. F. Kubis, 'Instrumental, chemical and psychological aids to the interrogation of witnesses', *Journal of Social Issues, 13* (1957) 40–9.
S. S. Levy, 'Hypnosis and legal immutability', *Journal of Criminal Law and Criminology, 46* (1955) 333–46.
D. T. Lykken, 'Psychology and the lie detection industry', *American Psychologist, 29* (1974) 725.
R. Mikesell, 'Hypnosis in the Conrey murder case', *Hypnosis Quarterly, 5* (1952) 1.

H. Münsterberg, *Psychology and Crime* (London: T. Fisher Unwin, 1909).

R. Reiff and M. Scheerer, *Memory and Hypnotic Age-Regression* (New York: International University Press, 1960).

J. H. Skolnick, 'Scientific theory and scientific evidence: analysis of lie-detection', *Yale Law Journal*, *70* (1961) 695–7.

J. Ungerman, 'Admissibility of scientific evidence – tactograph', *South Western Law Journal*, *14* (1959) 113.

P. Watson, 'Finding the bombers by hypnosis', *Sunday Times*, 8th December *1974*.

L. Wolberg, *Hypno-analysis* (New York: Grune and Stratton, 1945).

PART IV

LEGAL LANGUAGE AND COMMUNICATION

9: Is Legal Jargon a Restrictive Practice?

Patricia Wright

'Everything that can be said, can be said clearly'
Wittgenstein, *Tractatus Logico-Philosophicus*, 4.116

INTRODUCTION: THE IMPORTANCE OF CLEAR COMMUNICATION

Useful guidelines on writing well have been available for more than fifty years (e.g. Fowler, 1926). Yet many legal documents are a lexical steeplechase, in which intrepid readers surmount the hurdles of archaic terms only to stumble at the lengthy waterjumps of qualifying clauses packed end to end against each other. Such language inevitably restricts people's access to information. Moreover this style of language has been copied by many organisations dealing with the general public. The following example, from form SA101 issued by the Department of National Savings, is currently available in British post offices (January 1979). Paragraph 10 of the form explains what happens to those who join the Save as you Earn Scheme but die before making the full sixty payments:

> If repayment is made on or after the first anniversary of the starting date there shall be payable –
> (a) the total amount of the revalued contributions each contribution being revalued to reflect the difference between the Index figure applicable to the month beginning with the date following the due date of that contribution or, in the case of the first contribution, between the Index figure applicable to the month

in which the starting date falls and the Index figure applicable to the month of repayment; or . . .

Can many readers understand this without a struggle? Does the difficulty of such language restrict the number of people willing to join the scheme?

There are many similar examples. The use of legalistic phraseology undoubtedly restricts the range of holidaymakers who understand their travel insurance, just as it restricts the range of employees who understand their pension schemes. Within the range of people entitled to welfare benefits, it restricts to a small subset those who understand their rights and know how to obtain them (Ellis, 1978; Voysey, 1976). It even restricts the extent to which jurors understand their responsibilities and the range of options open to them (Sales, Elwork and Alfini, 1977). This in turn means that it sets limits to the justice available through the courts. Consumers may be restricted in many ways, as for example those who buy electricity without understanding the Code of Practice which explains the circumstances in which the supply will be cut off. The list of those affected by legal language could be extended further, but the critical issue is whether such restrictions are inevitable. Are they an inherent part of the explanation of any complex subject matter? This seems unlikely. In the United States President Carter has already initiated procedures to reduce the amount of unclear communication. One consequence has been the reduction of a 250 word paragraph to just thirty words (Leapman, 1978). Clearly the restrictions can be lifted.

It should not be thought that in a legal context the limitations arising from particular styles of language are confined to written communications. When lawyers give informal advice or an expert opinion, when they interview a client or cross-examine a witness the special words used can be critical. The hazards of leading questions are well known (e.g. Loftus, 1975) but many subtle aspects of language comprehension can result in 'misinterpretations' of questions and answers (Harris and Monaco, 1978). Even as small a change as replacing an indefinite article in a question can alter the accuracy of the answer obtained. Loftus and Zanni (1975) showed people a short film of a car accident and then asked either 'Did you see a broken headlight?' or 'Did you see the broken headlight?'. The questions were included in a written questionnaire, so avoiding any differential emphasis being given by the speaker. Nevertheless, more people reported having seen *the* headlight than thought they had seen *a* headlight. Similarly the choice of certain words in a question will restrict the way other parts of the question are interpreted. Loftus and Palmer (1974) asked people to estimate how fast two cars were going when an accident occurred. People's estimates of speed were higher when the question used words like 'smashed' rather than words like 'collided'. How often such effects occur is not yet clear. Read, Barnsley, Ankers and Wishaw (1978) failed to replicate this effect on estimates of speed, but found it on estimates of damage done. They have therefore suggested that such biases are most likely to arise when they are consistent with verbal associations. For example 'smashed' is associated with 'breakage', and hence when used in a question is likely to induce exaggerations of the amount of damage witnessed.

Accuracy is also affected by the syntactic structure of the question. Barnard (1979) has shown that passive questions encourage people to accept plausible, but not necessarily correct, implications of what they know. After people had read a statement such as 'John saw Mary drop the plate' there were more affirmative answers to the question 'Was the plate broken by Mary?' than to the question 'Did Mary break the plate?'. Wright (1969) found that people make three times as many mistakes when answering passive questions (e.g. 'Who was chased by the policeman?') than when answering active questions (e.g. 'Who did the policeman chase?'). Such evidence indicates that legal language may be restrictive in many subtle ways.

Oral communications involve many paralinguistic cues such as intonation pattern, pausing and gestures. For simplicity the following discussion will focus on the comprehensibility of written information, but many of the points raised are equally pertinent to spoken language. The next section will examine whether psychological research can help to improve the clarity of written communications. The third section will consider whether any other kind of help is needed when designing effective written information.

LEGAL LANGUAGE AND THE PSYCHOLOGICAL LITERATURE

The relevant psychological research is of two kinds. On the one hand there are psycholinguistic studies of the problems of comprehension (see the review by Clark and Clark, 1977). On the other hand there are psychological investigations of the design of information (see the review by Wright, 1977a). Together these studies offer guidelines on what to do and what to avoid when designing written information. A recent survey of such guidelines can be found in Hartley and Burnhill (1977), who summarize fifty rules of thumb that could be applied in the preparation of instructional texts. Many of these guidelines have relevance to the design of other kinds of documents.

In addition to producing indicative findings, there is a further way in which psychological research can be useful. The techniques used in behavioural research can often also be used during the preparation of a document in order to increase the chances of successful communication. The use of such techniques will be considered in greater detail while reviewing some of the research findings available in the literature. For convenience the studies will be related to three trouble spots in legal language: terminology, sentence structure and presentation.

TERMINOLOGY

It hardly needs experimental evidence to establish that people have problems with some of the words that are frequently found in legal language. Many of the terms are historical remnants of an English that we no longer speak (Partridge, 1957, p. 41). For example one mortgage application contains the following terms: 'hereinafter', 'severally', 'hereof', 'hereunder', 'hereafter', 'affixed', 'thereto', 'herein', and 'hereunto'. Some of these words are not needed at all. Consider the sentence 'This Legal Charge shall incorporate the agreements printed on pages 2 and 3'. In the context of a single document of four pages, such a sentence gains nothing useful from having 'hereof' tagged on the end of it. Where ambiguities might arise – for example, if pages 2 and 3 might be in some other document – the phrase 'of this document' would be one way of removing the ambiguity. Many others of the words listed above have much more familiar equivalents in contemporary English. Today when we mean 'hereunder' we say 'below'. When we mean 'hereafter' we say 'subsequently'. A phrase such as 'hereafter affixed thereto' probably means 'subsequently fixed to it'.

When people are solving reasoning problems, it becomes more

difficult to solve the problem if short, familiar words are replaced by unfamiliar, polysyllabic terms. Slight changes in wording can also have sizeable effects on the success with which candidates answer 'O' level chemistry questions (Johnstone and Cassels, 1978). Similar findings have been obtained in bilingual studies (e.g. Macnamara, 1966) which show that people have greater trouble thinking and reasoning in their weaker language. In effect, this is what the use of archaic terms is requiring the reader to do. Readers would benefit from a modern translation.

Problems with other kinds of technical terms require a different solution. If they cannot be replaced in the text, then explanations may need to be given. This can be done in a glossary, or sometimes in parentheses alongside the term itself. Bank customers uncertain who is the payee and who the drawer of a cheque might wish the bank would adopt this latter course.

Unfortunately, one man's jargon is another man's stock-in-trade. A writer can be unaware that he is using phrases and concepts unfamiliar to those outside his profession. One solution is to have the text critically evaluated by someone unfamiliar with the subject-matter. An example of this procedure can be found in the critique of some Open University textbooks which has been carried out by students in the department of typography and graphic communication at the University of Reading (Macdonald-Ross and Waller, 1975a and b). Other methods include surveys of the general public, to establish how well particular terms are understood. This method has been used by the Transport and Road Research Laboratory as a means of checking whether the Highway Code uses familiar and unambiguous terms (e.g. Cattell and Lewis, 1975). Using such a procedure to help produce a single document could obviously be expensive. But for organisations who will repeatedly be preparing written information relating to a specific subject-matter, such a survey of relevant vocabulary can be a sound, long-term investment. The information provided will almost certainly be illuminating to those who draft documents. This can be illustrated by just a couple of examples from the Cattell and Lewis report. The meaning of the word 'adequate' was understood by only thirty nine percent of the eleven year-old children in their sample. Only thirty two percent of the eleven year-olds understood the word 'priority'. A more recent survey carried out with adults shows a similar picture (Sheppard, personal communication). Although it was found that drivers did somewhat better than non-drivers, both groups understood fewer terms than the writers of road safety literature had imagined they would.

The problems of terminology apply with equal force to abbreviations. Less obviously, familiar words and phrases may also cause difficulties because they have different connotations for different members of the public. The phrase 'single woman and her dependants' conjures up for many people an image of a young, unmarried mother and her children. But in fact the national organisation that has this phrase in its title (The National Council for the Single Woman and her Dependants) is an organisation concerned to aid those single women who are caring for elderly parents. Familiar words like 'family', 'household', and 'income' are all further instances of terms which are not difficult to read, but whose precise meaning may vary from reader to reader. Again survey techniques may be a useful way of exploring such concepts. Alternatively, given that the interpretation of particular words may vary with the context in which the words are used, it may be preferable to 'trouble-shoot' the draft of a particular document.

SENTENCE STRUCTURE

Writers may fail to communicate successfully with readers not only because of the words being used but also because of the sentence structures chosen to express ideas. Everyone agrees that long sentences can be a problem. However, it has not always been clear just how one measures the length of a sentence, and doubts exist about the value of many formulae (Stokes, 1978). In the readability formulae of the 1940s, length was measured in numbers of words (e.g. Flesch, 1948). As a rough guide this can be useful: it certainly correlates with many other indices of reading difficulty. Many of the standard formulae for assessing the readability of text have the advantage that they can easily be computerised. Modern printing techniques often have text in a computer readable form from a fairly early stage. This makes it a simple procedure to check the approximate level of difficulty of the document by applying a formula (Macdonald-Ross, 1978).

However, sentence length is not the causal factor in generating comprehension problems. It is only a correlate. As such it acts as a filter rather than as a detector of difficult sentence structures (Rothkopf, 1976). Texts which do not pass through the filter almost certainly need revising. But a text which passes through the filter may still be very difficult to understand. These difficulties arise partly from the syntactic structure of the sentence and partly from the conceptual, or propositional, information in the sentence. A usefully succinct review of difficulties arising from the grammatical structure of sentences can be found in Sales, Elwork and Alfini (1977). A more detailed coverage of psycholinguistic research on many aspects of sentence comprehension is given by Clark and Clark (1977).

Analysis of the conceptual or propositional structure of sentences can be extended to deal with the relations between sentences. In recent years there has been an increasing number of well-developed models of the way people understand and remember paragraphs of text and short stories (e.g. Bower, 1976; Kintsch, 1976; Mandler and Johnson, 1977; Rumelhart, 1975). There are several differences among the models but they share a common claim that one of the major causes of comprehension difficulty, both within a sentence and between sentences, is the number of separate propositions and the way these propositions are related. Considerable evidence supports this view. For example, Kintsch and Keenan (1973) found that people took longer to read sentences containing more propositions, even though the sentences had roughly the same number of words in them. Thus, people were faster when reading 'Romulus, the legendary founder of Rome, took the women of the Sabines by force' than they were when reading 'Cleopatra's downfall lay in her foolish trust in the fickle political figures in the Roman world'. Vipond and Kintsch (1978) have shown that for some selected texts their propositional analysis can be a more reliable predictor of comprehension difficulty than the Flesch reading ease formula. In other studies it has been shown that texts are more difficult to remember, even though comparable in word length and number of propositions, if there is greater variety in the concepts being dealt with (Kintsch, Kozminsky, Streby, McKoon and Keenan, 1975). That is to say, a text which keeps talking about the same few things is easier to follow than a text which deals with a variety of different topics.

Clearly there is no simple rule of thumb which can be applied to guarantee that a particular sentence or paragraph structure will be easily understood. Sentence length is a useful rough guide but nothing more. Indeed one can find instances where the writer's attempt to shorten sentences has actually created ambiguities. This is particularly likely to happen when words are simply omitted. In conversation intonation pattern is used to help the listener grasp the meaning. It is less critical to provide all the function words such as relative pronouns ('who', 'which', 'that') which help to make the sentence structure clear. Written communications are much more dependent upon information being given explicitly in the text. This is particularly so for sentences involving complement constructions, where the inclusion of the word 'that' helps the reader (Hakes, 1971). For example, a sentence which begins 'I heard that the seminar . . . ' lets you know that the speaker/writer is going to say something about the seminar. Without 'that' the sentence begins 'I heard the seminar . . . ' This conveys a quite different meaning. Wright and Barnard (1975a) have discussed some of the exceptions to the rule about short sentences. Jones (1968) has discussed others.

Another example of the use of unhelpful deletion is to be found in section 4 of the leaflet *Guide to Legal Aid* (1976). The gist of the first sentence is that 'X' has a list of solicitors. The second sentence reads 'In difficulty, the offices of The Law Society throughout England and Wales can suggest . . . ' Who is in difficulty? It is not The Law Society, nor is it the solicitors on the list. It may not be 'X' either, since the writer probably hoped to indicate by the deletion that 'For anybody in difficulty, The Law Society can suggest . . . ' Although, in this instance, it does not take too much guesswork to arrive at the missing referent, it is a characteristic of clear communications that they do not have to rely on the reader's guesswork about the writer's intended meaning.

Studies of comprehension have shown that readers and listeners use a great deal of plausible guesswork in interpreting a message. This appears to be why more difficult sentence structures, such as the passive construction, can sometimes be understood quite easily (e.g. Glucksberg, Trabasso and Wald, 1973; Herriott, 1969). If there is only one plausible semantic relation between the major content words in a sentence (e.g. handbag – dropped – passenger), and the sentence has only one clause, then readers will probably manage without too much difficulty. But in most other circumstances passive sentences can cause comprehension problems. Another sentence from section 4 of the *Guide to Legal Aid* illustrates this. With the content words in the original replaced by 'X', 'Y' and 'Z' so as to emphasise the syntactic structure, the sentence reads 'If X is sought by Y, Z must be seen by his parent'. Whose parent? With this sentence structure the referent of the pronoun is ambiguous. Perhaps the most likely candidate is Z. Yet in the original version Z was *the solicitor*. It seems unlikely that the solicitor needed to see his own parents. The next most likely candidate would seem to be X, the topic of the sentence. The content of X in the original was *advice or assistance*. If 'his' cannot be referring to either X or Z then it must be referring to Y. Again the reader is invited to play with a semantic jigsaw in which the meaning can be grasped only if you know what the writer was probably trying to say.

This particular sentence could easily be restructured to remove the passive from both the first and second clauses. The original sentence read 'Where advice or assistance is sought by someone under the school-leaving age, the solicitor must be seen by his parent'. One version avoiding the passive altogether would have been 'The solicitor must see the parent of anyone under the school-leaving age who seeks advice'. Perhaps even better is a version which puts in the topic position the juvenile rather than the solicitor. For example, 'If someone under school-leaving age seeks advice, his or her parent must see the solicitor'.

In paraphrasing the original, another ambiguity became apparent. It is unclear whether the parental contact must take place *if* a juvenile seeks advice or *when* a juvenile seeks advice. This is not unusual. Once one conceptual muddle sets in, others follow fast on its heels.

In restructuring the last example, not only was the voice of the clauses changed from passive to active, but, in one version, the sequence of clauses was changed so that the main clause came first. There is experimental evidence that people find it easier to deal with sentences in which the main clause precedes the subordinate clause (e.g. Clark and Clark 1968). Hartley and Burnhill (1977) recommend that sentence length should be limited to only one subordinate clause. Certainly a writer who is introducing a second subordinate clause might do well to consider whether he is putting things in the most helpful way. No such question seems to have entered the thinking of whoever drafted the following explanation provided by the Eastern Electricity Board:

> If the meter for any reason has not been read on behalf of the Board at the relevant time the number of units supplied in the period concerned between the hours specified for the reduction of the rate of unit charge as aforesaid and the number of units supplied in that period at other times will be estimated having regard to previous or subsequent registrations.

This explanation has five clauses. To many readers it must feel more like fifty-five. One technique giving a rough idea of whether a sentence is too long, is to see if a reader can easily repeat it after having read it just once. Of course people can repeat things they do not understand. This is not a failsafe check on comprehension. It is just a convenient guide to staying within the tolerance range of the cognitive abilities of most readers.

The distinction between main and subordinate clauses has also been found relevant in experimental studies of negation. However, the distinction main/subordinate is often confounded with variation in the way information is negated. It is too soon to formulate general principles, but it does seem that people find it easier to deal with negative prefixes (such as in-, un-, dis-) than with negative particles such as *not* (Sherman, 1973). This may be because a negative prefix often conveys a rather more specific meaning than does the negative particle. For example, compare 'Jim is unhappy' with 'Jim is not happy'. If one imagines some dimension ranging from 'happiness' to 'unhappiness', the first statement clearly locates Jim well down at the 'unhappiness' end of the scale. This is less obviously the case in the second sentence. He might be, but he might also be near some neutral mid-point on the scale.

Studies by Clark and Lucy (1975) have stressed the importance of the conveyed meaning of an utterance. They have shown that this can be more critical than the presence or absence of explicit negative elements. For example when someone says 'The door is not closed' they are usually making a polite request for someone to shut the door. Such statements do not show the comprehension difficulties usually associated with negative statements. In contrast, explicit negatives in questions make them almost unanswerable. If someone asks 'Isn't the door closed?' does a truthful reply of 'Yes' mean the door was open or shut? The ambiguity arises because there are two quite different paraphrases of such a question. On the one hand, a tag question might have been used, to ask 'The door is closed, isn't it?' In this case the answer 'Yes' means that the door is shut. On the other hand, the negative particle could be cancelled out by changing 'closed' to 'open' giving 'Is the door open?' The answer 'Yes' now means the opposite of what it meant previously. Since there is no way of knowing how someone may have re-interpreted a negative question, no one can be certain what the answer means – unless they ask another question.

The comprehension of negatives occurring in instructions is again a complex issue. There is evidence that people more easily follow an instruction of the form 'Do something unless X' than an instruction 'Do not do something if X' (Wright and Wilcox, 1977). Indeed this sentence structure, in which the negative main clause is followed by a subordinate affirmative clause, was sometimes more difficult for people to understand than an instruction having two negatives ('Do not do something unless Y'). This is consistent with the Clark and Lucy finding that the meaning conveyed by the entire sentence is an important factor in determining comprehension difficulty, not just the number of negative elements. Although the relative difficulty of different kinds of negative may vary, research shows that performance remains significantly better with fully affirmative instructions, 'Do something if' (e.g. Wright and Wilcox, 1977).

Negatives do more than just convey information. They are also a means of adding emphasis, of focusing attention on specific information within a sentence. Their use can be highly appropriate in some contexts. An example quoted by Sales *et al.* is the sentence 'It is not a crime to smoke marijuana, but it is a crime to sell it' (Sales *et al.*, 1977, p. 44). Here the emphasis comes both from the use of the word 'not' and from locating the negative clause early in the sentence. There are other contexts where specific types of negation can be useful (e.g. Johnson-Laird and Tridgell, 1972; Wason, 1965; Wright and Barnard, 1975a). Nevertheless, there are many more contexts in which the use of negatives is neither necessary nor helpful.

Explicit negatives in sentences are easy to recognise. However there is a variety of other words which have negative connotations (e.g. reduce, prevent, deduct, forget, except). These may also be more difficult for the reader than their more positive antonyms, such as 'increase'. Wright and Barnard (1975b) compared people's ability to use the terms 'more' and 'less' to reach decisions about the information they were shown in a variety of numerical tables. They found that people were both faster and more accurate when the phrase 'more than' was involved. The indications are that 'less than' would be easier to deal with than its close paraphrase 'not more than'; but as yet empirical comparisons between these phrases have not been made. Perhaps when talking about income scales, the word 'below' might be even easier than 'less than'. It is a word which is acquired by young children quite early in their language development, and age of acquisition is often a good predictor of how easily adults can understand a particular word (Clark, 1977).

Psychological research has highlighted numerous comprehension problems caused by sentence structure and by the relations among clauses within a sentence. Nevertheless, it can be hazardous to generalise too glibly from this research. There are exceptions to almost every rule of thumb that one might care to formulate. Behavioural data require sensitive interpretation before being applied to a particular problem. This point is illustrated in a study of such examination rubrics as 'Answer ten of the following questions choosing at least two and not more than three from any one section' (Wright, 1975). This would seem to be a piece of complex prose in urgent need of simplification. To provide a baseline against which to measure comprehension difficulty, one group in the experiment were given the instruction 'Answer ten of the following questions'. With this very simple instruction, significantly more people answered the wrong number of questions than with the more complicated instructions! In fact the most common mistake was to go through and try answering all twenty of the available questions. Since some of the questions were very easy ('Do mice like cheese?') and some were very difficult ('What year was the Taj Mahal built?') it was quite inappropriate for people to disregard the option to select their questions. So there appear to be exceptions even to a guideline which urges writers to say things as simply as possible. This emphasises the need to supplement the findings available in the research literature with evidence about the reader's interpretation of the specific document being written.

PRESENTATION

Legal language creates problems for readers, not just because of the terminology it contains, nor just because of the sentence structures it uses, but also because of the way it is presented. The phrase 'the small print' has become part of our current idiomatic usage. For several years there have been recommendations concerning the usable range of type sizes (Tinker, 1965; Spencer, 1969). Print smaller than the normal text in newspapers becomes difficult to read. Yet the use of much smaller print persists. It has been known for some time that readers find it easier to read print that is set with an equal spacing between words, rather than using a variable spacing to create an even right-hand margin (Gregory and Poulton, 1970). Nevertheless two of the three leaflets currently available explaining legal aid are printed with an even right-hand margin.

Dr James Hartley of the University of Keele has recently illustrated how effectively space can be used in presenting written information to help the reader grasp the structure of a text (e.g. Hartley, 1978, 1980). There is also evidence from a number of sources that headings and subheadings can be extremely useful to the reader (e.g. Burnhill, 1970; Kozminsky, 1977). The following example illustrates how the use of headings and space can provide an alternative to legal prose. It originated somewhere inside the Medical Research Council, and is the first paragraph of a letter which was sent in July 1978 to all non-clinical scientists employed by MRC:

> You will remember that the terms of the option to transfer to MRC Pension Scheme from previous pensions arrangements allowed all service reckoning for the purposes of the MRC Supplementary Scheme to reckon in full in the new Scheme. Service not so reckoning has been allowed to count in the new arrangements at 9/10ths its actual length if it was FSSU service with an institution not participating in the supplementation arrangements; as service calculated in accordance with the public sector transfer scheme as at date of transfer to MRC Pension Scheme from premiums paid privately on FSSU policies accumulated with interest at the rate of 6% per annum; and in accordance with the transfer scheme as at date of joining the Council with transfer payments received from other schemes where these transfer payments did not allow the service to reckon for the purposes of the supplementation scheme.

This information could be presented so as to clarify the internal structure of the text, for example:

What account is taken of your past service when you join the MRC Pension Scheme?

1. Past service reckoning for the MRC Supplementary Scheme is transferred in full to the new scheme.
2. For other past service, the transfer depends on your previous pension scheme.
   a) FSSU with an institution outside the supplementation arrangements,
   9/10ths actual length of service will be transferred to the new scheme.

b) Premiums paid privately on FSSU policies, will be treated as per the 'public sector transfer scheme' operating on the date you joined the *MRC Pension Scheme*.

c) Other pension schemes, will be treated as per the transfer scheme operating on the date you *joined MRC*.

Once the idea takes root that written information does not have to be presented as paragraphs of flowing prose, then a variety of alternative presentation devices come to mind. Among the early studies which explored alternatives to prose was a presentation device called a 'logical tree' (Wason, 1962). This is a structured sequence of questions which can be presented either as a visual graph, sometimes called a flowchart, or as a series of 'jump' questions in which the answers given determine which questions are answered next. Elsewhere these flowcharts have been called 'algorithms' (e.g. Wheatley and Unwin, 1972), as well as 'logical trees' (e.g. Lewis, Horabin and Gane, 1967). All these studies have shown much better performance with flowcharts than with the prose version which had originally been the starting point for the study.

Just as prose comes in varying shades of opacity, so flowcharts can be drawn in a variety of different ways. Kamman (1975) included two rather different flowcharts among his comparisons, one of which gave better performance than the other. There were several differences between the two charts. One used binary yes/no decisions: the other had multiple options at decision points. In one the text was printed inside boxes with arrows joining the boxes: in the other the information was printed in white spaces set in a grey background, with captions set in white 'rivers' connecting various decision and action boxes. With so many differences it is difficult to know why one chart was better, but clearly some flowcharts may be more useful than others. As yet there is no behavioural research which clarifies just how a 'good' flowchart should be drawn. Nevertheless, in the hands of a skilled graphic designer flowcharts may be useful ways of dealing with conjunctive and disjunctive information. One recent example of their use has been the exposition of the rules of squash, which have just been published in flowchart form by the North-West Middlesex Squash League (Coe, 1977).

Flowcharts are not a universal solution to the problem of communicating complex subject matter of the 'if this, then that, otherwise . . .' variety. The advantages of flowcharts appear to be limited to helping readers solve fairly difficult problems (Blaiwes, 1974; Wright and Reid, 1973). For simpler problems, Wright and Reid found that the row and column headings of a two dimensional matrix were a useful way of dealing with conjunctive contingencies. As long as those using the table knew what to look up, tables were easier to use than any of the other versions compared. The advantage of the flowchart seems to be in providing people who are uncertain about the basic structure of a problem with a guided route to the solution. When such guides are not needed then flowcharts may not be the best answer. If the information must be memorised then neither tables nor flowcharts are particularly useful. Wright and Reid found that people remembered information better when it was given in the form of short sentences listed under subheadings. Indeed Blaiwes (1974) found that sometimes even on difficult problems performance was better with information presented as a list of short sentences.

When information is presented as a list, questions arise about the order in which the various items should be sequenced. Barnard, Morton, Long and Ottley (1977) showed that people find it easier to use lists which are structured so as to be compatible with their (the readers') conceptual groupings. Barnard *et al.* used items from categories such as fish, meat or fruit. In one list the items were arranged alphabetically irrespective of category membership; in the other list items were presented alphabetically within categories. This second arrangement was easier to use, even though the alternative, single alphabetic listing may have been more familiar to people from their experience with store directories, etc.

Problems of sequencing arise not only with lists but also with many other kinds of written information. Sales *et al.* (1977) examined a jury instruction which dealt with information in the following sequence: 1. Plaintiff's Claims, 2. Defendant's Defences, 3. Defendant's Counterclaim, 4. Plaintiff's Defences to Counterclaim. Each of these four sections was further subdivided into three or four sections. Sales *et al.* suggest that the information would be more comprehensible if the subsections became the main organising principle, so that everyone's claims and counterclaims were considered together, then everyone's burden of proof, and so on. Indeed one of the advantages of considering various non-prose options such as lists and flowcharts may be that they highlight useful ways of sequencing information. Wason (1968) illustrated this by constructing prose paragraphs directly from the flowchart he had drawn.

Perhaps two points come out strongly from these studies of presentation factors. One is that alternatives to prose are often worth considering. A range of such alternatives exists. Almost all of them would be an improvement on the standard type of legal language. The second point is that there is no single 'best way' of presenting written material. This means that there cannot be a simple cook-book of recipes for preparing written information for the consumer. Consequently other techniques must be explored for creating effective written communications.

PROCEDURES FOR CREATING CLEAR COMMUNICATIONS

Elsewhere it has been suggested that documents can be subjected to 'quality control' at various stages of the design process, in a way analogous to the use of such techniques in the manufacture of other products (e.g. Wright, 1978a). Three such control checks have been proposed, monitoring respectively the content, presentation and usability of the document. For each monitoring operation several different types of information will be useful. Wright (1978a) discusses in detail the kinds of information that can be obtained from observational field studies, from interviews and surveys, and from experimental comparisons within the laboratory. Some of these techniques have already been mentioned – for example the use of survey techniques as a means of checking whether readers will know certain terms. The following sections will examine ways of meeting the writer's need to have information about the reader; information about the research literature; and information about the communicative adequacy of his document.

INFORMATION ABOUT READERS

Two of the most important factors about readers are that they start the encounter with written material by looking for particular sorts of information, and that they interpret what they read on the basis of prior knowledge and expectations. Starting in the top left-hand corner and reading straight through to the end, is a reading strategy which most of us reserve for novels and short stories. Text-books are certainly not read this way (e.g. Waller, 1978). Nor are newspapers, nor explanatory leaflets (particularly the instruction leaflets accompanying domestic appliances). Observational studies of how a document is used will enable the writer to cater for the reader's needs. The document may require what Waller calls 'access structures'. These include indexes, headings, marginal annotations, and typographic variation within the text. If the written information has to be used from memory this may change the way it is best structured, and the writer may choose to make use of such aids as numbering systems. Where written material is used in conjunction with other documents, there is a need for compatibility between the two, for example, similarity in the sequencing of information.

Readers not only have expectations about which items belong together (Barnard *et al.*, 1977) they also have expectations about sentence structures. These expectations influence their decisions about the internal word groupings within a sentence. A quotation from a leaflet issued by the Department of Health and Social Security in January 1976 (Leaflet GR20A) illustrates this point:

> This leaflet explains the final statement and how the graduated pension you have earned will be preserved and paid when you retire at or after 65 (60 if you are a woman) or when you reach 70 (65 if you are a woman) whichever is earlier.

Many readers analyse the last clause of the sentence into the functional grouping:
(paid when you retire)(at or after 65 or at 70, whichever is earlier).
The writer had intended the grouping to be:
(paid when you retire, at or after 65)(or at 70)(whichever is earlier).
Such examples serve to emphasise that the reader's interaction with print differs from that of a passive radio receiver which faithfully transduces the signals from the transmitter. Once it is realised that reading is influenced by people's expectations it is easier to see that there will be issues about what information content the reader wants at all. Mention was made earlier of a 250-word paragraph being reduced to just thirty words. It would seem that much of what the writer felt he wanted to say was not what the reader wanted to read. Designers of documents need information about readers.

DECIDING TO APPLY RESEARCH FINDINGS

There are problems for non-psychologists both in finding and interpreting behavioural data. There are general reviews of typographic variables (e.g. Hartley, 1978; Spencer, 1969) and design-oriented summaries of research on linguistic factors (e.g. Macdonald-Ross, 1978) and other aspects of presenting technical communications (e.g. Wright, 1977a and b). Rather fewer reviews deal with the design of specific kinds of information, such as application forms (e.g. Wright, 1980). Consequently a writer may not know which options he should be considering at the design stage. When drawing up a contract, it is no use trying to look up the word 'contract' in an abstracting service such as *Psychological Abstracts*: the issues tackled in the research literature are much smaller than this. Enlisting the help of a researcher familiar with the area might be the simplest way out of this difficulty.

Once research has been located, the findings must be interpreted with respect to the design issues to hand. Factors which have to be evaluated include the extent to which the materials, readers and reading purposes of the experiment are comparable with those of the present document. Such interpretations are not always easy to make (Wright, 1978b). There is also a need to evaluate whether differences which were statistically significant in the laboratory will be of practical significance outside it. Take, as an example, the data reported by Jones (1968) and Wason (1968) on the relative abilities of civil service executive officers to understand and apply a set of regulations concerned with the use of private vehicles on official business. Performance with a prose excerpt of eleven paragraphs from these regulations, covering three pages of typed foolscap, was compared with performance on a 'jump' sequence of questions. On average it took two and a half minutes longer to solve a problem using the prose than using the sequenced questions. Whether saving a couple of minutes really matters depends on how often you save it. If only one person consults the rules once a year then it may not be too important. But if 1000 people look up the regulations once a month then 500 man hours are lost each year just from choosing the poorer way of presenting this information. Differences reported in the experimental literature often appear small. This is a function of the unit of measurement used in the study. Whether the differences are of practical significance is a decision which must be made by designers in the light of what they know about how their information will be used by readers.

REVISING DRAFT DOCUMENTS

So many causes of ambiguity exist that writers cannot hope to detect and avoid them all. Valuable help can be obtained by having the draft document critically evaluated, (Macdonald-Ross and Waller, 1975a and b). This critical appraisal cannot be carried out by a colleague down the hallway who knows the material as well as the writer. It requires either people from the relevant audience for the document or the experienced opinion of a 'good writer' as unfamiliar with the subject-matter as the readers will be. One of the difficulties in trying to get a critical appraisal of a draft is that many readers believe that it must be their fault if they cannot understand the text. This is curious. If the same people were having trouble following a conversation on a crackling telephone line they would not blame their hearing. Nevertheless there is a reluctance among many folk to point out sources of difficulty and confusion in a text.

One useful technique for getting round this problem is to try probing the reader's comprehension by using information presented in case study form. For example the reader can be given one of the leaflets explaining the provisions of legal aid, and then be asked whether various people whose details are provided should apply for legal aid. This technique enables trouble-spots to be located with some precision. It also enables the document to be vetted 'on behalf of' a range of potential readers. This trouble-shooting technique for assessing comprehension goes beyond the verbatim repetition of words in the original text, which can often be all that more direct question and answer techniques require. For example, assume a text says that 'Principal Clinical Executives are entitled to a transport allowance'. If readers are asked 'Who gets a transport allowance?' they will reply 'Principal Clinical Executives'. But it does not follow they have any idea what such an executive is. With the case study technique it could soon become apparent that people were uncertain whether or not Dr Smith, Mr Brown or Sister were entitled to a transport allowance.

One other procedure, perhaps less sensitive than the previous one, is to number small units of the text (e.g. clauses) and ask people to rate the ease of understanding of these clauses on a five or six-point scale. The success of this technique can be improved by having people make the ratings on behalf of some other group such as pensioners or school-leavers. This gets round the problem of people being reluctant to admit that they themselves have comprehension difficulties. It allows them to say, 'Of course I understand it, but I think 'X' will have trouble'. The ratings from different people can then be averaged to give a clause-by-clause profile of people's subjective estimate of the difficulty of the text. This technique is quick and easy to employ, but, as with readability formulae, trouble-spots may be missed. For example, without a specific need to interpret it, many raters may not realise that they do not know what a Principal Clinical Executive is.

TEAM APPROACH TO DOCUMENT DESIGN

Wason (1968) pointed out the need for collaboration between different kinds of specialists if the potential advantages of having well designed information were to be realised. More recently a similar argument has been put forward by Waller (1977 and 1978) who suggests that the production of written information requires the integration of diverse talents in the same way that the production of a radio or television programme does. It requires reaching a compromise between the preferences of the subject-matter expert, the experience of the printing and typographic experts, the findings of research by psychologists and information designers, and the limitations of available time and budget.

If a team approach to document design is desirable, a range of practical questions arise. Who should fund such teams? Who should have access to them? Should they be continually re-constituted on an *ad hoc* basis for specific documents or should there be a central core of team members who are joined by others as the occasion requires? Such questions cannot be answered here, and of course there are documents which may not be of sufficient importance to warrant the skills of a design team. Nevertheless the case could be made that if parliamentary bills could be more easily understood then the social benefits would far outweigh the costs of maintaining the design teams.

MIGHT BADLY DESIGNED INFORMATION BECOME ILLEGAL?

The central concern in this discussion has been legal language. However, other poorly designed documentation can easily be found. The instructions issued by manufacturers often leave room for improvement. The Institute of Scientific and Technical Communicators issued a press release in 1977, which cited a case where the documentation accompanying a £25 valve was so poor that the valve was fitted incorrectly. The result was £800 of damage to the plant. If ever such mishaps result in litigation then perhaps writers may find it necessary to ensure that what they write is an effective communication.

A similar case would seem to arise with forms. A local authority can take legal action against a form-filler for giving false information. But where the questions or explanatory notes exceed the cognitive abilities that can reasonably be expected of the form-filler, then to be held 'guilty' for misunderstanding them seems contrary to justice. A number of local authorities now qualify their warnings and say that an offence is committed only if the form-filler *knowingly* gives false information. From the language on some forms, it may be very difficult to establish whether the form-filler's misunderstanding was genuine or deliberate.

The Trade Descriptions Act stipulates that certain communications should be truthful. Perhaps the day will come when certain communications must be comprehensible.

CONCLUSIONS

This discussion has ranged a long way from the opening remarks about the subtle influences that the phrasing of questions can have on the accuracy of the answers obtained. It has been shown that psychological research on comprehension processes can highlight forms of expression to be avoided. Similarly behavioural research on the design of information has indicated that alternatives to prose offer useful solutions to the problems of communicating complex subject-matter. It has been emphasised that the findings of behavioural research are not suitable for rote application. Rather, they require intelligent integration with a number of other factors which affect particular design decisions. One way of achieving such integration is through a design team.

Let me finish with a personal speculation about why legal language still exists. A colleague received a letter from a civil servant. It was a short, friendly letter in which the writer said that as he was now doing Bill's job he expected he would be in touch more often. The intention and tone were definitely friendly. The structure was a single sentence of ninety-seven words. It seems plausible that the writer was suffering from an occupational disease. Perhaps this is also true of those who write legal language. If so, then the prognosis is good. The disease is probably curable with just a little effort from the patient. Without such effort the disease may become increasingly restrictive.

REFERENCES

P. J. Barnard, 'Presuppositions in memory for the pragmatic implications of sentences and in the interpretation of active and passive questions', Paper submitted for publication (1979).

P. J. Barnard, J. Morton, J. B. Long and E. A. Ottley, 'Planning menus for displays: Some effects of their structure and content on user performance', in *Displays for Man Machine Systems*, Institute of Electrical Engineers Conference Publication No. 150 (1977) 130–3.

A. S. Blaiwes, 'Formats for presenting procedural instructions', *Journal of Applied Psychology, 59* (1974) 683–6.

G. H. Bower, 'Experiments on story understanding and recall', *Quarterly Journal of Experimental Psychology, 28* (1976) 511–34.

P. Burnhill, 'Typographic education: Headings in text', *Journal of Typographic Research, 4* (1970) 353–65.

R. Cattell and G. D. Lewis, 'Children's understanding of words used in road safety literature', Supplementary Report 155UC (Crowthorne, Berkshire: Transport and Road Research Laboratory, 1975).

E. V. Clark, 'First language acquisition', in J. Morton and J. C. Marshall (eds.), *Psycholinguistic Series, 1* (London: Elek Science, 1977).

H. H. Clark and E. V. Clark, 'Semantic distinctions and memory for complex sentences', *Quarterly Journal of Experimental Psychology, 20* (1968) 129–38.

H. H. Clark and E. V. Clark, *The Psychology of Language: An Introduction to Psycholinguistics* (New York: Harcourt, Brace, Jovanovitch, 1977).

H. H. Clark and P. Lucy, 'Understanding what is meant from what is said: A study in conversationally conveyed requests', *Journal of Verbal Learning and Verbal Behavior, 14* (1975) 59–72.

B. Coe, *A guide to the rules of squash* (London: Royal College of Art, 1977).

K. Ellis, 'We shouldn't have to fight to understand our rights', *Good Housekeeping, 113* (1978) 57.

R. F. Flesch, 'A new readability yardstick', *Journal of Applied Psychology, 32* (1948) 221–33.

F. W. Fowler, *A Dictionary of Modern English Usage* (Oxford: The Clarendon Press, 1926).

S. Glucksberg, T. Trabasso and J. Wald, 'Linguistic structures and mental operations', *Cognitive Psychology*, 5 (1973) 338–70.

M. Gregory and E. C. Poulton, 'Even versus uneven right-hand margins and the rate of comprehension in reading', *Ergonomics*, 13 (1970) 427–34.

D. Hakes, 'Does verb structure affect sentence comprehension?', *Perception and Psychophysics*, 10 (1971) 229–32.

R. J. Harris and G. E. Monaco, 'Psychology of pragmatic implication: information processing between the lines', *Journal of Experimental Psychology, General*, 197 (1978) 1–22.

J. Hartley, *Designing Instructional Text* (London: Kogan Page Ltd., 1978) (a).

J. Hartley, 'Space and structure in instructional text', in R. A. Easterby and H. Zwaga (eds.), *Visual Presentation of Information* (London: Wiley, 1980).

J. Hartley and P. Burnhill, 'Fifty guide-lines for improving instructional text', *Programmed Learning and Educational Technology*, 14 (1977) 65–73.

P. Herriott, 'The comprehension of active and passive sentences as a function of pragmatic expectations', *Journal of Verbal Learning and Verbal Behavior, 8* (1969) 166–9.

P. N. Johnson-Laird and J. M. Tridgell, 'When negation is easier than affirmation', *Quarterly Journal of Experimental Psychology*, 24 (1972) 87–91.

A. Johnstone and J. Cassels, 'What's in a word?', *New Scientist*, 77 (1978) 432–3.

S. Jones, *Design of Instruction*, Training Paper 1, Department of Employment and Productivity (London: HMSO, 1968).

R. Kamman, 'The comprehensibility of printed instructions and the flow-chart alternative', *Human Factors*, 17 (1975) 183–91.

W. Kintsch, 'Memory for prose', in C. N. Cofer (ed.), *The Structure of Human Memory* (San Francisco: W. H. Freeman, 1976).

W. Kintsch and J. M. Keenan, 'Reading rate as a function of the number of propositions in the base structure of sentences', *Cognitive Psychology*, 5 (1973) 257–74.

W. Kintsch, E. Kozminsky, W. J. Streby, G. McKoon and J. M. Keenan, 'Comprehension and recall of text as a function of content variables', *Journal of Verbal Learning and Verbal Behavior*, 14 (1975) 196–214.

E. Kozminsky, 'Altering comprehension: The effect of biasing titles on text comprehension', *Memory and Cognition*, 5 (1977) 482–90.

J. Leapman, 'Leapman in America', *The Times* 13 March, 1978.

B. N. Lewis, I. S. Horabin and C. P. Gane, *Flowcharts, Logical Trees and Algorithms for Rules and Regulations* (London: HMSO, 1967).

E. F. Loftus, 'Leading questions and the eyewitness report', *Cognitive Psychology*, 7 (1975) 560–72.

E. F. Loftus and J. C. Palmer, 'Reconstruction of automobile destruction: An example of the interaction between language and memory', *Journal of Verbal Learning and Verbal Behavior*, 13 (1974) 585–9.

E. F. Loftus and G. Zanni, 'Eyewitness testimony: The influence of the wording of a question', *Bulletin of the Psychonomic Society*, 5 (1975) 86–8.

M. Macdonald-Ross, 'Language in texts: A review of research relevant to the design of curricular materials', in L. S. Shulman (ed.), *Review of Research in Education*, 6 (Itasca, Ill.: Peacock, 1978).

M. Macdonald-Ross and R. Waller, 'Criticism, alternatives and tests: A conceptual framework for improving typography', *Programmed Learning and Educational Technology*, *12* (1975) 75–83. (a)

M. Macdonald-Ross and R. Waller, '*Open University Texts: Criticism and Alternatives*', (Milton Keynes: The Institute of Educational Technology, The Open University, 1975). (b)

J. Macnamara, *Bilingualism and Primary Education* (Edinburgh: The University Press, 1966).

J.M. Mandler and N. S. Johnson, 'Remembrance of things parsed: Story structure and recall', *Cognitive Psychology*, *9* (1977) 111–51.

E. Partridge, *Usage and Abusage*, revised (Harmondsworth: Penguin, 1957).

J. D. Read, R. H. Barnsley, K. Ankers and I. Q. Wishaw, 'Variations in severity of verbs and eyewitnesses' testimony: An alternative interpretation', *Perceptual and Motor Skills*, *46* (1978) 795–800.

E. Z. Rothkopf, 'Writing to teach and reading to learn: A perspective on the psychology of written instruction', in *Seventy-fifth Yearbook of the National Society for the Study of Education, Part I* (Chicago, Ill.: The University Press, 1976).

D. E. Rumelhart, 'Notes on a schema for stories', in D. G. Bobrow and A. M. Collins (eds.), *Representations and Understanding: Studies in Cognitive Science* (New York: Academic Press, 1975).

B. D. Sales, A. Elwork and J. J. Alfini, 'Improving comprehension for jury instructions', in B. D. Sales (ed.), *Perspectives in Law and Psychology, I, The Criminal Justice System* (New York: Plenum Press, 1977).

M. A. Sherman, 'Bound to be easier? The negative prefix and sentence comprehension', *Journal of Verbal Learning and Verbal Behavior*, *12* (1973) 76–84.

H. Spencer, *The Visible Word* (London: Lund Humphries, 1969).

A. Stokes, 'The reliability of readability formulae', *Journal of Research in Reading*, *1* (1978) 21–34.

M. A. Tinker, *Bases for Effective Reading* (Minneapolis: The University of Minnesota Press, 1965).

D. Vipond and W. Kintsch, 'A process approach to text comprehension and readability', Paper presented at the International Congress of Applied Psychology, Munich (1978).

H. Voysey, 'Computer analysis shows up welfare deficiencies', *New Scientist*, *69* (1976) 507.

R. Waller, *Notes on Transforming* (Milton Keynes: Institute of Educational Technology, The Open University, 1977).

R. Waller, *Typographic Access Structures for Educational Texts* (Milton Keynes: Institute of Educational Technology, The Open University, 1978).

P. C. Wason, *Psychological aspects of negation* (London: Communication Research Centre, University College London, 1962).

P. C. Wason, 'The contexts of plausible denial', *Journal of Verbal Learning and Verbal Behavior*, *4* (1965) 7–11.

P. C. Wason, 'The drafting of rules', *The New Law Journal*, *118* (1968) 548–9.

D. M. Wheatley and A. W. Unwin, *The Algorithm Writer's Guide* (London: Longman, 1972).

P. Wright, 'Transformations and the understanding of sentences', *Language and Speech*, *12* (1969) 156–66.

P. Wright, 'Presenting people with choices: The effect of format on the comprehension of examination rubrics', *Programmed Learning and Educational Technology*, *12* (1975) 109–14.

P. Wright, 'Presenting technical information: A survey of research findings', *Instructional Science*, *6* (1977) 93–134. (a)

P. Wright, 'Behavioural research and the technical communicator', *The Communicator of Scientific and Technical Information*, *32* (1977) 3–13. (b)

P. Wright, 'Quality control aspects of document design', Paper presented at the International Congress of Applied Psychology, Munich (1978) (a). Reprinted in *Information Design Journal*, *1* (1979) 33–42.

P. Wright, 'Feeding the information eaters: Suggestions for integrating pure and applied research on language comprehension', *Instructional Science*, *7* (1978) 249–312. (b)

P. Wright, 'Strategy and tactics in designing forms', in R. A. Easterby and H. Zwaga (eds.), *Visual Presentation of Information* (London: Wiley, 1980).

P. Wright and P. Barnard, 'Just fill in this form – a review for designers', *Applied Ergonomics*, *6* (1975) 213–20. (a)

P. Wright and P. Barnard, 'Effects of "more than" and "less than" decisions on the use of numerical tables', *Journal of Applied Psychology*, *60* (1975) 606–11. (b)

P. Wright and F. Reid, 'Written information: Some alternatives to prose for expressing the outcomes of complex contingencies', *Journal of Applied Psychology*, *57* (1973) 160–66.

P. Wright and P. Wilcox, 'When two no's nearly make a yes: A study of conditional imperatives', Paper presented at the Conference on Processing of Visible Language, Eindhoven (1977). To appear in P. A. Kolers, M. Wrolstad and H. Bouma (eds.), *Processing of Visible Language*, *1* (New York: Plenum Publishing Corp., in press).

PART V

APPLICATIONS OF PSYCHOLOGY IN AREAS OF SUBSTANTIVE LAW

10: The Limits of Law and Psychology in Decisions Concerning the Welfare of Children

Michael King

A short time ago when I was wandering around the ruins of the Mayan civilisation in Mexico, the thought occurred to me that the role of the Mayan priests was not so different from that of lawyers and psychologists in our civilisation. These priests existed as a ruling élite, by seizing what amounted to a virtual monopoly over all forms of knowledge including the computation of the calendar, divination and prophecies, the cure of diseases and even reading and writing. They were, I should add, also responsible for human sacrifices and the most common victims for these sacrifices were children – mainly orphans and the offspring of unmarried mothers (Coe, 1971, pp. 179–80).

Now I do not wish to draw any facile analogies between the Mayan methods for disposing of their unwanted children and our own. My point is somewhat more complex; it concerns the relationship between knowledge and power and in particular the way in which what passes for knowledge is often no more than an ideology or value system which some social group seeks to impose in order to maintain the existing social order or to change society in the direction which the group considers appropriate.

Since Victorian times the high priests of our society have claimed to know what was best for children (see Skolnick, 1975). Whether it was compulsory education, restrictions of child labour or protection from moral corruption, these so-called 'advances' in our civilisation often did more to forward the interests of power groups within our society than to promote the welfare of children. A real break-through for the child evangelists, however, took place this century with the advent of Freudian psychoanalytic theory and Skinnerian behaviourism. Both these psychological theories proposed that what happened to a child during infancy and early childhood to a greater or lesser degree determined what sort of adult that child would grow up to be. The way was now clear for a new science of child development and for new experts to tell the world what was and what was not good for children. From that time on, self-respecting judges in the field of family law could no longer rely upon the judicial value system – which normally meant a mixture of biblical morality, male chauvinism and the protection of capital – in their decisions concerning the placement of children. It was no longer possible to give the child to the wealthiest or the most morally deserving (or at least the judgement could not be expressed in those terms). Instead, they had to consider the long-term trauma that might result from their decisions, the risks of children becoming depressive, delinquent, psychopathic or sexually deviant as a result of the wrong decision being made.

Who then were these experts? Perhaps one would have expected them to emerge from the ranks of the philosophers, philanthropists and the educationalists who had dominated much of the thinking about children in the nineteenth century. Instead, they came somewhat surprisingly from the medical profession. It was as if the massive advances in medicine, and in particular the prevention of infant disease and mortality, had presented doctors with the right to pronounce on every aspect of a child's development, physical, intellectual and emotional. So Benjamin Spock told American parents how to bring up their babies and John Bowlby shocked the western world with his revelations of what might happen to a child separated from its mother during a critical phase of its development, (Bowlby, 1951).

Meanwhile, the courts struggled to keep pace with this new knowledge about children that was being churned out by child psychiatrists. In America the whole juvenile court scene was transformed so that court hearings came to resemble clinical consultations, with lawyers, social workers, psychiatrists and psychologists all working together to find solutions to the child's 'problems' (see Platt, 1969). Psychiatric reports were almost obligatory for any child who appeared before the courts and some courts even installed a clinic staffed by child psychiatrists and child psychologists within the court's precincts. In Britain, thanks mainly to scarcity of resources and an inherent resistance to change, the courts succeeded in avoiding the worst excesses of the child-saving movement. Instead a strange, symbiotic relationship developed between the courts and the ever-growing ranks of child specialists. By describing anyone who was qualified in child psychology as a 'medical expert' and their evidence as 'scientific', the judiciary was able to present psychologists and psychiatrists not only with a new status, but also with the opportunity to apply their theoretical knowledge to the real world of decision- and policy-making.[1] In return, judges have been able to use the experts to relieve some of the pressure which impossibly difficult cases impose upon them. If they can show the rest of the world that they have followed the advice of 'the experts' in their decisions, they are able to absolve themselves of much of the responsibility for unpopular decisions or for child-placements which subsequently went wrong.

However, such indirect influence over the policy of the courts through the medium of 'experts' has not satisfied some critics of the legal system mainly, I suggest, because the 'experts' often have to compromise (some would say prostitute) their 'scientific' knowledge in order to gain acceptance from the courts. The most extreme of these critics have called for the complete removal of judges and lawyers from decisions concerning children and their substitution with a panel of experts in the field of child development.[2] These extreme proposals have included a network of family courts where the role of professional counsellors, including child experts, would be equal to that of the lawyers. (See, for example, *The Report of the Departmental Committee on One-Parent Families* (DHSS, 1974); and Mortlock, 1972, pp. 189–205). More recently, two child psychiatrists and an American law professor wrote a book called *Beyond the Best Interests of the Child* which severely took to task the way in which English and American courts reach decisions concerning children as well as the whole theoretical basis for such decisions (Goldstein *et al.*, 1973). This book has proved highly influential in the United States and it would appear from articles and reviews I have read in English legal journals that there are many people in this country who consider the work sufficiently serious for judges and legislators to be swayed by its arguments. Having myself given this book a favourable review some time ago (King, 1974) I am now of the opinion that both theoretically and in terms of the changes it proposes in social policy, much of it is highly suspect. I would like

now to take a little time in examining in some detail the issues of
theory, social policy and practice arising from this book. My reason
is not simply to provide a counterweight to the unrestrained
enthusiasm which has greeted this book in some circles but, more
importantly, to use the book to identify some of the pitfalls that lie in
wait for psychologists and lawyers who trespass beyond the limits of
scientific knowledge and successful legal action.

First, then, the theoretical position of these authors: they ask,

> How can the law assure for each child a chance to be a member of
> a family where he feels wanted and where he would have an
> opportunity on a continuing basis, not only to recieve and return
> affection, but also to express anger and to learn to manage his
> aggression . . . [the law] is confronted with a highly complex
> decision which involves, implicitly, if not explicitly, a prediction
> about who, among available alternatives, holds most promise for
> meeting the child's psychological needs.
>
> Psychoanalytical theory confirms the substantial limitations in
> our capacity to make such a prediction, yet it provides a valuable
> body of generally applicable knowledge which may be translated
> into guidelines to facilitate making decisions that inevitably must
> be made (pp. 5–6).

The authors therefore expect us to accept psychoanalytic theory
without any prior discussion of its credentials. We are asked to
ignore the critics of Freudian theory who have, for example, pointed
out that a theory which is based upon the behaviour of middle-class,
neurotic Austrian families around the turn of the century is hardly
likely to have universal application. We must turn a deaf ear to the
many critics who deny the claim that psychoanalytic theory is
scientific, at least in Popper's sense of the term. These critics argue,
of course, that since the theory deals largely with undetectable
mental events, it is not amenable to direct empirical testing. In
other words, it cannot be disproved. It is worth pointing out in this
context that *Beyond the Best Interests of the Child* does not contain a
single reference to any empirical study on adoption or foster-
placement. Moreover, the only studies quoted in the book cited to
support any of the author's assertions and proposals are those
carried out by researchers of a similar psychoanalytic orientation to
their own.[3] Nowhere is any reference made to the extensive surveys
on the effects of parent-child separation carried out by such

researchers as Michael Rutter (1971) in this country and the McCords (1959) in the United States. Where the results of psychoanalytic studies are quoted, they are presented as if they were scientific facts with no hint of the controversy that surrounds many of these findings.

Perhaps one would be more ready to accept the evidence of these authors purely on the basis of their extensive accumulated experience in the field of child development, were it not for the fact that they appear at times to disregard the logical limits placed upon the drawing of general inferences from limited data. At one point, for example, they state categorically, that

> Multiple placement of school-aged children is the direct cause of behaviour which schools experience as disrupting and the courts label dissocial or even criminal (p. 34).

Quite apart from the fact that the only evidence given to support this statement is a single case study, the authors make an error that one would not expect from a first-year psychology student, that of confusing causation with correlation. The most that can be inferred from the association between multiple foster-placement and anti-social behaviour is that the child who experiences such placements is more likely than other children to be disruptive. To establish that the multiple fostering actually caused the behaviour would require a large number of cases where such factors as race, class, poverty and intelligence were held constant and only the number of foster-placements varied.

Worse still, on another occasion, the authors actually fly in the face of available empirical evidence by stating that 'the prolonged absence or death of one parent may place the child at risk' (p. 16). The evidence from almost all the studies that have been carried out stresses that the absence of a parent on its own is unlikely to be harmful and that the crucial factors are the relationships the child experiences before and after the separation rather than the mere absence of a parent. (Rutter, 1971; McCord and McCord, 1959).

At another point, Goldstein, Freud and Solnit write of the need for suitable models for identification and maintain that 'the sexual identities of the parents may be insufficiently resolved so as to create confusion in the child as to his own sexual identity' (p. 34). And later, that a visiting non-custodial parent 'has little chance to serve as a true object of love, trust and identification' (p. 38). Yet there is absolutely no evidence to suggest that the children of homosexual parents are any more likely to become homosexual themselves than are the children of heterosexual parents: nor is there any reason why a visiting non-custodial parent should not, given sufficient goodwill from the custodial parent, be able to serve as an adequate model for his or her child.

It turns out, therefore, that far from being firmly based upon tested, scientific evidence, the authors' 'knowledge' of the needs of children is not even grounded on factual data which could be described as unequivocal or uncontroversial (see Ainsworth, 1962; Clarke and Clarke, 1976). The most that can be said for this 'knowledge' is that it represents the views of three wise and experienced people. Apart from that, it is no more and no less valid than the views of any other wise and experienced people. Moreover, psychoanalytic theory is no more and no less valid a framework for analysing and predicting human social behaviour than any other value system, be it religious, political, philosophical or psychological.

A short anecdote will illustrate this point. In a recent custody case which took place in New Haven, Connecticut, a mother who sought to convince the court of the dangers of separating her from her young children, produced as evidence the testimony of a child psychiatrist from the Yale University Child Study Center with which both Joseph Goldstein and Albert Solnit are closely associated. The father, however, countered by presenting the court with a psychologist from the State University of New York Community Psychology Center who argued that there was no evidence that the children would suffer any long-term effects from being separated from their mother; that in his view the only factor which consistently correlated with success and happiness was wealth; and that since the father was in a far better economic position than the mother, the children should be given to him.[4]

Turning now to the social policy issues raised by the book, the authors preface their discussion of these issues by stating their recognition that in such matters

the law for the most part is a relatively crude instrument. It may be able to destroy human relationships but it does not have the power to compel them to develop (pp. 49–50).

This is a sentiment with which I wholeheartedly agree as I do with the authors' preference for the 'private ordering of inter-personal relationships over state intrusion on them' (p. 50). But to use this modest position as a springboard for the proposals that 'all placements be unconditional and final' (p. 101) that 'the court shall not retain continuing jurisdiction over the parent-child relationship', and that 'the non-custodial parent should have no legally enforceable right to visit the child and the custodial parent should have the right to decide whether it is desirable for the child to have such visits' (p. 38) seems to ignore the fact that parents, even psychological parents as identified by psychoanalysts, cannot always be relied upon to act unselfishly in the best interests of their psychological children. When it comes to destroying human relationships, parents, particularly those in the throes of emotionally charged divorce proceedings, are as capable as any court of law. It also ignores the fact that, in some cases at least, the legal system with its ultimate threat of sanctions is able to act as a restraining influence to prevent children suffering unduly at the hands of unthinking or selfish parents.

Furthermore, it seems to me a great mistake for anyone discussing such complex social policy issues to concentrate their attention entirely upon the needs of children while giving little or no consideration to the interests and rights of the adults involved in custody and care proceedings. I, for one, would not want to be in court when a final and irreversible judgement was announced in favour of a foster parent retaining all rights over a young child whose mother, a single parent, had been forced to place her child in care while she went into hospital. Nor would I like to be there to see the reaction of a blameless divorced father as the court deprived him of any right to see his children. It is clear that in the vast majority of cases the well-being of children is inexorably linked to the well-being of the adults who have care of those children. To attempt to consider children's needs and interests in almost total isolation from those of their adult caretakers seems to be asking for trouble. Moreover, not only would the courts be forced to take draconian measures to enforce orders depriving parents of any contact with their children, but any adult who is likely to be the victim of such an order would use every device possible to avoid bringing the issue before the court. Some of these devices, such as child-snatching and the refusal to place children in voluntary fostering situations, far from providing satisfactory 'private ordering of inter-personal relations', will often make matters far worse than judicial intervention, however clumsy this may be.

My final objection on the level of general social policy to the analysis and proposals in *Beyond the Best Interests of the Child* is that by concentrating attention at the level of interpersonal relationships between adults and children, the authors turn a blind eye to all the other factors which might affect a child's development and welfare, such as money, race, housing conditions, the extended family and educational opportunities. Their narrow focus of attention also causes them to ignore all those social forces such as the organisational interests of social work and adoption agencies and the adversary ethos of the legal profession which play an important part in determining which children's cases actually reach the courts and the way in which they are dealt with by the legal system.

It is abundantly clear that in writing their book the three authors have gone far beyond the limits of scientific psychological knowledge and have entered the realms of ideology and social values. This would not matter if they had been content to present their analysis and proposals for reform more modestly, but instead they chose to wrap up their values in pseudo-scientific rhetoric and, like the Mayan priests, chose to claim for themselves a virtual monopoly of knowledge concerning the welfare of children. Yet it would be a mistake to point the accusing finger solely at these authors, when there is a large number of psychologists, psychiatrists and social workers who, armed with different theories, are prepared to pontificate both inside and outside the courtroom on what is and what is not in the best interests of children. For the benefit of anyone who still clings to the view that what these pontificators are involved in is the dissemination of scientific knowledge rather than the imposition of class and cultural values, Rudolph Schaffer (1977) in his book *Mothering* tells of observations carried out by Leonard Rosenblum (Rosenblum, 1971) of two species of monkey, the pigtail and the bonnet, who have very different child-rearing habits. While the bonnets are gregarious creatures the pigtails are rarely in close physical contact with one another. When a bonnet mother gives birth she almost immediately reunites with the group and permits other adults to touch and handle the newborn. Among pigtails, by contrast, one finds only close-knit family units of mothers and children. After giving birth the pigtail mother vigorously attacks any animal that approaches her infant. When the infant attempts to leave the mother to explore his surroundings, the mother restrains him. Schaffer writes that 'these differences in group living become absorbed into the overall differences in infant experience' (p. 109). Pigtails have a much more enduring and selective relationship with their mothers than bonnets. The birth of a sibling also shows up similar differences. While the bonnet reacts only minimally, the pigtail becomes disturbed and even more clinging. Even in play the bonnets have many opportunities to interact with other young, whereas the pigtails engage mainly in non-social exercise play. Schaffer adds,

It is not difficult to translate these observations into human terms and find the equivalent situations where a child is, respectively, wholly in the hands of one mother-figure or distributed among several (p. 109).

Moreover, humans are much less restrained biologically than lower animals and thus freer to choose among different types of social settings in which to rear their children. There is therefore a wide variety in family life and a rather different personality structure results from group rearing as opposed to traditional family-oriented rearing.

'Do we want bonnet children or pigtail children?' asks Schaffer (p. 110). 'Which is better?' The answer to this question is not scientific. It involves a value judgement which must be made by society, not psychologists. As Schaffer points out,

Unfortunately in the past value judgments have commonly been dressed up as mental health judgments; children had to be brought up as pigtails or their capacity for social living was said to be stunted. That might be true, but only so long as society was commited to the pigtail type of social living. A bonnet-reared child is unlikely to become an effective pigtail parent . . . . (p. 110).

Different forms of child rearing may result in differences in child personality, but they are not better or worse than one another in any absolute sense. Indeed Arlene Skolnick (1975) has demonstrated how, during the course of recent history, psychological theories about child development have tended to reflect the prevailing social ideology of childhood.

Are the courts then to reject altogether all psychological evidence in their decision-making concerning children? Certainly not, but lawyers and the judiciary must learn to cut the child developmental experts down to size. They must know how to define the limits of genuine psychological knowledge. May I suggest the following guidelines:

1. Lawyers should assume that psychologists and psychiatrists are no better qualified than they to determine on the basis merely of short interviews over a limited time period during divorce or care proceedings which of the competing adults should have care of the child. Cases in which they have treated or observed the parent or child over a long period prior to the court proceedings, present a very different situation where the experts might very well be able to provide the court with useful information concerning the likely responses of the particular child and adults to different placement alternatives.

2. Child experts can play a useful rôle in interviewing young children who are the subject of court proceedings. They may be far better able than lawyers and judges to find out how the child sees the world and in particular how he or she responds to the relationships with the various adults who are involved in the proceedings.

3. Child experts are also able to play a useful rôle in counselling both children and adults throughout periods of family reorganisation. Children in particular often lack anyone other than confused and anxious parents to whom they can turn for guidance and support during this disruptive period of their lives. Perhaps an equally important rôle for psychologists and psychiatrists lies in sensitising the legal profession and judiciary to the immediate and possible long-term effects of the court proceedings themselves. Despite all the criticism I have directed at *Beyond the Best Interests of the Child*, Goldstein, Freud and Solnit have made a valuable contribution in this direction.

4. On a more general level, psychiatrists and psychologists have over the past fifty years been successful in identifying environmental factors which may affect a child's development. Often psychiatrists have overstated the risks involved because their contact has been with people who have suffered in adult life as the result of childhood experiences rather than those who have recovered unscathed from the same types of

experiences. More reliable indicators of the nature and extent of the relationship between childhood events and mental disturbance in adult life are longitudinal studies or normative surveys involving large numbers of families. However, it is highly dangerous to apply these general findings to individual cases.

5. The rôle of the child expert as educator should also extend to providing lawyers and judges with the necessary critical techniques for assessing the validity and applicability of psychological and psychiatric studies and the testimony of experts. Instead of telling lawyers what to think, as Goldstein, Freud and Solnit do, psychologists should teach them how to think.

Finally, I wish to return to *Beyond the Best Interests of the Child* to look at some of the practical implications of the book's proposals and in doing so to identify what in practice are the limits of a successful legal intervention in relationships between adults and children. The book recommends that in any case involving the placement of a child the courts should determine who is the child's psychological parent, that is the parent who

> on a continuing day to day basis, through interaction, companionship, interplay and mutuality fulfills the child's psychological needs for a parent as well as the child's physical needs (p. 98).

The court must also decide what is the least detrimental alternative for the child, namely, that

> child placement and procedure for child placement which maximises, in accordance with the child's sense of time the child's opportunity for being wanted and for maintaining on a continuous, unconditional and permanent basis a relationship with at least one adult, who is or will become the child's psychological parent (p. 99).

Yet, nowhere do these authors begin to consider the problems of identifying the psychological parent. Indeed, how is it done? It is clear that one cannot simply assume that a person who has physical possession of a child qualifies for the position of psychological parent. It seems, therefore, unavoidable that in every disputed case one would need expert testimony (presumably from someone psychoanalytically trained) and that this evidence could only properly be obtained by observations of the interaction between child and competing adults over a fairly long period.

What happens, one might well ask, if it is found that one adult provides some of the child's needs and another adult provides others? Would it then be up to the court to decide which amongst these needs are more important? And what happens when each parent is equally capable of meeting the child's needs? At this point Goldstein, Freud and Solnit give up all pretence that the court is involved in making rational decisions and propose 'a judicially supervised drawing of lots', (note 12, p. 153).

Whatever the solution, it is quite clear that the fact-finding efforts demanded of the court before it makes any decision regarding the placement of children would involve a long drawn-out process which would run quite contrary to another of the Goldstein, Freud and Solnit proposals – that placement decisions should reflect the child's sense of time. It seems difficult, therefore, to understand how the court could possibly act 'with all deliberate speed either to restore stability to an existing relationship or to facilitate the establishment of new relationships to replace old ones' (p. 42).

But it is not only the time factor in the court's fact-finding process that Goldstein, Freud and Solnit ignore. Nowhere in the book is there any indication that these authors are aware of the realities of the courtroom. Courts are imperfect places for fact-finding even if the facts are capable of being found. Where one is dealing with such nebulous concepts of 'needs', 'attachments' and 'relationships', in custody cases, the court process is likely to resemble less a scientific inquiry than a contest in which each party attempts to convince the court of his or her value as a parent while portraying the other party as incompetent, uncaring or immoral. Furthermore, are judges the real world's independent fact-finders and decision-makers? Are they not dependent upon the skills of the advocate? Do they not have prejudices and preconceptions? Are they not influenced by the advice of social workers and probation officers attached to the court who themselves will probably have developed value-laden theories about what is best for children?

Moreover, the authors do not at any stage turn their attention to the problems of enforcement. With all placement orders being final and irreversible and with the custodial parent being the sole determiner as to whether the other parent sees the child, one would expect the instances of refusal to comply with court orders to increase drastically. The image of the court bailiff forceably dragging the Stone children away from their mother[5] should be sufficiently fresh in our memory to make us realise the degree to which respect for the courts and the law in children's cases depends upon the willingness of the parties to submit to the court's authority. Once that authority is challenged the whole edifice begins to crumble. One dares not predict how many more Stone cases there would be if the proposals of *Beyond the Best Interests of the Child* were accepted by this country's legislators.

The practical implications of providing child advocates for every case involving a child's interests are complex and controversial (see King, 1975). Suffice it to say that the species of child advocate proposed by Goldstein, Freud and Solnit will have 'no other goal than to determine what is the least detrimental alternative for his client' (p. 66). Not only does this rôle appear to pre-empt the task of the court, but it also may make ridiculous demands upon lawyers in asking them to make decisions which even child experts find difficult or impossible. Furthermore, one could anticipate that each child advocate might well be faced on occasion with the difficult ethical problem of reconciling their own assessment of what is in the child's best interests with the instructions they receive from their young clients. A child may, for example, wish to remain with a parent who spoils him horribly rather than be placed with a parent who is less indulgent but probably better for him.

From all this there should emerge the recognition that there are severe limits on what can be achieved by legal intervention in children's cases and that to exceed these limits probably creates more social harm than doing nothing at all, as well as bringing the law and the courts into disrepute. As long ago as 1916 in an article entitled 'The Limits of Effective Legal Action', Roscoe Pound set out what he considered these limits to be[6]. They include (1) the inability of the law to protect against purely mental suffering because of the problems of producing evidence of such suffering and the ease with which false testimony may be introduced without detection; (2) the inability of the law to enforce duties which morally may be of great importance but legally defy enforcement. These include duties to do with care for the health, morals and education of children; (3) the inability of the law to rectify subtle infringements of individual interests such as the alienation of affection or contravention of the 'right of privacy'; (4) the inability of the legal machinery to rule and remedy many phases of human conduct, many important relations and some serious wrongs; and (5) the ineffectiveness of the law where it entails the necessity of appealing to individuals to set the law in motion. Laws do not enforce themselves. Human beings must execute them and there must be some motive to set the individual in motion beyond the abstract content of the rule and its conformity to an ideal justice or ideal social interests.

I need hardly point out that if Goldstein, Freud and Solnit's proposals were accepted, the law would be exceeding almost all these limits. Moreover, quite irrespective of these authors' recommendations, the existing scope of state intervention in the relationships between children and adults in many respects goes far beyond Pound's formula for successful legal action. The state has through legislation and the creation of several welfare agencies set itself up as arbitrator of what is best for children and uses the courts, often quite inappropriately, to enforce its will. While there is not time now to consider in detail how the scope of legal intervention might be reduced, let me as a final word suggest some general guidelines.

The first point relates to the protective rôle which the law assigns to the court, (the *parens patriae*). Ours is a pluralistic society in which there exists no consensus of what is and what is not psychologically harmful to children. Given that this is so, the law should respect the right of the parents to bring up their children free from State interference unless the State can prove *beyond reasonable doubt* that *observable harm* has been or is likely to be caused to the child. Furthermore, no child should be removed from its home unless the State can prove beyond reasonable doubt that less harm is likely to result from removing the child than leaving it where it is. These formulae would not only place a more stringent burden of proof upon the State than exists at present. They would also, to a large extent, rule out the removal of children from their parents for moral reasons short of physical or sexual abuse, or because of supposed psychological damage inflicted by the parent which is at present undetectable but which may or may not reveal itself when the child has grown older[7].

Secondly, it would be necessary to restrict wherever possible the court's discretion, for discretion is often synonymous with the imposition of values. I am in favour, for example, of rigid time limits for dispensing with parental consent to adoption. I also favour the law in some American states which deprives a parent of parental rights where he or she has had no contact with the child for a specified period of time.

In the difficult area of custody disputes, I believe it is far preferable that parents should work out their own solutions and only have recourse to the courts as a last resort. I would support almost any solution, therefore, which restricts the use of lawyers and the courts in this delicate area of interpersonal reorganisation. This includes informal counselling and attempts to reconcile the differences between the adults concerned and also decision-making by non-judicial arbitrators such as priests, rabbis or even psychoanalysts who might well be selected by the parties. These decisions, once made, could be incorporated in a court order and enforced through the legal system (see Coulson, 1969; Kubie, 1964).

In general, I believe we should be moving in the direction of less intervention rather than more intervention by the law. It is hardly fair to blame psychologists such as Anna Freud and Albert Solnit for exceeding the limits of successful legal action when many lawyers themselves are still suffering from the delusion that the law is capable of doing almost anything.

NOTES

1. P. Bromley, in his textbook *Family Law*, writes 'Medical evidence may be of vital importance in estimating the effect which living with a particular parent may have on the child. Much more is now known about the effects of change of care and control on the child's development and future mental and physical health . . . . Although medical evidence is rarely accepted as decisive, the courts are undoubtedly paying much more attention to it' (1971, p. 277).
2. This is one of the reforms proposed by the organisation 'Fathers Need Families'.
3. For further discussion of this point see Katkin *et al.* (1974).
4. This episode was taken from Murray Levine's (unpublished) account of his experiences as an expert witness in the case.
5. See the *Guardian* 30th November, 1973 and 1st December, 1973.
6. For a more recent discussion, see D. J. Danielski, 'The Limits of Law', in J. Pennock and J. Chapman (1974).
7. See M. Wald, (1975). For an excellent examination of the issues involved in fostering decisions, see R. H. Mnookin (1977).

REFERENCES

M. Ainsworth, *Deprivation of Maternal Care: A Reassessment of its Effects*, Public Health Papers No. 14 (Geneva: WHO, 1962).

J. Bowlby, *Maternal Care and Mental Health*, Monograph No. 2 (Geneva: WHO, 1951).

P. Bromley, *Family Law*, 4th ed. (London: Butterworths, 1971).

A. M. Clarke and A. D. B. Clarke, *Early Experience: Myth and Evidence* (London: Open Books, 1976).

M. D. Coe, *The Maya* (Harmondsworth: Penguin, 1971).

R. Coulson, 'Family arbitration – an exercise in sensitivity', *Family Law Quarterly*, 3 (1969) 22.

Department of Health and Social Security (DHSS), *The Report of the Departmental Committee on One-Parent Families*, (London: HMSO, Cmnd. 5629 1974).

J. Goldstein, A. Freud and A. J. Solnit, *Beyond the Best Interests of the Child* (New York: Free Press, 1973).

D. Katkin, B. Bullington and M. Levine, 'Above and beyond the best interests of the child', *Law and Society Review* (Summer, 1974) 681–7.

M. King, Review of 'Beyond the best interests of the child', *Legal Action Group Bulletin* (July, 1974).

M. King, 'Do children really need their own lawyers?', *The Times*, 18th July, 1975.

Z. S. Kubie, 'Provisions for the care of children of divorced parents: A new legal instrument', *Yale Law Journal*, 73 (1964) 1197.

W. McCord and J. McCord, *Origins of Crime: A New Evaluation of the Cambridge – Sommerville Youth Study*, Youth Study, (New York: Columbia Press, 1959).

R. H. Mnookin, 'Foster care – in whose best interests?', *Harvard Educational Review*, 43 (1977) 599–638.

B. Mortlock, *The Inside of Divorce* (London: Constable, 1972).

J. Pennock and J. Chapman (eds), *The Limits of Law*, Nomas XV (New York: Atherton, 1974).

A. Platt, *The Child Savers* (Chicago: Chicago Press, 1969).

R. Pound, 'The limits of effective legal action', *International Journal of Ethics*, 27 (1916) 150–1 and 161–7.

L. Rosenblum, 'Infant attachment in monkeys', in H. R. Schaffer (ed.), *The Origins of Human Social Relations* (London: Academic Press, 1971).

M. Rutter, 'Parent – child separation: Psychological effects on the children', *Journal of Psychology and Psychiatry*, (1971) 233–60.

H. R. Schaffer, *Mothering* (London: Fontana/Open Books, 1977).

A. Skolnick, 'The limits of childhood: Conceptions of child development and social context', *Law and Contemporary Problems* (1975) 38–72.

M. Wald, 'State intervention on behalf of neglected children: A search for realistic standards', *Stanford Law Review*, 27 (1975) 1007.

11: Family Violence: Interpretations and Solutions

Michael D. A. Freeman

In the last two decades we have gradually become aware of the phenomenon of family violence (see Freeman, 1979a). Child abuse was the first aspect of the problem to surface to public attention. The earliest discoveries date from the late 1940s but it was H. Kempe's address to the American Academy of Paediatrics in 1961 which first attracted major attention to the problem (Kempe, 1962). The earliest sociological and psychological studies date from the mid-1960s (Elmer, 1967; Young, 1964). Wife abuse 'arrived' a decade later. It had previously been seen as a problem in the mid-nineteenth century: Erin Pizzey's work in Chiswick and her book *Scream Quietly or the Neighbours will Hear* (Pizzey, 1979a) plus the fact that a women's movement was active were largely instrumental in bringing it again to public attention. Only now are inter-sibling violence, 'granny-bashing' and husband battering beginning to be seen as problems (see Steinmetz, 1977; 1978). Social problems are more than just an objective state of affairs. They require interpretation and entrepreneurial activity before we hear of them and before they acquire meaning – or a meaning of sorts (Fuller and Myers, 1941). Putative solutions to social problems are integrally related to the definitions of those problems which have been constructed and to the questions which have been posed about them. These same definitions have a way of influencing subsequent research, and definitions and solutions which challenge those which are in control have a difficult time trying to displace the traditional theories (see Kuhn, 1970).

Our understanding of family violence has been governed by a

psychiatric approach. This has concentrated on the personality of the offender, examined features of his psychopathology and proposed solutions in terms of what could be done to punish or cure him. This traditional approach ignores interaction between participants and the socio-cultural context of the behaviour in question. Despite its deficiencies it has proved immensely influential and social and legal policies remain under its spell. As lawyers and psychologists we can, I think, learn much from the way this has happened. Dealing with family violence has not been a particularly successful collaborative activity.

In this chapter I discuss the psychopathological interpretations of family violence which have dominated the literature; I examine the limitations in this approach and put forward alternative suggestions as to ways of understanding the phenomenon. I discuss both child and wife abuse though limitations on space mean that discussion of child abuse is somewhat fuller.

THE PSYCHOPATHOLOGICAL INTERPRETATION OF FAMILY VIOLENCE

As Gelles (1973) shows, throughout the literature on child abuse there runs a common theme: 'anyone who would abuse or kill this child is sick'. It is commonly suggested that there is a psychological pathology which accounts for child abuse. The traditional model of child abuse assumed that child abusers have distinctive personality traits and that these are typical of the psychopathic personality. Commonly the cause of this psychopathy is traced to the abuser's early childhood when he or she was abused.

Two examples of this model will elucidate its parameters and philosophy. One of the most authoritative and widely quoted of psychiatric studies of abusive parents is that of Steele and Pollock (1974). They studied intensively sixty families in which significant abuse of infants or small children had occurred. Their clinical study was supplemented by interviews and home visits by a social worker. The patients were a cross-section of the white population, and all socio-economic strata were covered. 'In respect to psychopathology' the authors note, 'they were equally heterogenous' (p. 94). They suggest there is a wide spread of emotional disorders so that instead of trying to associate the problem with a specific type of psychiatric disorder, they searched for what they call 'a consistent behaviour pattern which can exist in combination with, but quite independently of, other psychological disorders' (p. 95). They emphasise the unreal demands that the parents make of their children. 'It is hardly an exaggeration', they write 'to say the parent acts like a frightened, unloved child, looking to his own child as if he were an adult capable of providing comfort and love' (p. 95). The key, as they see it, is the fact that the abusive parents themselves had been deprived of 'basic mothering'. They list also secondary elements of parental psychopathology: intense, unresolved sibling rivalry; an obsessive compulsive character structure; and unresolved Oedipal conflicts with excessive guilt. They do not altogether ignore the child's rôle in instigating abuse: characteristics such as sex, time of birth, health status and behaviour are noted as factors which may contribute to the parent's behaviour. One aspect of an interactional approach is thus present but its implications remain dormant.

A second illustration of the psychopathological model is contained in the NSPCC Battered Child Research Department publication entitled *At Risk* (NSPCC, 1976). The sample was a small one (twenty-five families) and contained severe biases in that it was the product of references to the Department. The authors concede that their sample is too small to allow generalisations regarding the psychosocial pathology of child batterers. They content themselves with listing 'suggestive pointers'. They refer to 'immaturity, impracticality and a tendency to flee into fantasy in the face of real problems' (p. 194). The fathers are said to have 'introverted schizoid personalities', and to be unable to support the mothers in their time of need so that the mothers turn to their small children for 'emotional replenishment' (p. 195). The authors of *At Risk* do not ignore the factor of environmental stress, but it figures only marginally in their explanation.

The psychopathological model probably represents what the man in the street thinks of the parents of battered children. It is also the mainspring for much of our social policy on the question. That we should want to think of abusing parents as 'sick' may tell us something about ourselves. I find Gil's comment on this most persuasive. 'Is it possible', he asks, 'that the illness-as-cause hypothesis is accepted readily because it soothes society's conscience, as well as the conscience of individual parents who may be subject to abusive impulses?' (Gil, 1970, p. 17). The labelling of abusing parents as deviants, particularly as 'sick' deviants, is an important functional mechanism for the rest of us (Box, 1971; Gusfield, 1967). It fills us with a sense of security. It obviates the need for us to examine the social circumstances and cultural trends which may be major factors in child abuse.

When we turn to wife abuse the concerns and interpretations are very similar. It is most commonly hypothesised that wives are battered by husbands who have sick or inadequate personalities. The tendency is to isolate particular pathological characteristics and then assert their existence in statistically significant numbers of husbands who have battered their wives. The behaviour is then attributed to possession of the particular pathological characteristic in question. Attention is concentrated on behavioural characteristics of those whom Box (1971) has called 'official deviants'. Thus it is commonly asserted that battering husbands are alcoholics or drug addicts or have 'personality disorders' or that they are psychopaths. Their violent behaviour is said to be irrational rather as other deviance – industrial sabotage, football hooliganism or racism – is categorised as 'mindless' or 'meaningless' (cf. Cohen, 1971).

Erin Pizzey, the most influential of publicists of the plight of the battered woman, subscribes to this view. She has described battering husbands as 'deeply immature', (Pizzey, 1974), as 'aggressive psychopaths', (Pizzey, 1975, p. 2). They are 'outside the law', beyond the pale of 'democratic society'. They act 'instinctively, not rationally', (Pizzey, 1975). Remedies accordingly lie, she believes, in the hands of the medical profession. Gayford, one of the earliest of researchers in this area, has emphasised the 'pathological jealousy' of the husbands, produced by alcohol and not susceptible of being removed by 'logical reasoning' (Gayford, 1975, 1978, 1979). Faulk (1974) concluded that younger men who assaulted their wives were more psychopathic and older men more likely to suffer from a psychiatric disorder (see also Hanks and Rosenbaum, 1977).

How useful an explanation is the psychopathological model? It has, I think, marginal value only. Of course, some batterers have personality disorders but this does not explain their behaviour. Often the model offers an exceptionalistic explanation of a universalistic problem (Ryan, 1976). It implies that the problem is unique to a specially defined category of persons, rather than a function of the social arrangements of the society (see also Wright Mills, 1943). More particularly one may note that most of the studies do not test specific hypotheses, that they tend to use samples which are not truly representative and that practically all the psychological research in both child and wife abuse is *ex post facto*, and thus offers little analytic understanding of its genesis (see Gelles, 1973; Spinetta and Rigler, 1972).

Gelles has commented that the model cannot 'account for the majority of cases of child abuse because it posits a single causal variable . . . and ignores other factors' (Gelles, 1973, p. 611). It does not explain why, for example, a parent himself abused as a child should express this experience in child abuse as opposed to other forms of dysfunctional behaviour. It does not explain why many people who are immature or impulsive or possessed of other character traits which psychologists impute to child abusers do not act violently towards their children. It assumes an act of abuse cannot occur unless the psychological potential is present. It would thus seem to account for both too much and too little abuse. Furthermore, there is little agreement in the literature as to the make-up of the psychopathy. Gelles noted nineteen traits referred to in a cross-section of the literature he surveyed, but only four figured in the diagnoses of more than two authors.

The evidence tends to be produced by clinicians using data gathered from interviews with patients. But, as not all abusers find their way to clinics, the samples are inevitably biased. In the case of child abuse we need to know much more about how abusive caretakers get referred to the helping professions. Studies of referral in relation to other problems demonstrate the importance of this (for example, Daniels, 1970; Freidson, 1966; Scheff, 1966; Scott, 1969). Certain individuals quite clearly are more likely to be defined as 'abusers' than others. The greater the social distance between the typer and the person singled out for typing, the more quickly the typification may be applied (see Rubington and Weinberg, 1977, p. 164). Once the label of 'abuser' has been attached it is difficult to remove it. When a parent comes to a psychiatrist as an 'abuser' the psychiatrist is thus apt to engage in what Schur has called, 'retrospective interpretation' of facts (Schur, 1971, p. 52). In Lofland's words, 'the *present evil* of current character must be related to *past evil* that can be discovered in biography' (Lofland, 1969, p. 150). As Goffman (1968) has noted, a function of case records is to support current diagnoses. The pathological model requires that parents be studied in terms of what is 'wrong' with them. But it may be that the attachment of the label 'abuser' produces the very personality characteristics which in due course are diagnosed as the causes of the abuse in question (see Lemert, 1972).

The psychopathological interpretation of family violence leads necessarily to solutions which bear its imprints. Parents, since they are abnormal or 'sick', require extensive psychiatric treatment to enable them to overcome their 'illness'. Predictive screening questionnaires must be developed to identify potential high-risk cases (Schneider *et al.*, 1972). But these pose considerable methodological and ethical problems. Light (1974) has shown that errors may be as high as eighty-five per cent with the result that many parents will be mistakenly stigmatised. Labelling may, of course, interfere with the resocialisation process. Abusive or potentially abusive parents also require social work intervention. But, as an NSPCC study noted, the recidivism rate amongst parents known to a protective agency was more than twice the rebattering rate where there was no social work intervention (Skinner and Castle, 1969). It is a sad fact that in all the *causes célèbres* of recent years – Colwell, Auckland, Meurs, Godfrey, Peacock – the cases were not new referrals which had not been investigated quickly enough, but cases known to a department (more often several) for a considerable period (see Jordan, 1975).

Solutions to wife abuse also tend to follow from the dominant psychopathological understanding of the problem. This is hardly surprising for to the general public, no less than to the legislature, Erin Pizzey is assumed to have the last word on the subject. Solutions, therefore, are primarily treatment-orientated: social work intervention, better medical provision, more refuges.

ALTERNATIVE VIEWS OF FAMILY VIOLENCE

Both child abuse and wife abuse must be seen in the context of the norms of the community. Both terms are culturally determined labels, the result of an imputation or judgment by an observer, usually a social control agency, such as the police, social welfare agency or the medical profession. They are not absolutes and are essentially problematic. Whether the imputation is made or not may depend on a large number of contingencies.

Two rather obvious examples may make this point clearer. In our culture physical attacks on children are legitimate techniques employed in the socialisation process: we call them corporal punishment. Such attacks are sanctioned by statute (see Children and Young Persons Act 1933, Section 1(7). The Newsons' Nottingham studies show how prevalent they are (Newson and Newson, 1978). By the time children are seven they found that twenty-two per cent have received corporal punishment from their parents via some implement (middle-class parents favouring a cane and working-class parents a strap or belt) and a further fifty-three per cent have been so threatened. The humbug of the situation is revealed in all its glory when a social services committee can, as Nottinghamshire and one or two others have recently done, re-introduce corporal punishment in its community homes when children who are to be on the receiving end may well be in the homes because they have been abused by their parents. The House of Commons Select Committee on Violence in the Family did not question the practice of corporal punishment. A bill to abolish corporal punishment of handicapped and deprived children failed to get a second reading (see *Social Work Today*, 1979). Secondly, despite our concern with battered wives, moves to remove a husband's immunity from prosecution for raping his wife have been unsuccessful. An attempt to do this whilst the Sexual Offences (Amendment) Bill 1976 was before Parliament failed (see House of Commons Standing Committee F, 24 March 1976 and H.C. Deb., Vol. 911, col. 1952 *et seq.*). In England, therefore, a husband cannot be prosecuted successfully for raping his wife. The immunity has been abolished in several American states and elsewhere, but the first American prosecution has just failed (see *The Guardian*, 29th December, 1978). By definition rape cannot exist within marriage, though, of course, the behaviour itself, forced sexual intercourse, may be functionally equivalent to comparable behaviour com- mitted outside the bounds of marriage and given the official label of rape (Freeman, 1979c).

Some child abuse, therefore, is not so regarded because it is legitimised as corporal punishment. Other acts are not stigmatised as abuse because they attract the classification of being 'accidents'. This concept tends to be treated as unproblematic. One of the few discussions of intentionality is that by Kelley (1973). The label 'abuser' is applied by high status personnel, and is less likely to be applied if the doctor and suspected abuser share similar socio- economic status and other characteristics. Injuries found in the children of higher status families are more likely to attract the classification of being regarded as 'accidents'. So the same injury regarded as abuse in one situation, for one child or in one social class, may not so be regarded for another child or in another social class (Freeman, 1979b; Newberger and Bourne, 1978).

How is one then to understand violence within the family? No single explanation can be found and personality factors cannot be completely ruled out. As far as child abuse is concerned the cultural acceptance of corporal punishment is a significant contributor. This is the view of Gil (1970) and Farson (1978). In other cultures where physical punishment of children is not sanctioned incidents of child abuse are not reported. One example is China (see Sidel, 1972). Whether child abuse still takes place and whether, if it does not, its absence may be attributed to a reluctance to use physical force on children has not been determined. Further, in trying to understand family violence, levels of violence in society generally should not be ignored. Exposure to violence on television must not be underestimated for it often demonstrates that violence is a way of achieving a goal or resolving conflict (see Belson, 1978).

An understanding of why parents use violence also requires an understanding of their own upbringing. Information about child-rearing is culled from many sources. The most influential, it seems, remains the parent's own child-rearing experiences. There are clear findings of a relationship between exposure to physical punishment and aggression (Feshbach and Feshbach, 1976). Many violent parents were themselves abused as children (Hyman, 1978). Gelfand *et al.* (1974) found, in a recent experiment, that a child disciplined by an adult with punitive tactics was more likely to use such tactics himself when given the chance to train another child. Despite this evidence eminent psychologists like Bettelheim still urge that children should learn about violence in order to learn how to handle it (Bettelheim, 1974, p. 299).

Many discussions of child abuse relate it to experiences of the parent when he was a child. But relating abuse to physical punishment *simpliciter* does not take us very far. Recent psychological findings (Young, 1964), not dissimilar from those of an earlier era relating to delinquency (McCord *et al.* 1961), do, however, note a relationship between intermittent punishment and a child's aggression. These indicate that intermittent punishment administered by a single agent is less effective than consistent punishment. Furthermore, inconsistency between socialising agents is noted to be ineffective. Deur and Parke (1970) note that boys who were inconsistently disciplined persisted in aggressive behaviour longer than those who were treated with consistency. So far as is known no investigation has sought to make the link between the quality (that is its consistency) of punishment in childhood and subsequent abusive tendencies. A correlational study of this relationship would clearly be worth doing. Looking at these data another way, it seems possible that an agent whose punishment is ineffective may resort to more intensive punishment and that this is an explanation of how culturally sanctioned punishment declines into culturally pro-scribed abuse. If that is so, it would suggest that abusive parents are influenced not only by their own experiences in childhood but also by interactive relationships with their own children.

This leads to the question of what rôle a child plays in his own abuse. The development of a 'science' of victimology (there is now a journal called *Victimology*) has made us focus attention on the part played by victims in crimes (see Viano, 1976). Early research on child abuse concentrated on the parent, his personality and his action: the child was seen passively. Of late it has been noticed that certain children may be more at risk than others (Friedrich and Boriskin, 1976). There is evidence of an association between prematurity, low birth-weight and abuse (Lynch, 1975). There is some evidence of an association between physical handicap and abuse (Birrell and Birrell, 1968). Children who are 'slow-to-warm-up' or moody or hyperactive may, it seems, also be more prone to abuse than more 'normal' children (Herbert and Iwaniec, 1977). An abused child attracts negative reactions thus inviting further abuse (Bakan, 1971). Indeed, Dion (1974) discovered in a recent experiment that an unattractive child receives more severe punish-ment than an attractive one. In parenthesis one may note that similar processes have been noted by Landy and Aronson (1969) and others (for example, Nemeth and Sosis (1973)) in a jury's reaction to an attractive defendant.

The part that the other spouse plays in child abuse has hardly been questioned. Leontine Young's *Wednesday's Children* saw the non-abusing parent as a prisoner of the other marriage partner, more as another child than a parent (Young, 1964, pp. 49–50). Others have been doubtful as to the non-abusing parent's non-involvement. The likelihood that a parent will abuse both his child and his spouse has frequently been noted. But how often, one may wonder, is child abuse the result of a battered wife aggressing against a child when unable, for whatever reason, to strike back at her husband? There is some support for this hypothesis in research by Fenigstein and Buss (1974): subjects preferred to demonstrate intense aggression against someone who was not associated with the experimenter than to deliver a mild noxious stimulus to his confederate.

Interaction between parent and child and between parents is, then, an important factor in explaining child abuse and one on which considerable psychological research is still needed. Interplay between the family and its social context is another interactional process which no theory of child abuse (or wife abuse) can ignore. Explanations in these terms have tended to concentrate on environmental stress. Thus, Gil (1975) has argued that a major cause of child abuse is the stress and frustration which result from 'multi-faceted deprivations of poverty and its correlates, high density in overcrowded, dilapidated, inadequately served neighbourhoods, large numbers of children especially in one-parent, mainly female-headed households, and the absence of child-care alternatives', (p. 352), to which he adds poor education and the alienating circumstances of most work places. Gil does not suggest that poverty in itself is a direct cause of child abuse: rather, it operates through an intervening variable, *viz.*, 'concrete and psychological stress and frustration experienced by individuals in the context of culturally sanctioned use of physical force in child rearing' (p. 352). Gil's thesis does not explain why abuse occurs at all in higher-income families and why it does not occur even more commonly in families who suffer multiple deprivation and stress.

The environmental stress view of child abuse finds some support in Garbarino's (1976) research in New York State. He found that socio-economic stress, exacerbated by the unavailability of adequate support systems for the family from the community, accounted for thirty-six per cent of the variance in rates of child abuse/maltreatment across New York counties. Economic conditions more generally affecting the family accounted for sixteen per cent of the variance. There is considerable evidence of deprivation amongst child abusers (Gil, 1970). Parents tend to be poor, very young, socially isolated, the father to be unemployed. Many have accommodation problems. It is common to find fathers with a criminal record. Mothers have often had to cope alone. Many mothers were pregnant or recently confined at the time of abuse. But this does not explain why abuse takes place.

Part of the answer to this may lie in social learning: perhaps the child who grows up in an environment where he learns that violence is a major resource in tackling life's problems resorts to similar techniques himself. A life of poverty or a ghetto existence tends to generate the sort of stressful experiences that may trigger abuse by weakening the parent's psychological mechanisms of self-control. In this setting resort to violence is greater, so that a tendency to use violence may well be learned through lower-class socialisation in circumstances of environmental stress. Murray Straus (1977), found a consistent tendency for more violence to have occurred in marriages of blue-collar husbands as compared to the white-collar occupation group. He noted that 'although about as many white-collar husband families have experienced at least some violence during the course of the marriage as blue-collar families, the frequency and seriousness of family violence is considerably greater in the blue-collar sector of the society' (p. 3). When he examined attitudes there was no difference between the two groups in the proportion viewing violence as 'good' and almost no difference in the extent to which violence is regarded as 'normal'. But the blue-collar rate of viewing violence as 'necessary' is considerably higher than the white-collar rate. This suggests, he argues persuasively:

> that the basis for the wide belief in social class differences in attitudes towards violence . . . is the fact that lower class people live in a situation where violence is present and often necessary for self-preservation. They do not favour violence any more than middle class people. But the blue-collar group seems to differ in regarding violence as an inevitable – even though disliked and disapproved – aspect of life' (p. 5).

Explanations of child abuse (and wife abuse) are thus complex. Nonetheless, the problem of child abuse revolves round our definition of children: the way we perceive them; children as the property of their parents, as non-persons, as objects of rather than participants in the social process (see Freeman, 1980; Gerzon, 1973; Gottlieb, 1973). Striking another adult is frowned upon: not so striking a child. One thing that psychology's interest in law has already achieved is research to establish that children can understand the legal and moral basis of social rights at earlier ages than was once thought (see Tapp, 1971; Tapp and Levine, 1974). Knowledge such as this may help to remould a concept of childhood which ultimately may make assaults on children in the name of socialisation less acceptable.

In the same way the move away from abuse of women demands a redefinition of male-female relationships. Violence against women is a necessary concomitant of woman's generally oppressed position in the social structure. The purpose of male violence is to control women (see Smart and Smart, 1978). It is the result of a 'macho' ideology which supports the male's use of violence to maintain dominance over his mate. Women are battered because they are powerless and dependent (see Dobash and Dobash, 1977). Not only do husbands possess greater power but many women believe they ought to do so (Bell and Newby, 1976). They believe in the authority of their husbands and that it is right to defer to them. Deference derives from power but becomes in time a moral position. Both the social security system and the law regulating marriage reflect this asymmetry of power (see Land, 1978; Weitzman, 1974; Wilson, 1977). So do the activities of institutions like the police, business practices such as those concerned with credit and housing policies, and various legislative provisions and judicial pronouncements (see Mayo, 1977). Violence is used to control women both within and outside the home. A survey by Whitehurst (1974) showed that threats of violence are frequent among husbands as a means of controlling wives. He describes a case where a husband catching his wife *in flagrante delicto* 'set upon the two of them in a jealous rage'. He interprets this reaction in terms of the 'husband's own need to control his wife and feel superior', and explains that this was 'too much of an emotional burden for him to handle without recourse to violence' (Whitehurst, 1974, p. 80). Outside the home women are taught to avoid certain areas, so that, as Jalna Hanmer has put it, 'urban space for woman is compartmentalised, to deviate from women's alloted space is to run the risk of attack by men' (Hanmer, 1978, p. 228). The fear of violence, particularly rape, has the effect of driving women to seek protection from men, and increasing their dependency. Ironically, women feel safer in the company of husbands and boy friends though they are more likely to be attacked or raped by them than by the dangerous strangers whom they are taught to fear (Amir, 1971).

CONCLUDING COMMENTS – CAN FAMILY VIOLENCE BE ELIMINATED?

Family violence, it has been argued in this chapter, is essentially learned behaviour. This should give us greater hope for the future for what is learned can be unlearned and future generations can be socialised differently. The key to the immediate future lies in resocialisation, in teaching families to function and to interact more constructively. The law may well have a part to play here. Thus measures which compel parents to learn parenting practices which are acceptable to the community as a whole might be a useful way in which lawyers and psychologists could combine to tackle the problem of child abuse. Bevan (1970) makes a similar suggestion. Lawyers and the courts cannot, however, act *in vacuo*. It is up to psychologists to develop such training programmes. One that does exist (in the USA) was developed by Patterson (1974). This concentrates on retraining parents of aggressive children and is based on social learning principles, particularly operant conditioning concepts. It appears to have been fairly successful, and it is economical.

In the longer term it is redefinitions that are required. Greater attention must be given to equality between spouses and increased recognition of the personality and rights of children. Here legal reforms can help – the abolition of corporal punishment, the removal of the husband's immunity from prosecution for rape of his wife, a fairer tax and social security system, more teeth for the anti-discrimination legislation. Seen in this way the task is not hopeless. Examined from the psychopathological perspective the prospects were dim indeed. Perhaps now there is at least light at the end of the tunnel.

REFERENCES

M. Amir, *Patterns in Forcible Rape* (Chicago: University of Chicago Press, 1971).

D. Bakan, *Slaughter of the Innocents* (San Francisco: Jossey-Bass, 1971).

C. Bell and H. Newby, 'Husbands and wives: The dynamics of the deferential dialectic', in D. L. Barker and S. Allen (eds.), *Dependence and Exploitation in Work and Marriage* (Harlow, Essex: Longman, 1976).

W. Belson, *Television Violence and the Adolescent Boy* (Farnborough, Hampshire: Saxon House, 1978).

B. Bettelheim, 'Children should learn about violence', in S. Steinmetz and M. Straus, *Violence in the Family* (New York: Dodd, Mead, 1974).

H. K. Bevan, *Child Protection and the Law* (Hull: University of Hull Press, 1970).

R. Birrell and J. Birrell, 'The maltreatment syndrome in children: A hospital survey', *Medical Journal of Australia*, *2* (1968) 1023–9.

S. Box, *Deviance Reality and Society* (New York: Holt, Rinehart and Winston, 1971).

S. Cohen, *Images of Deviance* (Harmondsworth: Penguin, 1971).

A. Daniels, 'Normal mental illness and understandable excuses: The philosophy of combat psychiatry', *American Behavioural Scientist*, *14* (1970) 167–84.

J. L. Deur and R. D. Parke, 'Effects of inconsistent punishment on aggression in children', *Developmental Psychology*, *2* (1970) 403–11.

R. Dobash and R. Dobash, 'Love honour and obey', *Contemporary Crises*, *1* (1977) 403–18.

K. K. Dion, 'Children's physical attractiveness and sex as determinants of adult punitiveness', *Developmental Psychology*, *10* (1974) 772–8.

E. Elmer, *Children in Jeopardy* (Pittsburgh: University of Pittsburgh Press, 1967).

R. Farson, *Birthrights* (Harmondsworth: Penguin, 1978).

M. Faulk, 'Men who assault their wives', *Medicine, Science and The Law*, *14* (1974) 180–3.

A. Fenigstein and A. H. Buss, 'Association and affect as determinants of displaced aggression', *Journal of Research in Personality*, *7* (1974) 306–13.

N. D. Feshbach and S. Feshbach, 'Punishment: Parent rites versus children's rites', in G. P. Koocher (ed.), *Children's Rights and the Mental Health Professions* (New York: Wiley, 1976).

M. D. A. Freeman, *Violence in the Home – A Socio-Legal Study* (Farnborough, Hampshire: Saxon House, 1979). (a)

M. D. A. Freeman, 'Child welfare: law and control', in M. Partington and J. Jowell (eds.), *Welfare Law and Policy* (London: Pinter, 1979). (b)

M. D. A. Freeman, 'Rape by a husband?', *New Law Journal*, *129* (1979). (c)

M. D. A. Freeman, *The Rights and Wrongs of Children* (London: Pinter, 1980).

E. Freidson, 'Disability as social deviance', in M. Sussman (ed.), *Sociology and Rehabilitation* (Washington D.C.: American Sociological Association, 1966).

W. Friedrich and J. Boriskin, 'The role of the child in abuse: A review of the literature', *American Journal of Orthopsychiatry*, *46* (1976) 580–9.

R. Fuller and R. Myers, 'Some aspects of a theory of social problems', *American Sociological Review*, *6* (1941) 24–32.

J. Garbarino, 'A preliminary study of some ecological correlates of child abuse: The impact of socio-economic stress on mothers', *Child Development*, *47* (1976) 178–85.

J. J. Gayford, 'Wife battering: A preliminary survey of 100 cases', *British Medical Journal*, (25th January, 1975) 194–7.

J. J. Gayford, 'Battered wives', in J. P. Martin (ed.), *Violence and the Family* (Chichester: Wiley, 1978).

J. J. Gayford, 'The aetiology of repeated serious physical assaults by husbands on wives (wife battering)', *Medicine, Science and the Law*, *19* (1979) 19–24.

D. M. Gelfand, D. P. Hartmann, A. K. Lamb, C. L. Smith, M. A. Mahan, S. C. Paul, 'The effects of adult models and described alternatives on children's choice of behavior management techniques', *Child Development*, *45* (1974) 585–93.

R. Gelles, 'Child abuse as psychopathology: A sociological critique and reformulation', *American Journal of Orthopsychiatry*, *43* (1973) 611–21.

M. Gerzon, *A Childhood for Every Child* (New York: Outerbridge and Lazard, 1973).

D. Gil, *Violence Against Children* (Cambridge, Mass.: Harvard University Press, 1970).

D. Gil, 'Unraveling child abuse', *American Journal of Orthopsychiatry*, *45* (1975) 346–56.

E. Goffmann, *Asylums* (Harmondsworth: Penguin, 1968).

D. Gottlieb, (ed.), *Children's Liberation* (Englewood Cliffs, New Jersey: Prentice Hall, 1973).

J. Gusfield, 'Moral passage: The symbolic process in public designations of deviance', *Social Problems*, *15* (1967) 175–88.

S. E. Hanks and C. P. Rosenbaum, 'Battered women: A study of women who live with violent alcohol-abusing men', *American Journal of Orthopsychiatry*, *47* (1977) 291–306.

J. Hanmer, 'Violence and the social control of women', in G. Littlejohn, B. Smart, J. Wakeford and N. Yuval-Davis (eds.), *Power and The State* (London: Croom Helm, 1978).

M. Herbert and D. Iwaniec, 'Children who are hard to love', *New Society*, *21* (April, 1977).

C. A. Hyman, 'Some characteristics of abusing families referred to the NSPCC', *British Journal of Social Work*, *8* (1978) 171–81.

B. Jordan, 'Is the client a fellow citizen?', *Social Work Today*, *6* No. 15 (1975), 471–5.

C. H. Kempe, 'The battered child syndrome', *Journal of the American Medical Association*, *181* (1962) 17–24.

H. Kelley, 'The process of causal attribution', *American Psychologist*, *28* (1973) 107–28.

T. Kuhn, *The Structure of Scientific Revolutions*, revised ed. (Chicago: University of Chicago Press, 1970).

H. Land, 'Sex-role stereotyping in the Social Security and Income Tax Systems', in J. Chetwynd and O. Harnett, *The Sex Role System* (London: Routledge and Kegan Paul, 1978).

D. Landy and E. Aronson, 'The influence of the character of the criminal and his victim on the decisions of simulated jurors', *Journal of Experimental and Social Psychology*, *5* (1969) 141–52.

E. Lemert, *Human Deviance, Social Problems and Social Control*, 2nd ed. (Englewood Cliffs, New Jersey: Prentice Hall, 1972).

R. Light, 'Abused and neglected children in America: A study of alternative policies', in Harvard Educational Review, Reprint Series No. 9, *The Rights of Children* (Cambridge, Mass Harvard University Press, 1974).

J. Lofland, *Deviance and Identity* (Englewood Cliffs, New Jersey: Prentice Hall, 1969).

M. A. Lynch, 'Ill health and child abuse', *The Lancet*, 7929 (1975) 317–19.

M. Mayo (ed.), *Women in the Community* (London: Routledge and Kegan Paul, 1977).

W. McCord, J. McCord and A. Howard, 'Familiar correlates of aggression in non-delinquent male children', *Journal of Abnormal and Social Psychology*, *62* (1961) 79–93.

C. Wright Mills, 'The professional ideology of social pathologists', *American Journal of Sociology, 49* (1943) 165–80.

C. Nemeth and R. H. Sosis, 'A stimulated jury study: Characteristics of the defendant and the jurors', *Journal of Social Psychology, 90* (1973) 221–9.

E. H. Newberger and R. Bourne, 'The medicalization and legalization of child abuse', in J. Eekelaar and S. Katz (eds.), *Family Violence* (Scarborough, Ontario: Butterworths, 1978). (Also in *American Journal of Orthopsychiatry, 48* (1978) 593–607).

J. Newson and E. Newson, *Seven Years Old in the Home Environment* (Harmondsworth: Penguin, 1978).

National Society for the Prevention of Cruelty to Children (NSPCC), *At Risk* (London: Routledge and Kegan Paul, 1976).

G. R. Patterson, 'Intervention for boys with conduct problems: Multiple settings, treatments and criteria', *Journal of Consulting and Clinical Psychology, 42* (1974) 471–81.

E. Pizzey, Article in the *Spectator* 23 November, 1974.

E. Pizzey, quoted in *Minutes of Evidence, House of Commons Select Committee on Violence in Marriage* (London: HMSO, 1975).

E. Pizzey, *Scream Quietly or the Neighbours will Hear*, revised ed. (Harmondsworth: Penguin, 1979).

E. Rubington and M. Weinberg, *Deviance: The Interactionist Perspective*, 3rd ed. (London: Macmillan, 1977).

W. Ryan, *Blaming the Victim*, revised ed. (New York: Vintage Books, 1976).

T. Scheff, 'Typification in rehabilitation agencies', in M. Sussman, *Sociology and Rehabilitation* (Washington D.C.: American Sociological Association, 1966).

C. Schneider, R. E. Helfer and C. Pollock, 'The predictive questionnaire: A preliminary report', in C. H. Kempe and R. Heifer (eds.), *Helping the Battered Child and His Family* (Philadelphia: Lippincot, 1972).

E. Schur, *Labeling Deviant Behavior* (New York: Harper and Row, 1971).

R. Scott, *The Making of Blind Men* (New York: Russell Sage, 1969).

R. Sidel, *Women and Child Care in China* (New York: Hill and Wang, 1972).

A. Skinner and R. Castle, *Seventy-Eight Battered Children: A Retrospective Study* (London: NSPCC, 1969).

C. Smart and B. Smart, *Woman, Sexuality and Social Control* (London: Routledge and Kegan Paul, 1978).

Social Work Today, 12, (news item) (1979) 5.

J. J. Spinetta and D. Rigler, 'The child-abusing parent: A psychological review', *Psychological Bulletin, 77* (1972) 296–304.

B. Steele and C. Pollock, 'A psychiatric study of parents who abuse infants and small children', in R. Helfer and C. H. Kempe (eds.), *The Battered Child*, 2nd ed. (Chicago: University of Chicago Press, 1974).

S. Steinmetz, *The Cycle of Violence: Assertive, Aggressive and Abusive Interaction* (New York: Praeger, 1977).

S. Steinmetz, 'Sibling violence', in J. Eekelaar and S. Katz (eds.), *Family Violence* (Scarborough, Ontario: Butterworths, 1978).

M. Straus, 'Normative and behavioral aspects of violence between spouses', unpublished paper, 1977.

J. L. Tapp (ed.), 'Socialization, the law and society', *Journal of Social Issues, 27* (1971).

J. L. Tapp and F. J. Levine, 'Legal socialization: Strategies for an ethical legality', *Stanford Law Review*, 27 (1974) 1–72.

E. C. Viano, *Victims and Society* (Washington D.C.: Visage, 1976).

L. Weitzman, 'Legal regulations of marriage: Tradition and change', *California Law Review*, 62 (1974) 1169–1283.

R. N. Whitehurst, 'Violence in husband-wife interaction', in S. Steinmetz and M. Straus (eds.), *Violence in the Family* (New York: Dodd, Mead, 1974).

E. Wilson, *Women and the Welfare State* (London: Tavistock, 1977).

L. Young, *Wednesday's Children* (New York: McGraw-Hill, 1964).

12: The Legal and the Psychological View of Gambling

David Miers

In 1978, the Royal Commission on Gambling, under the Chairmanship of Lord Rothschild, presented its report. Its general terms of reference were 'to inquire into the existing law, and practice thereunder, relating to betting, gaming, lotteries and prize competitions . . .' (Rothschild, 1978, p. iii). Four particular areas of concern were enumerated:

1. the adequacy of existing legal regulation of the different forms of gambling;
2. the financial structure of the gambling industry and the degree of commercial exploitation of the market;
3. the provision of information about the odds against winning in any particular form of gambling;
4. the contribution made, and which should be made, from the proceeds of gambling, to other activities, particularly sport.

In addition to these, I would say that there are at least half a dozen other reasons why the Royal Commission was set up;

5. the recurrent fear that there exists in Britain a growing population of addicted gamblers;
6. the relative paucity of hard data on the incidence of the various forms of gambling;
7. the desire to review the progress of the Gaming Board as the main administrative-regulatory instrument of policy;
8. the suspicion that despite the relatively intense level of

administrative control, there exists in some gambling outlets, notably lotteries, a high level of abuse and inadvertent non-compliance with the law;

9. the lack of a comprehensive and integrated approach to all forms of gambling, which has come about in part as a result of changes in fiscal and social policies in the past twenty years;

10. concern that there are still opportunities for infiltration into gambling activities by professional criminal organisations.

Gambling is an activity which is regulated in a number of different ways by the law. Fiscal, penal and administrative-regulatory techniques are deployed in various combinations to control firstly the quantity and quality of gambling outlets, and secondly the disposition of the finance generated by the activity (and hence its profitability to the Exchequer, the entrepreneur and the punter). Law has been used for centuries in the pursuit of these two strategies, not always with success. One possible reason for this is the existence of discrepancies between legal expectations about, and the reality of, individuals' gambling behaviour. Hitherto, in the enactment of laws regulating gambling, some assumptions have been made about the behaviour which are psychologically questionable.

Implicit in this criticism is an instrumentalist perspective towards law creation, at least in legislative contexts. Where laws are being enacted to serve an instrumental purpose, divergences between legal understandings and social-scientific explanations of the affected behaviour (be they psychological, sociological, economic, etc.) are likely to result in inappropriate responses being made by a legislator at any or all of the stages which precede that enactment. These include perception and diagnosis of a problem to be solved, formulation of policy, choice of law as the appropriate instrument of control, choice and implementation of a specific legal technique(s) giving effect to such policy, and prediction of consequential behavioural change.

I propose to approach the matter in two ways. First I shall consider the rôle which the 1978 Royal Commission envisaged for psychology in the formulation of legal policy. Second I shall examine some of the assumptions about gambling behaviour which are apparently operative in the selection of specific legal controls.

Before proceeding to these discussions, I wish to make two preliminary points.

1. I am concerned here only with the psychological dimension to

gambling and with its implications for legal control of the behaviour. Of course there are other social-scientific dimensions to gambling. Two of the more obvious of these are the economic and the sociological. Economics may elucidate some aspects of legal control by offering theoretical and methodological frameworks within which to test the consequences of gambling within an economy, and models with which to explain risky decision-making and the probabilities affecting given preferences. Sociology can provide data, which currently are badly needed, on such basic matters as the distribution of participation in all forms of gambling according to such variables as social class, as well as offering alternative explanations of the development and maintenance of gambling behaviour in individuals and social groups.

Both economics and sociology, like psychology, offer certain falsifiable hypotheses about gambling. But there are also significant normative dimensions, most notably the religious and the moral. I do not propose to pass any comment upon the goodness or badness of gambling, although I naturally recognise that such considerations may play a part in the enactment of law.

2. So far I have referred to gambling as 'activity' and as 'behaviour'. When we can describe a plurality of activities with one word, it is tempting to look for a single set of conditions which uniquely characterise them, and this temptation is often aggravated by the way in which issues relating to the subject are posed. Questions like, 'why do people gamble?' imply and encourage assumptions about those activities and about the determinants which occasion participation. First, they encourage the assumption that all forms of gambling, despite superficial differences, share some essential quality. Second, they encourage an explanation of the etiology of gambling which is largely person-centred, and which seeks to ascribe gambling behaviour to a small number of personal predispositions. Both oversimplify complex and perplexing aspects of behaviour. The first ignores the differing structural characteristics of gambling outlets: quite different considerations apply to the long-odds, low-frequency gambling typified by the football pools and by lotteries, and to the short-odds, high-frequency gambling typified by casino games. The second, which suggests that, by reason of their behaviour alone, 'people who gamble' can be singled out as a group whose members share certain characteristics and differ from non-gamblers in respects other than gambling, ignores

environmental determinants of the initial decision to gamble and the rôle of learning in the decision to continue.

Moreover, emphasis on person-centred accounts supports the commonly-held assumption that addictive gambling is a deviant extension of moderate gambling (Herman, 1967). Recent research on the rôle of learning in the acquisition and entrenchment of behavioural traits suggests that this assumption is misguided. But as I shall discuss below, it has had a profound influence upon the choice of legal controls for different gambling outlets.

ROTHSCHILD AND THE ROLE OF PSYCHOLOGY

As I have already observed, law has been used for centuries to regulate gambling, from the simple prohibitions enacted during Henry VIII's reign to the complex structures of the three principal statutes governing gambling, the Betting, Gaming and Lotteries Act, 1963, the Gaming Act, 1968 and the Lotteries and Amusements Act, 1976. But for all this legislative activity and the succession of Royal Commissions, the Rothschild Report is, so far as I can tell, the first occasion on which there has been official explicit reference to the contribution that psychology can make to an understanding of gambling behaviour and to the selection of appropriate legal techniques to control it.

The Rothschild Commission had proposed to include a chapter in their report on the psychology of gambling, but as a Home Office review (Cornish, 1978) was in an advanced stage of preparation, and as its recommendations accorded with those the Commission was considering, it was decided instead to treat the review and its principal suggestions as a kind of supplementary third volume. I propose now to discuss briefly two aspects of the Commission's approach to the relevance of psychology to the legal regulation of gambling; first, their conception of the rôle of psychology in data collection, and second, their attitude towards explanations of gambling.

A constant theme of Cornish's review is the relative paucity of hard data on gambling. With the exception of two recent surveys of specific types of gambling behaviour by Dickerson (1975) and Downes *et al.* (1976), there are only isolated repositories of information. Some of these are held by the various commercial organisations, which are principally concerned with gambling's financial aspects; some by the Gaming Board, which is additionally concerned with the quantity and quality of gambling outlets; and some by the Churches' Council on Gambling, which is one of the few non-commercial or non-official organisations which has an interest in the incidence of gambling. Apart from the submission of the Churches' Council on Gambling (1967) few attempts have been made, outside experimental situations, to explain how and why individuals are recruited to participate in different forms of gambling, and how and why this initial decision may differ from, if indeed it does, the subsequent decision to continue participation (Oldman, 1974; Seager, 1970; Zola, 1963). In particular, the need is clearly established for epidemiological studies of addictive gambling. Although this is a subject which attracts considerable attention, there are significant gaps in the existing data on its incidence, prevalence and development in individual cases. One of the primary obstacles has been disagreement as to what constitute appropriate criteria for defining addictive gambling. Broadly speaking the disagreement lies between those who emphasise person-centred tests, such as the individual gambler's feeling of compulsion (Bergler, 1958), and those who employ quantative diagnostic techniques, such as frequency or duration of gambling (Dickerson, 1974).

To remedy this situation, the Rothschild Commission has recommended that a government organisation be set up:

> We therefore believe it both essential and urgent for the Government to establish a Gaming Research Unit to monitor and study the incidence, sociology and psychology of gambling. This Unit, which should be responsible to the Social Science Research Council, should be inter-disciplinary and consist of about six 'professionals' . . . The Unit should be funded by the Home Office for a minimum of ten years (in principle) with a review after year 5; and it should make an annual report to parliament. (Rothschild, 1978, paras. 4.5–4.6).

A similar suggestion was made at the conclusion of Cornish's survey. Although both authors envisage that their respective organisations would requisition what Rothschild terms 'routine information' about gambling, there is a divergence of emphasis between them, which in the case of the Royal Commission affords an insight into its policy orientation towards the role of psychology in formulating strategies for controlling gambling.

Essentially, the Royal Commission is concerned with the efficient regulation of commercial gambling. To this end it concentrates on the mechanics of the gambling market, the elimination of abuse and maladministration on the part of its entrepreneurs, and the refinement of bureaucratic control. Psychological investigations of gambling are required to serve these goals by producing quantitative rather than interpretative analyses of particular forms of participation. When discussing pathological gambling, the Royal Commission observes simply that there is insufficient work undertaken on how many pathological gamblers there may be, and when, in the chapter on licensed bingo clubs, there is an explicit reference to the potential of the Gambling Research Unit, the hope is expressed merely that data can be collected on spending patterns. In this, the Royal Commission casts psychology in a subservient rôle.

The last point is reinforced, I think, by the Royal Commission's attitude to explanations of gambling behaviour offered by psychology, which can best be described as ambivalent. Clearly it recognises that psychology may have something to say, but it appears unwilling to embrace the notion that one should begin by understanding the behaviour to be controlled and then select suitable legal techniques of control, rather than by accepting the existing legal policy and looking to psychology to produce data within its parameters.

In the two-page chapter on psychology and gambling, the Commission briefly discusses Cornish's review, but in the most non-committal fashion. Cornish himself describes his explanation of gambling as follows:

(a) . . . the initial decision to participate is influenced by factors arising from a wide variety of personal, social and situational circumstances, many of which are of a non-specific and temporary nature; and (b) . . . continued gambling, as well as reflecting the operation of these variables, is determined not so much by the influence of deep-seated motivations (though some sort of more general and necessary personal contribution will be proposed) as by a process of learning which is heavily influenced by the salient characteristics of particular forms of gambling and by those of the environment in which it takes place. (Cornish, 1978, p. 90).

The Royal Commission evidently finds this approach attractive, but it is not committed to a behaviourist explanation of gambling, as the following quotation concerning addictive gambling (which additionally demonstrates a sceptical attitude towards psychoanalysis, Halliday and Fuller, 1974) indicates:

> As laymen we find [the behaviourist explanation] rather more appealing than the view of the psychoanalytic school that compulsive gambling is caused by a repressive urge to kill one's father, but it does seem to us that the behaviourist explanation for excessive gambling must at best be incomplete. It does not explain, for example, why all persons exposed to the stimuli of a betting office do not become similarly conditioned nor why pathological gambling is frequently associated with other symptoms of a disordered personality like excessive drinking, criminality and depression. (Rothschild, 1978, para. 7.37).

There are indeed gaps in the behaviourist explanation of gambling, as Cornish recognises, but there are other diagnoses, such as the psychiatric, which treat pathological gambling as a condition which can be medically treated (Bolen and Boyd, 1968; Moran, 1975). Rothschild's failure to consider these prompted criticism from this quarter (Moran, 1978; Rankin 1978).

It would be naive, however, to expect a single agreed explanation of gambling behaviour. Clearly there is no unique set of determinants which can account for all its aspects. The plurality of explanations poses problems for observers and policy-makers not conversant with the various schools within the broad scope of psychological theory and research. In defence of the Royal Commission, it must be recognised that it would be a near impossible task for it to present an agreed account of the behaviour. It is perhaps not surprising that the Commission opts in part for Cornish's account, with its multi-causal explanation of the initial decision to gamble and its emphasis on the role of learning and the significance of environmental cues in continued participation, but falls back on a person-centred orientation towards addictive gambling.

ASSUMPTIONS ABOUT THE PSYCHOLOGY OF GAMBLING AND THEIR LEGAL EXPRESSION

In this section I propose to identify four assumptions upon which, it seems to me, much legislation concerning gambling is predicated, and then examine briefly how each is given specific legal expression and to what extent the assumptions are supported by psychological research evidence. Some of the assumptions have an affinity one to another, while others conflict. I have confined myself to these four because they strike me as being good representatives of the person-centred/behaviourist orientation implicit in Rothschild; because each can be well illustrated by specific legal prescriptions; and because they seem to go to the basis of existing legal policy. The four are:

1. gambling is 'instinctual';
2. all gamblers are engaged in basically the same activity;
3. the instinct to gamble can be reinforced;
4. most gamblers are ignorant of the realities of chance-based outcomes.

1. Gambling is instinctual, and therefore the law would operate dysfunctionally if it sought to suppress it entirely
This view I take to be the basis of much of the current legislation. Introducing the controversial and far-reaching Betting and Gaming Bill, 1960 in a House of Commons debate, the Home Secretary, Mr. R. A. Butler said,

> In framing our modern legislation, we must realise that in human nature gambling is a constant instinct, and we must decide what aspects of conduct can appropriately be regulated by the criminal law. (Butler, 1959, column 805).

A corollary of this view, then, is that it would be fruitless for the law to be used as an instrument of complete suppression of the behaviour, but that given the recognisably mischievous consequences of totally unregulated gambling, it can be appropriately used to channel and direct the manifestations of that instinct.

This finds expression in the policy (which has been pursued by the Gaming Board since its inception, and which was implicit in the Gaming Act, 1968), of offering facilities which respond only to the 'unstimulated demand' for a particular form of gambling. The notion of 'unstimulated demand' is by no means susceptible of easy objective definition, and indeed carries with it a degree of subjective evaluation on the part of those determining the existence or strength of a demand. It is employed principally to justify measures to restrict recruitment to gambling, by the exercise of rigorous controls over the creation of opportunities to gamble. I shall illustrate this by reference to the law concerning the licensing of gaming clubs.

The 1960 Act, which implemented in part the recommendations of the 1950 Royal Commission, proved to be a sorry failure in its control of gaming clubs. Casinos flourished unchecked. Many of them engaged in practices of dubious legality which the enforcement agencies could do little to prevent. The development of commercial gaming led to considerable public and parliamentary disquiet and this culminated in the enactment of the Gaming Act, 1968. Its prime object was 'to establish a strict but flexible system of control capable of containing all forms of gaming which were liable to be commercially exploited and abused', (Rothschild, 1978, para. 17.1). Casino gaming – typically roulette, craps, blackjack and other card games of unequal chance – is generally designated 'hard gaming'. This is because the inherent structural characteristics of these games conduce to high levels of consumption – high event-frequency, rapid payout and a wide range of odds and stakes. These conditions can be regulated only marginally if the essential nature of the game is to remain unaltered, and so it was thought that there should be correspondingly greater control over the conditions of recruitment than with other, 'softer' forms of gambling. This in turn led to the adoption of the notion of 'unstimulated demand' and to a policy which seeks to keep recruitment to hard gaming as low as is consistent with the realisation of the objective of eliminating illegal gaming.

Four specific controls deserve mention. First, and perhaps most important, is the control exercised by the Gaming Board over the number and geographical location of casinos. Over 1000 existed prior to the 1968 Act. But drastic measures, namely the selection of certain 'permitted areas' from within which applications for certificates of consent to operate a club would be entertained, reduced that number to 125 at the end of 1977. These were distributed throughout forty-six of the fifty-three permitted areas, but mostly in London, and involved no more than 300,000 members. No really clear criteria were established to ascertain what would be designated 'permitted' areas, save that they were confined 'to large towns where the principal demand appears to exist, and certain tourist and holiday centres where casinos had already become established' (Rothschild, 1978, para. 18.35). This produced arbitrary and quixotic decisions, but more questionable was the complete absence of any attempt to sample the demand for gaming facilities. Recent Gaming Board reports reiterate that 'unstimulated demand' has been met, but it is not easy to determine the basis for this conclusion. The Gaming Board reports for the four years 1973–7 show that in 1973–4, sixteen certificates of consent were issued from thirty-eight applications; in 1974–5, twelve from thirty-five; in 1975–6, twenty from fifty-three and in 1976–7, twenty-one from forty-five. (Gaming Board, 1975, 1976, 1977, 1978). These figures are not necessarily inconsistent with the judgement that unstimulated demand has been met, for some of the applications may represent repeated attempts which have hitherto been unsuccessful, while others are withdrawn. The number of outright refusals each year was five, nine, thirteen and seven respectively, but the point is that the Board can only refuse a consent certificate on the grounds that the applicant is unsuitable in certain specified ways – not because there is a lack of demand. It is true that acquisition of a consent certificate does not entitle the holder to open a club – he must first obtain a gaming licence from the local justices. When a certificate holder applies to the licensing justices for a gaming licence, the Board may object on the ground that there is no demand, but its Reports show that it has done so in only two cases within the past four years. It is difficult, then, to see upon what evidence the Gaming Board has adjudged that unstimulated demand has been met.

The other three environmental controls can be disposed of more quickly. First, there is a general prohibition, subject to a few exceptions, on the advertisement of gaming facilities. Second, an individual can participate in casino gambling only when forty-eight hours have elapsed since his application for membership. The object of the 'forty-eight hour rule' is quite obviously to serve as a buffer between the possibly ephemeral desire to gamble and its fulfilment. As the Rothschild Report says, 'the principle of unstimulated demand is not infringed by requiring that the demand should be strong enough to survive a forty-eight hours delay', (Rothschild, 1978, para. 18.27). Last, there is a general prohibition on live entertainment within casinos. The purpose of this will be clear enough also: individuals attracted to a club by facilities ancillary to gaming may in time be recruited to gambling. It should be observed that this prohibition is also directed to the situational conditions which reinforce the initial decision to gamble, and which encourage continued participation. It is commonplace to associate opulent and sumptuous surroundings with gaming establishments, surroundings which encourage the suspension of normal judgment. Live entertainment would contribute to these conditions.

Although these four control techniques are regarded by the Gaming Board as contributing significantly to a successful policy of containment in recruitment to gambling, the premise on which they were based – that gambling is instinctual – remains problematic. Mr Butler's use of the term 'instinct' is anyway probably incorrect in this context. A more likely claim would be that gambling is the product of a relatively stable set of predispositions inhering in the individual, but this would lead one to expect that the majority of legal controls would be aimed at the individual with a pre-disposition to gamble, rather than at gambling environments. Such an expectation faces two problems. First, the available evidence does not support the basic claim. Second, even if it were possible to identify with sufficient precision the nature of those predispositions, the legal controls required would be unacceptably intrusive, and being specific to the individual, would invoke excessive costs.

Thus, a legislative programme based upon a person-centred account of recruitment to gambling would probably be legally impossible to devise, which may explain in part why the existing controls were selected. Even if only fortuitously, they accord with the view, for which there is considerable support in the literature, that the regulation of the environmental conditions which determine the visibility of gaming will have an important influence on the likelihood of recruitment in individual cases (Dickerson, 1974; Newman, 1972; Paley and Glendinning, 1963).

2. *All gamblers are engaged in basically the same activity, and thus if legal controls can be employed to restrict opportunities for repeated gambling, the potential population of addictive gamblers will be reduced*

This view follows from the person-centred account of gambling which I discussed earlier. It implies a direct connection not only between different varieties of gambling, but also between moderate and addictive gambling, and suggests that it would be appropriate to use legal techniques to minimise the risk of moderate gamblers becoming addictive through repetition of behaviour. In so far as this view relies on a process of generalisation to explain the graduation from moderate to addictive gambling, by analogy with explanations of alcohol abuse (Popham, 1975) and drug abuse, it is open to question. These kinds of escalation hypotheses are notoriously hard to prove: it is easy to confuse coincidental with causal relationships between behaviours. In the specific instance of gambling, the evidence, while not necessarily inconsistent with a generalisation process, by no means establishes it (Borrill, 1975; Downes *et al.* 1976; Kemsley and Ginsburg, 1951). On the other hand, this view does accord with behaviourist accounts of the rôle of learning in the entrenchment of patterns of behaviour (Akers, 1973; Kazdin, 1975).

For those, like the members of the Rothschild Commission, who prefer a person-centred account of gambling, a crucial question is, why do some individuals exposed to given conditions learn to be addicted, while others do not? Social learning theorists can answer this by suggesting that the difference may be accounted for by the operation, in the case of the non-addicted individual, of other conditions which inhibit involvement, but reliance on person-centred accounts leads to the conclusion that addiction is the result of some personality variable not present in the non-addicted population. This conclusion in turn leads to assumptions about the appropriateness of using legal controls to reduce the potential population of addictive gamblers, since this aim is to some extent in conflict with the assumption already made. That is, it will have been assumed that because addiction is the result of factors inhering in some individuals, there is a limit on the efficacy of legal controls on general opportunities for repeated gambling to protect the individuals at risk. I shall illustrate this conflict by looking at the controls on the conduct of betting shops.

The introduction of legal off-course cash betting in 1960 was a major social innovation, and it was not surprising that Parliament moved with some caution, following the 1951 Royal Commission which recommended a strict system of licensing. But not all of that Commission's recommendations were implemented. In particular, their concern with what they saw as a necessary correlation between continuous betting and addictive gambling was not heeded. Of the specific proposals designed to prevent continuous betting, the two most important, that winnings should not be paid out during racing hours and that loitering within a betting shop should be an offence, were rejected. Parliament evidently thought that the punter would be deterred from continuous betting by the spartan regime within the shop – no television, radio (except for the Extel race commentaries) music, dancing or refreshments – and by the 'dead' frontage which follows from the rules on advertising and on visibility of the interior from the street. The reality is quite different from the aspiration. Apart from the restrictions on advertising and live television, betting shops provide all the facilities necessary for continuous betting. Indeed, the 'atmosphere of the racecourse', which the 1951 Royal Commission thought conducive to continuous betting, is very nearly recreated in betting shops, and because a considerably longer and fuller programme can be offered than on a racecourse, so more varied and intensive betting practices are encouraged.

Forms of gambling which offer opportunities for continuous play are most likely to be the setting for addictive gambling, (Weinstein and Deitch, 1974), but because the Rothschild Commission believes that the addiction arises from a 'disordered personality', it subscribes to the view that there is a serious limit on the efficacy of legal controls on such opportunities. For this reason, they conclude that some of the rules governing the facilities in betting shops are unlikely 'to have even a marginal effect on the incidence of compulsive gambling', and that there is no justification for the imposition of further controls.

This attitude is in marked contrast to that of the Churches' Council on Gambling. Although much of their analysis of addictive gambling is based upon the view that gamblers are of a kind, and that addiction follows a process of generalisation, they have also turned to behaviourist accounts of reinforcement to justify additional restrictions on the conduct of betting shops – in particular, a ban on the Extel race commentary. They claim, in short, that 'a psychologist who set out to create laboratory conditions for turning people into compulsive gamblers could hardly hit upon a more suitable scheme than the arrangements in any ordinary British betting office', (Rothschild, 1978, para. 7.32). The Rothschild Commission is dismissive both of the Churches' Council and of behaviourist theory. In its view, a ban on the race commentary would certainly result in a fall in continuous betting but not because the behaviour of the gambler is no longer the object of reinforcement, but because the adictive gambler will simply transfer his addiction to some other gambling outlet.

It is unfortunate that Rothschild takes such a dismissive attitude, because the lengthy research by Dickerson (1974) on betting shops is one of the few instances of the application of learning theory to real gambling. He suggests that the Extel commentary acts as reinforcement for the punter, who passes through various stages of excitement and anticipation prior to the 'off', and that in time, in tandem with the variable ratio schedule of reinforcement that comes from winning, the fixed-interval schedule of the pre-race commentary will train him to place his bet nearer to the 'off', and to bet more heavily. The corollary of this, quite clearly, is that betting shops do teach punters to gamble.

3. *The instinct to gamble can be reinforced, and so the law can be used to minimise the effect of reinforcers*

As a general proposition, the suggestion that behaviour can be reinforced is unexceptionable (Skinner, 1953). A problem arises, however, when we attempt to determine what particular be-haviours are reinforced by what particular reinforcers. One specific area in which the law is used to minimise the effect of monetary gain as a reinforcer is in the control of jackpot machines.

The structural characteristics of gaming on machines are con-ducive to a high level of consumption. They have a very rapid event frequency, and high payout ratios. Because they involve continuous or 'action' gambling, gaming machines are always considered a danger to the financially vulnerable – those who have most to lose in terms of their available gambling capital but for whom the utility of a win is very high. For this reason the controls on gaming by means of machines are very severe. They are also very complicated, but in essence the legal position is as follows:

(a) Jackpot machines, which have no financial limit other than their physical capacity, can only be installed in premises licensed or registered under the Gaming Act, 1968. This includes casinos, bingo clubs and miners' welfare institutes.
(b) 'Amusements with prizes' machines, which are subject to a limit of £1, can be installed in public houses, cafes and restaurants and similar establishments.

When the Gaming Act, 1968 was being prepared it was thought appropriate to distinguish not between different kinds of machines, but between different kinds of premises upon which gaming by means of machines could take place. Thus, the kind of gaming which offers the greatest rewards can take place only in clubs licensed or registered under the Act. Members of the public have no right of access to such premises, and persons under eighteen are excluded. These clubs are themselves subject to close scrutiny by the Gaming Board, and are restricted to two jackpot machines each. On the other hand, petty gaming (in terms of the prizes awarded) is permitted on a variety of premises not so strictly controlled. In these ways the law is used to control access to the financial reinforcers which jackpot machines offer.

This still leaves the questions, what behaviour is being reinforced and in what way? Gambling provides financial rewards for successful play, and it is therefore not surprising that the behaviour is often regarded as being prompted by economic motivations. There is of course a considerable literature which examines gambling in terms of various expectation theories (Kogan and Wallach, 1967; Payne, 1975; Rapoport and Wallsten, 1972). It seems that in its control of access to jackpot machines, the law too proceeds from this perspective. It is difficult, however, to determine accurately the precise impact of money as a reinforcer (Kazdin, 1975), a difficulty which is complicated by the very obvious fact that many individuals lose when they gamble. Although persistence in the face of repeated losses may be explained in terms of the operation of expressive motivations to gamble, the problem which then arises when formulating legal policies is how to select the reinforcers which are to be the objects of legal control.

An obvious candidate for legal control is the financial rewards offered by jackpot machines. However, the evidence suggests that such controls are unlikely to affect the incidence of the behaviour. Experiments show that the kind of reinforcement schedule typified by jackpot machines – variable in both extent of reward and the intervals between rewards – have a most powerful effect on promoting continued gambling (Lewis and Duncan, 1956, 1957, 1958). These experiments indicate that even if economic expectations are aroused by the opportunity to gamble, the fact that they are not realised does not act as a disincentive to gamble – on the contrary, intermittent reinforcement may even promote persistence (Levitz, 1971). It may be that the law could be more usefully employed if it were directed against some of the design features of jackpot machines which act as reinforcers. In particular, features such as 'hold' and 'nudge' buttons introduce to the punter the impression that what is a chance-based outcome can be controlled to some degree by his own skill. This reinforces the behaviour by encouraging an illusion of control over, and the excitement of participation in, the outcome. Similarly, the 1–2–3 order in which the wheels stop can create an anticipation of winning which can be enhanced by having a large proportion of potentially winning symbols on the first wheel, while the impression that the gambler has achieved a 'near win' can be created by displaying the lines above and below the winning line (Strickland and Grote, 1967).

These kinds of reinforcers could quite easily be controlled by law, as the Gaming Board has suggested, but the Rothschild Commission was more concerned with the maxima for stakes and prizes.

4. *Most gamblers are ignorant of the realities of chance-based outcomes*
I turn now to the last assumption which I have identified as underlying legal policies on gambling, and it is one upon which there is quite clearly a concordance between legal understanding and psychological findings. First, considerable evidence shows that in assessing the utility of different payoffs, gamblers do not necessarily choose the bet which objectively offers the best return. Expectation theories have been proposed and modified to take account of the subjective evaluation of bets (Edwards, 1955, Rapoport and Wallsten, 1972), but no one model can explain the varieties of preferences exhibited by gamblers faced with different payoff permutations. Of course, some gamblers may choose what are objectively poor bets – in particular long-odds betting associated with the football pools – because there are other inducements to gamble, but there is also widespread ignorance of the utility of different gambles.

Second, gamblers are on the whole poor judges of the probabilities of winning in the chosen medium (Devereux, 1968). For example, those who prefer combination bets on horse or dog racing can be shown to overestimate quite seriously the probability of a series of events coinciding. Gamblers can also display many fundamental misconceptions about random events. A common misconception is the belief that the more frequently one kind of result recurs, the more likely the opposite result becomes; a misconception generally known as 'the gamblers' fallacy' (Epstein, 1967). And, as is probably well known, a great deal of superstition and ritual surrounds the playing of chance-based games, much of which purports to improve the chances of the player, implying control over what in fact remains a chance outcome (Henslin, 1967; Langer, 1975).

Until recently, the consumerist notion of 'value for money' has not been applied to gambling. This is probably because of an ambivalence, in some influential quarters at least, about the propriety of gambling, despite the law's facilitation of it. An example which comes readily to mind is the continued non-enforceability of gambling contracts. In addition, it has generally been thought that it is only discretionary income which is expended on gambling, and therefore that there is less need or urgency to have rigorous value for money controls than in the case of essential spending. However, there is a good deal of evidence that some forms of gambling – in particular, long-odds gambling typified by lotteries, the pools and combination and accumulator bets – are very poor value for money; and that these are typically the kinds of gambles preferred by lower socio-economic groups. As a result, the poor have to invest more than the rich to secure the same return, and so, partly through their own ignorance of payoffs and probabilities and partly through gambling promoters' manipulation of that ignorance, the poor to a degree subsidise gambling by other, more discerning, punters.

There are two main strategies that could be employed to promote value for money. The first is that the law could be used to prevent the grosser forms of exploitation and manipulation of the various gambling outlets. It is well known that entrepreneurs manipulate gamblers' expectations of winning by reinforcing, in particular, their misconceptions about probabilities. In addition, most commercial promoters are aware that certain options are more appealing than others to a large proportion of punters. Coincidentally, these options do not give an especially good return, and so are known colloquially as 'mug bets'. Since the 1968 Act, legal controls have been used to reduce the incidence of both forms of manipulation. The former has been the object of general control through bodies such as the Gaming Board and the Horserace Betting Levy Board, and of specific control via prohibitions on advertising and promotion of specific odds. In the case of the latter, the most comprehensive control was introduced in 1970, which removed the 'mug bets' from casino games (Downton and Holder, 1972; Gaming Clubs (Bankers' Games) Regulations, 1970).

The second strategy is controversial. It involves a deliberate policy of educating the gambling public about the odds against winning in specific contexts. This appears to be a policy agreed upon within the Home Office at any rate, for the terms of reference of the Rothschild Commission included 'the publication of information about gambling activities and the methods of selecting winners or fixing odds . . .' In response, the Rothschild Commission devoted a thirty-page annexe to a comprehensive account of the odds against winning in the most popular forms of gambling. But such a strategy is controversial in that it may stimulate demand, and thus run counter to the policy of responding only to unstimulated demand discussed earlier.

The Rothschild Commission noted this possible conflict in connection with the suggestion that meters displaying all stakes and payouts made should be incorporated into jackpot machines as a means of checking that the gaming public is receiving the minimum payout ratio over a given interval:

> If the meters were visible in the interests of self-policing, it is arguable that they would stimulate people to play more, by analogy with the "sucker" who, when black has come up ten times consecutively at roulette, backs red. (Rothschild, 1978, para. 24.41).

As I previously indicated, the Rothschild Commission was not unduly concerned with the propriety of gambling. Its attitude was more pragmatic. It expressed its commitment to the view 'that those who gamble should have the right to know what is or what may be going to happen to their money' (Rothschild, 1978, para. 24.47). Of course, the fact that information is provided to potential gamblers does not mean that it will be used in choosing between uncertainties. If the law were to be used as an educative device, it might be insufficient merely to require, for example, all gambling outlets to display prominently an official version of the odds against winning. The extent to which law should be used to intervene between the punter and the entrepreneur involves difficult policy decisions, and I do not wish to enter that debate here.

CONCLUSION

Gambling is an activity which has long been recognised by psychologists as posing difficult questions concerning individual and group decision-making under conditions of risk. It is also an activity which has long been controlled by law. It is, however, only recently that there has been official recognition of the contribution that psychology can make to the formulation of legal policy and the selection of specific legal controls to regulate the activity. There is no reason to suppose that what is psychologically verifiable can necessarily be translated into legal prescription, but this recognition, though belated, could at the least mean that legal decisions would be better informed.

I have endeavoured to show the nature and possible consequences of this recognition in two ways. Firstly I discussed, in a general way, the potential relationship between law and psychology as this is perceived by the Rothschild Commission on Gambling. That this is a fragile relationship is illustrated by Rothschild's acceptance of 'common-sense' explanations of pathological gambling, and by its occasionally dismissive attitude towards psychological research. Secondly, I examined four assumptions about gambling upon which some aspects of the current legislation are based. I concluded that in some cases there is a concordance between legal understanding and psychological reality; in other cases there is a fortuitous coincidence between preferred legal techniques and the available psychological evidence; and in yet other cases there are some discrepancies between the two.

A rational legislator should generally seek to introduce legal prescriptions which are likely to be efficacious. If laws are to be used to control gambling, then their efficacy must in part be determined by theoretical and experimental criteria supplied by psychology.

REFERENCES

R. L. Akers, *Deviant Behaviour: A Social Learning Approach* (California: Wadsworth, 1973).

E. Bergler, *The Psychology of Gambling* (London: Harrison, 1958).

D. W. Bolen and W. H. Boyd, 'Gambling and the gambler', *Archives of General Psychiatry*, *18* (1968) 617–30.

J. Borrill, 'Study of gamblers and drug-takers in H. M. prison Pentonville', (London: Consultation on Compulsive Gambling, 1975).

Rt Hon. R. A. Butler, vol. 613 *H.C. Debs* Column 805 (16th November 1959).

Churches' Council on Gambling, Submissions of Evidence to the Royal Commission on Gambling 1976 (1976).

D. B. Cornish, 'Gambling: A review of the literature and its implications for policy and research', *Home Office Research Unit Report No. 42* (1978).

E. C. Devereux, 'Gambling in psychological and sociological perspective', *International Encyclopedia of the Social Sciences*, 6 (1968) 53–62.

M. C. Dickerson, 'The effect of betting shop experience on gambling behaviour', Ph.D. Thesis, University of Birmingham (1974).

M. C. Dickerson (ed.), *Gambling: Associated Problems* (London: Consultation on Compulsive Gambling, Report No. 1, 1975).

D. M. Downes, *et al.*, *Gambling, Work and Leisure: A Study Across Three Areas* (London: Routledge and Kegan Paul, 1976).

F. Downton and R. Holder, 'Bankers' games and the Gaming Act 1968', *Journal of the Royal Statistical Society, Series A 135* (1972) 336–64.

W. Edwards, 'The prediction of decisions among bets', *Journal of Experimental Psychology, 51* (1955) 201–14.

R. Epstein, *The Theory of Gambling and Statistical Logic* (New York: Academic Press, 1967).

Gaming Board for Great Britain, *Report*, 1974, H.C. paper 318 (1975).

Gaming Board for Great Britain, *Report*, 1975, H.C. paper 237 (1976).

Gaming Board for Great Britain, *Report*, 1976, H.C. paper 253 (1977).

Gaming Board for Great Britain, *Report*, 1977, H.C. paper 278 (1978).

J. Halliday and P. Fuller (eds.), *The Psychology of Gambling* (London: Allen Lane, 1974).

R. D. Herman (ed.), *Gambling* (New York: Harper and Row, 1967).

J. Henslin, 'Craps and magic', *American Journal of Sociology, 73* (1967) 316–30.

A. Kazdin, *Behaviour Modification in Applied Settings* (Illinois: The Dorsey Press, 1975).

W. Kemsley and D. Ginsburg, *Betting in Britain* (London Central Office of Information, Social Survey – Consumer Expenditure Series, 1951).

N. Kogan and M. Wallach, 'Risk-taking as a function of the situation, the person and the group', in T. Newcomb (ed.), *New Directions in Psychology* (New York: Holt, Rinehart and Winston, 1967).

E. J. Langer, 'The illusion of control', *Journal of Personality and Social Psychology, 32* (1975) 311–28.

L. Levitz, 'The experimental induction of compulsive gambling behaviours', *Dissertation Abstracts International, 32B* (1971) 1216–17.

D. Lewis and C. Duncan, 'Effects of different percentages of money reward on extinction of a lever-pulling response', *Journal of Experimental Psychology, 52* (1956) 23–7.

D. Lewis and C. Duncan, 'Expectations and resistance to extinction of a lever-pulling response as functions of percentage of reinforcement and amount of reward', *Journal of Experimental Psychology, 54* (1967) 115–20.

D. Lewis and C. Duncan, 'Expectation and resistance to extinction of a lever-pulling response as a function of percentage reinforcement and number of acquisition trials', *Journal of Experimental Psychology, 55* (1958) 121–8.

E. Moran, 'Pathological Gambling', *British Journal of Psychiatry*, Special Publication No. 9: Contemporary Psychiatry (1975).

E. Moran, 'Instant lotteries', letter to *The Times* 3rd June, 1978.

O. Newman, *Gambling, Hazard and Reward* (London: Athlone Press 1972).

D. Oldman, 'Chance and skill: A study of roulette', *Sociology, 8* (1974) 407–26.

H. D. Paley and J. A. Glendinning, 'Pattern for New York? A report on off-track betting in England', (New York Assembly, 1963).

J. W. Payne, 'Relation of perceived risk to preference among gamblers', *Journal of Experimental Psychology, 104* (1975) 86–94.

T. Popham, 'The prevention of alcoholism', *British Journal of Addiction, 70* (1975) 125–44.

H. Rankin, 'The pathological gambler', letter to *The Times* 20th July 1978.

A. Rapport and T. Wallsten, 'Individual decision behaviour', *Annual Review of Psychology, 23* (1972) 131–76.

Royal Commission on Betting, Lotteries and Gaming (1949–51): *Final Report* (London: HMSO, Cmd. 8190, 1952).

Royal Commission on Gambling: Final Report (The Rothschild Report) (London: HMSO, Cmnd 7200, 1978).

C. P. Seager, 'Treatment of compulsive gamblers using electrical aversion', *British Journal of Psychiatry, 117* (1970) 545–54.

B. F. Skinner, *Science and Human Behaviour* (New York: Macmillan, 1953).

L. H. Strickland and F. Grote, 'Temporal presentation of winning symbols and slot machine playing', *Journal of Experimental Psychology, 74* (1967) 10–13.

D. Weinstein and L. Deitch, *The Impact of Legalised Gambling* (New York: Praeger, 1974).

I. K. Zola, 'Observations on gambling in a lower-class setting', *Social Problems, 10* (1963) 353–61.

LEGISLATION

Betting, Gaming and Lotteries Act, 1963.

Gaming Act, 1968.

Gaming Clubs (Bankers' Games) Regulations 1970, S.I. 1970 No. 803.

Lotteries and Amusements Act 1976.

13: The Traffic Offence as a Rational Decision: Exposure of a Problem and Suggested Countermeasures

Ivan D. Brown

It is well established that the frequency of conviction for road traffic offences depends, to some extent, on the age and the sex of the offender (e.g. see Campbell, 1972; Konečni *et al.*, 1976; Pelz and Schuman, 1971; Schuman, 1970). There is also evidence that the perceived seriousness of traffic offences is a function of motorists' age and sex (see Brown and Copeman, 1975). The extent to which these individual differences in behaviour and beliefs are causally related, and which is cause and which effect, represent an area of concern in which psychologists may be expected to have professional expertise to offer the legislators and the judiciary. At the Applied Psychology Unit (APU), Cambridge, we have collected data on the determinants of perceived seriousness of traffic offences. The main objective of this chapter is to discuss some of these and earlier data in relation to the design and imposition of penalties against driving offences.

The origins of this research at the APU clearly illustrate some of the problems at the interface between law and psychology. Some eight years ago I was invited to join a Council of Europe Working Group on Road Traffic Offences. Its task was to advise a Committee of legal experts, charged with the harmonisation of penalties against traffic offences throughout the member countries of Europe. The Committee had progressed to the point where agreement was reached on a 'points system' of penalties. Offences had been defined, ranked and grouped into four categories carrying penalties of from one to four 'points'. A 'totting-up' procedure was planned, under which drivers would be warned, reprimanded, referred for additional training or group counselling, disqualified from driving, fined, or imprisoned commensurate with the seriousness of their single or accumulated offences.

One laudable aim of this exercise was to provide more comprehensible feedback to motorists on the seriousness of their offences, and thus better to inform offenders of the behaviour society expected from them within the shared road transport system. However, the social and applied psychologists on the Working Group disputed the Committee's rank-ordering of offences. There were two main reasons for this disagreement.

Firstly, the Working Group conceptualised the operation of the feedback mechanism at the individual level. In other words, offenders would evaluate the justice of their own penalties in the light of the seriousness they attached to the behaviour in question under the environmental conditions obtaining at the time of their offence. The Committee took a broader, societal view, which placed a high deterrent value on penalties against certain technical offences that cause problems for society because of their prevalence, rather than their importance for road safety *per se*. To the Working Group, this latter view seemed likely to impair the effectiveness of the proposed points system, because individual offenders would regard some penalties as unduly harsh and others as over-lenient. Neither bias would be conducive to the reforming of offenders' attitudes, nor to the reshaping of their behaviour along acceptable lines.

The second reason for disagreement between the lawyers and judges on the one hand and the psychologists on the other, derived from their different conceptual approaches to traffic problems. As would be expected, for example from Stephenson's (1977) review of this issue, the former group tended to speak in terms of criminality, morality, responsibility, culpability, punishability, etc. The latter group tended to seek *explanations* for socially undesirable road-user behaviour and use these to advance more supportive methods of dealing with conduct that could not otherwise be reshaped by, say, ergonomic-type changes to the traffic environment.

Clearly, some empirical data were needed on which to resolve some of these operational and conceptual differences between lawyers and psychologists. I was fortunate in being able to initiate research in this area, as part of a study of accident causation among younger drivers.[1]

I have introduced my subject in the above detail for three reasons, which bear on our present concern with the resolution of interface problems between lawyers and psychologists:

1. To illustrate, by personal experience, the enormous conceptual differences existing between law and psychology. These are not only of some theoretical interest: they impede improvements in the effectiveness of legislation, particularly with regard to influence on behaviour at the level of the individual.
2. To draw attention to the many groups of legal experts who are currently attempting to harmonise European legislation. Such groups seem likely to produce a host of interesting problems for empirical research. They are also likely to comprise the major consumer groups for research findings at this interface between law and psychology.
3. To draw attention, more specifically, to road user attitudes and behaviour as an important subject for research by lawyers and psychologists. Traffic offences represent the most common source of contact between law enforcement authorities and the general public. Psychological interest derives from the breadth of research possibilities in this field, including, as it does, a variety of individual characteristics such as age, sex, personality, temperament, risk-perception, decision-making, and a number of others.

I shall be discussing here the way in which certain of these personal characteristics might interact to influence rational decision-making by drivers in the road traffic system.

THE TRAFFIC OFFENCE AS A RATIONAL DECISION

If, for the moment, we consider the driver as a rational person whose offences result from a weighing-up of the costs and payoffs attached to alternative actions, then the process may be modelled in the manner illustrated in Figure 13.1.

In order to maximise his expected gain, the potential offender

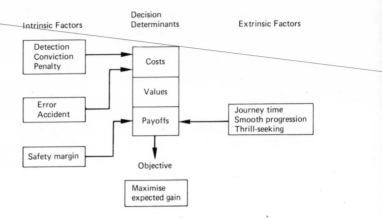

Figure 13.1   The traffic offence as a rational decision

must consider the *payoffs* likely to result from his decision. These will include factors such as decreased journey time, smooth progression through the traffic system, being head of the queue, etc., as well as more personal payoffs, such as increased pleasure or excitement. In practice, there may well be occasions when a driver considers his traffic offence to have a positive value, or payoff, in terms of road safety (e.g. passing a red traffic light to avoid being in collision with an inattentive following motorist). However, for the more experienced driver, these occasions will be rare.

The potential offender must also consider the likely *costs* of actions taken on his decision. He may be detected in his offence, convicted and punished. His actions may incur abuse, assault, or some other retribution from offended road users. It may result in an accident, or an alarming near-miss for himself or other road users. It may impede traffic flow, or inconvenience the public in some other way.

All the alternative costs and payoffs will be weighted on the individual's personal value system, in order to maximise the expected gain. The set of specific values used will have been acquired with experience of driving in traffic, but it will be based upon the individual's moral code. Clearly, individuals' value systems represent a vitally important area for research by lawyers and psychologists, being the central determinant in the process of rational decision. Legislation has little chance of operating effectively if it makes incorrect assumptions about public values. As Wilde (1976) has pointed out, there are differences between the 'legal' norms and the 'social' norms which a driver might use to evaluate alternative behaviours. In addition, there are many pressures on road users' value systems which are inimical to the appropriate evaluation of safe behaviour on the roads. For example, a certain model of car has been advertised as 'Virtually uncatchable along winding country lanes': a statement which implicitly values vehicle speed and handling far higher than the safe avoidance of common rural hazards, such as mud on the road, or humans and animals walking against the flow of motor traffic. However, I raise this issue of conflicting values simply as an indication of its mutual importance for lawyers and psychologists. It is not my purpose to pursue this issue in detail here.

Perhaps the most important point illustrated by Figure 13.1 is the difference in origin between the costs and the payoffs of a decision to offend against traffic legislation. The majority of the payoffs likely to result from an offence are factors *extrinsic* to the traffic environment. Shortened journey times may be desirable for business or domestic reasons. Smooth progression through traffic and payoffs classifiable as 'thrills' are purely personal experiences. All these factors result from motivational pressures which an individual imports into the traffic system from his everyday life. By contrast, most of the costs associated with a decision to offend are highly specific *intrinsic* factors. That is, they are viewed within the immediate context of the offending act. Naturally, involvement in an accident may have consequences outside the traffic system, but these are not likely to weigh heavily in the driver's decision (see the discussion of intrinsic factors below).

One immediate implication of the origins of costs and payoffs in intrinsic and extrinsic factors, respectively, is that the potential offender will tend to value costs on quite different criteria from payoffs. It will therefore be extremely difficult for him to maximise his expected gain by the rational process of decision. In addition, a number of particular conceptual and perceptual errors the driver may make in estimating these two sets of factors have been highlighted by research, as follows:

Extrinsic factors
1. Drivers overvalue the effect of high-speed 'bursts' on overall journey time (see, for example, Svenson, 1976). Their speeding offences may therefore not be producing the expected effect on average trip speed. A limited amount of research effort has been

directed at changing intuitive estimates of time-savings (e.g. by Svenson, 1971) and propaganda has been employed in the U.K. to persuade drivers of the limited time-savings obtainable in practice should they exceed maximum speed limits by given amounts over well-known routes. There appears to be scope for further research in this area, but it must of course be recognised that not all speeding offences are motivated by time-saving.

2. Drivers undoubtedly overestimate time lost by traffic delays, because human time perception depends upon concurrent activity (Woodrow, 1951). Intervals spent inactively in traffic jams will therefore tend to be overestimated, compared with similar intervals spent driving at high speeds. Thus drivers may overvalue the need to maintain a smooth progression through traffic in order to reach their destination on time. This misperception may result in offences committed unnecessarily in order to avoid delay.

Intrinsic factors

1. Drivers initially overestimate the probability of detection and conviction for offences committed against new legislation. This has been established in a small (unpublished) study by the Transport and Road Research Laboratory, and is the most plausible explanation of the initial dramatic fall in convictions for 'drinking and driving' offences committed following the use of breathalysers by the police, under the Road Safety Act, 1967 (see the Report of the Department of the Environment Committee on *Drinking and Driving*, 1967, App. 2, Fig. 3). The slow return to previous levels of detection and conviction, and beyond, identified by the same study, suggests that there is substantial learning of detection probabilities over quite prolonged periods. Therefore, at any given moment in time, the costs of detection and conviction associated with a decision to offend may be widely divergent from the true costs based on objective probabilities.

2. Drivers often underestimate the serious practical consequences of certain penalties against traffic offences, such as disqualification. They may therefore undervalue certain costs because of ignorance of the impact of the law, rather than moral turpitude.

3. Drivers find it difficult to conceptualise accident probabilities, because the risk of involvement for the individual is extremely low (see Michon, 1973). Therefore the cost of accident involve-

ment probably figures negligibly in their decision-making on offences.

4. Drivers appear to experience zero level of subjective risk in the traffic system (Näätänen and Summala, 1976). This is probably because they have confidence in their ability to match their driving to traffic demands (Taylor, 1964). Thus the probability of error will also figure negligibly in their costing of offences.

5. Drivers can make substantial personal gains in convenience from offences which, in isolation, cost society very little; e.g. parking offences. However, this leads to undervalued costing of such offences by individuals, producing more prevalent offending by motorists as a group, thus resulting in problems for society in general. This indicates a need for convergence between the value systems of individuals, or groups of motorists, and society as a whole. There are clear analogies here with other moral problems, such as whaling, environmental pollution by industry, staff thefts within large organisations, and so on, indicating a general problem for law and psychology. These 'social dilemmas', involving conflict between 'individual rationality' and 'group rationality' have been reviewed more formally by Dawes (1975) and Slovic *et al.* (1976).

REMEDIAL MEASURES

How can the model illustrated in Figure 13.1, and the above research findings on intrinsic and extrinsic factors, help in the design of more effective measures against traffic offences?

Firstly, they emphasise the importance of correctly diagnosing problem behaviour in terms of the costs, payoffs, or values which are its cause; thus leading to the design of more specific countermeasures. It may be quite ineffective, for example, to improve enforcement tactics if the resultant increased cost of detection is still heavily outweighed by the payoff for that particular behaviour. Far better, in such a case, to manipulate the payoff directly, wherever possible.

Secondly, they suggest that drivers' decision-making will more easily be directed along socially desirable lines if more immediate feedback on the costs of offending is built into the traffic system. In other words, one must balance immediately perceived payoffs by immediately perceived costs, rather than relying on heavily delayed feedback such as fines, disqualification, or imprisonment. We are already familiar with some examples of this approach. They include the use of road humps ('sleeping policemen') to control speed in residential areas. This device forces the motorist to balance the advantage of high speed against the disadvantage of ride discomfort, or even vehicle damage. Another familiar example is the synchronisation of urban traffic lights to permit steady progress only if drivers adhere to a predetermined speed. Clearly there is considerable additional scope for highway engineers, ergonomists and psychologists to collaborate in the design of other built-in devices which provide road users with immediate feedback of the costs of their proposed actions.

Thirdly, the discussion of intrinsic and extrinsic factors in drivers' decision-making highlights the fact that costs and payoffs are usually not explicit. In most instances they have to be derived by means of a perceptual process which is limited in its capacity for processing information and biased by its reliance on personal skills and experience. Thus information relating to costs and payoffs may be completely overlooked by the driver, or it may be misconstrued. This suggests that there is considerable scope for the reduction of traffic offences by (a) the *addition of information* on costs and payoffs, and (b) the *provision of better information* on costs and payoffs. *Additional* information on costs may take the form of propaganda emphasising the consequences of certain accidents: for example, recent seat-belt campaigns have presented statistics on the relative risks of being restrained in a vehicle by a belt, or thrown out, during a collision. Alternatively, the additional information may be built into the traffic system: for example, signs warning of police radar checks, which allow drivers to recost excessive speeding. Additional information on payoffs is more difficult to achieve because, as the model in Figure 13.1 shows, they are mostly determined by extrinsic factors. However, some examples are currently in use, such as the advance notice of a dual carriageway, which allows drivers to anticipate the payoff from a deferred overtaking and perhaps avoid a risky premature manoeuvre. *Better* information, too, can often be built into the traffic system: for example, advisory speed signs for bends may resolve ambiguity, say, when an easy-looking curve includes an adverse camber, and thus assist in the assessment of both costs and payoffs from fast cornering.

The provision of additional and better information by these means usually alters only the *perceived* costs and payoffs of offending behaviour. There are, however, alternative methods of achieving this same end by altering the *actual* costs and payoffs. For example, the probability that speeding offences will be detected can be greatly increased by optical and electronic devices such as vehicle-borne radar which measures and records vehicle speeds without requiring offenders to be followed by a police patrol car; or static roadside equipment employing infra-red photography and preset to record, automatically, specific offences such as excessive speed or close car-following in fog. The improved probability of obtaining convictions when offences are detected by these 'objective' devices, plus the spread of knowledge that they are in common use, should eventually alter the *perceived* costs of committing those offences against which they operate.

There remains the question of how the individual offender values these costs and payoffs. This appears to present the most intriguing, although perhaps the most intractable, problem for lawyers and psychologists. Representatives of the police and other authorities concerned with road safety have often attempted to change values by exhortation and simple moralising. The apparent hope is that entreaty and/or admonition will appeal to the offender's (or potential offender's) sense of justice or duty and thus instil in him the relevant, socially desirable, principles of conduct. Now it is true that moralising can alter individuals' value systems under certain conditions. For example, Dawes *et al.* (1976) report a study in which taxpayers were interviewed either (a) with an emphasis on the positive moral aspects of tax payment, or (b) with an emphasis on the legal penalties for non-payment of taxes. Subsequently, the former group paid, on average, $243 more in tax than they had contributed during the previous year, whereas the latter group paid only $11 more than previously! However, moralising can be effective only if the recipient clearly perceives his inadequate adherence to the values being promulgated. Now there are some situations on the road in which the normal limitations of human perception will provide drivers with imperfect information on the costs of their behaviour. It follows that such misperceived costs will be inappropriately valued in the overall decision, which may result quite unintentionally in the commission of socially undesirable acts. For example, Brown (1970) has summarised evidence that speed and distance perception are highly unreliable in foggy conditions and he thus concludes that 'motorway madness' (driving too fast and too close to others) may be attributable to the driver's inability to assess safety margins when visibility is poor. In other words, the problem could, at least partially, result from perceptual rather than moral failures. They may be a number of comparable traffic situations where exhortation to drive safely will be ineffective because, on the evidence of their own senses, drivers think they *are* driving safely. The appropriate remedial measure against such difficulties will involve perceptual aiding, by the use of optical and electronic devices, or special training in hazard perception, rather than a simple reliance on moralising.

This consideration of the traffic offence as the product of a rational decision thus allows us to clarify the essential determinants of offending and hence pose the following important practical questions:

1. How can the various *payoffs* likely to accrue to individual offenders be constrained, without seriously inconveniencing other users of the traffic system?
2. How can the true costs of their behaviour, to themselves and other road users, be made more *perceptible* to offenders?
3. How can the values attached to these costs and payoffs by offenders be made more realistic and congruent with the values of society in general?

THE APPLIED PSYCHOLOGY UNIT STUDIES

Research at the APU to date has concentrated on the second and third questions above. The objectives have been:

1. To study the value systems of drivers in relation to traffic offences, as a function of age and sex differences which are known to affect road accident involvement.
2. To explore the extent to which any differences in evaluation of the costs of offending result from a misperception of the true costs, rather than from the use of different values.

I. AGE AND SEX DIFFERENCES IN PERCEIVED SERIOUSNESS OF TRAFFIC OFFENCES

The young male driver is over-represented in road accident statistics and is a major offender against traffic legislation (see Pelz and Schuman, 1971). Although the causal relationship between these findings remains to be quantified, it was considered important, with respect to road safety, to investigate the extent and type of any differences in costs and associated values attached to offences by this group of road users, as compared with females and older males. A full account of this research has been published by Brown and Copeman (1975), but a recapitulation of the relevant main points seems in order here.

Briefly, 224 subjects were asked to complete a questionnaire, in which thirty-one examples of offensive driving behaviour had to be assessed for seriousness on a magnitude rating scale. Each offence was specified clearly in lay terms, e.g. 'overtaking on a pedestrian crossing'; 'driving with a blood-alcohol level just over the legal limit'; 'passing a red traffic light'; 'driving with bald tyres'; and so on. The standpoint from which seriousness had to be judged was given by instruction. A 'Control' group of subjects was given no specific instructions (the NI group), beyond the standardised information on the imaginary driving conditions under which all subjects operated. A 'Personally Involved' (PI) group was asked to rate seriousness as if they were the person most likely to be inconvenienced or injured, should the offences result in an accident. A 'Personally Responsible' (PR) group was asked to rate seriousness as if they were tempted to commit the offences in question themselves. A 'Social Consequences' (SC) group was asked to rate the seriousness of the offences in relation to the consequences for society in general. Each group consisted of fifty-six volunteers with current driving licences. A balanced experimental design was used, in which these four groups were comprised of equal numbers of younger, older, male and female subjects. (For this purpose, 'younger' subjects were drawn from the high-risk age-group of eighteen to twenty-four year-olds: 'older' subjects came from the low-risk age-group of thirty-five to fifty-five year-olds).

Table 13.1 shows the main findings on the effects of age and sex subgroup differences and of instructed standpoint from which seriousness was judged. As expected, younger males generally valued the costs of offending lower than did the other three groups. This raises the question of how to design a system of penalties which is perceived to be equitable by all sections of the population to which it applies? However, across the four different 'instruction' groups, there was a significant overall level of agreement among the subjects on the rank-ordering of offences for seriousness (Kendall's Coefficient of Concordance $W = 0.48$, $p < 0.001$). In other words,

Table 13.1 Mean rated seriousness of offences for each age, sex and instructed standpoint subgrouping (N = 14 in each of the 16 subgroups)

Instructed standpoint	Age/sex subgroup				All age and sex subgroups combined
	Younger		Older		
	Male	Female	Male	Female	
No specific Instructions (NI)	6.48*	6.97	6.88	7.71*	7.01
Personally Involved (PI)	6.86*	6.68	7.09	7.63*	7.07
Personally Responsible (PR)	5.75*†	6.42†	7.37†	7.88*	6.86
Social Consequences (SC)	6.58*†	7.52†	7.46†	8.02*	7.40
All standpoints combined	6.42	6.90	7.20	7.81	7.08

Significant differences (Mann-Whitney U-tests)

* Younger males gave reliably lower ratings of seriousness than older females under all instructed standpoints ($p < 0.002$ for NI, $p < 0.05$ for PI, $p < 0.001$ for PR and SC).

† Younger males gave reliably lower ratings of seriousness than younger females and older males from standpoints PR ($p < 0.01$) and SC($p < 0.004$).

the value systems used by the younger, older, male and female drivers to cost the possible consequences of each offence relative to the others were congruent. This suggests that it would be possible to construct a finely-graded points system of penalties against traffic offences, which would operate effectively as feedback of societal values to all sections of the population.

Two additional findings are of incidental interest here. Firstly, the rank-order of seriousness obtained from these subjects correlated poorly with the points system of penalties for those offences devised by legal experts, as mentioned earlier. Certain offences regarded by the subjects as intrinsically dangerous (e.g. driving with a vehicle which was defective to some specified extent) were regarded by the experts as of minor importance, statistically. Other offences (e.g. driving with blood-alcohol concentrations just above the legal maximum) were considered by the subjects to carry a low risk of accident, whereas the experts considered the risk to be of great practical significance. Secondly, there was a clear discontinuity at the less serious end of the ranked offences, highlighting a number of minor technical offences which might be 'decriminalised'. This could improve the credibility of traffic penalties and also unburden the courts of the need to process technical offences having little bearing on road safety.

Although these results confirm that younger males differ from older males and from females in their evaluations, they leave several questions unanswered. The results are open to alternative explanations. For example, younger males gave atypically low ratings of seriousness when asked to judge offences as if they were tempted personally to commit them. A plausible explanation here is that the younger driver's lack of experience leads him to underrate the probability of error attached to his own decisions and actions. The costing of offences by younger males, in terms of accident probabilities, may thus be unrealistically low. However, an equally plausible alternative explanation is that younger males value the costs of offences differently from females and older males. Similar alternative explanations could be advanced for the finding, in Table 13.1, that younger males gave atypically low ratings of seriousness when instructed to judge the social consequences of offences. We therefore need to answer the question: are younger male drivers perceptually insensitive to the possible consequences of traffic offences; or are they using different criteria on which to value these possible consequences; or are both factors involved in their decision making? Clearly, different remedial measures are appropriate to these different explanations. Perceptual insensitivity might be countered by training in hazard perception, for example, whereas inappropriate criteria might be susceptible to change by moral exhortation, group counselling, or similar therapy. The second study to be reported here attempted to answer these important questions.

2. FACTORS UNDERLYING THE YOUNG MALES' LOW RATINGS OF SERIOUSNESS

This study was initiated by my colleague, Dr C. J. Colbourn (1975). He observed that fifteen of the offences used in the previous questionnaire approach (Brown and Copeman, 1975) could clearly be classified as 'overt' and fifteen could equally clearly be classified as 'covert'. Overt offences were those which would be readily observable by any nearby road user, whereas covert offences would not. Examples of overt offences are failing to stop at a red traffic light, or overtaking on a pedestrain crossing. Examples of covert offences are driving with defective brakes, or whilst excessively fatigued. Colbourn argued that covert offences are inherently more dangerous, because nearby road users cannot take them into account when setting their own margins of safety, as they can with overt offences. Thus the cost of, say, being too close to a fatigued driver could probably not be taken into account, whereas the cost of being too close to a driver who persistently ignored red traffic lights could clearly be perceived and, presumably, allowed for by drivers of adjacent vehicles.

In order to explain the previous findings of deviant ratings of seriousness by young male drivers, Colbourn set out to test the following hypotheses, using our earlier data:

1. Motorists in general will rate the consequences of covert offending as more serious than overt.
2. Young males are relatively insensitive to the greater potential cost of covert offences.
3. Young males employ a different criterion for the acceptance of overt and covert offences as relatively safe or unsafe, and will tend to regard many of the latter category of offence as relatively safe.

A re-analysis of the data, subdividing the offences into overt and covert, provided clear support for the first hypothesis. Overt offences received a mean seriousness rating of 6.65, compared with 7.40 for the covert offences. The difference is not large, but it is statistically significant ($p < 0.001$). Thus the cost assigned to an offence does appear to be generally related to its visibility to adjacent motorists, which is somewhat encouraging from the viewpoint of road safety.

In order to test hypotheses 2 and 3, Colbourn employed the analytical techniques of Signal Detection Theory (SDT). A complete exposition of the theory would be inappropriate here. (See Swets *et al.*, 1961, also Swets, 1964, for basic details. For a specific application to road safety, see Newsome, 1974). Suffice it to say that the theory deals with the way in which choices are made on the basis of evidence which does not unequivocally support one hypothesis from a number of alternatives. Its advantage is that it allows us to separate two aspects of the decision process. Firstly, it provides a measure of perceptual sensitivity, d' (d-prime), which tells us how well the person makes correct judgements and avoids incorrect ones. Secondly, it provides a measure of response bias, β (beta), which indicates the extent to which the person favours one hypothesis over the alternative(s).

Hypothesis 2, advanced above, asserts that the young male drivers' relatively low ratings of seriousness derive from their insensitivity to the greater danger inherent in covert offending. We would therefore expect an SDT analysis of the data to produce a lower value of d' for this subgroup.

Hypothesis 3 asserts that the young male drivers' deviant ratings derive from bias: in other words, the criterion (β) they use to rate offences as serious is less strict than that used by older and female drivers and will thus more often assign lower ratings to covert offences.

In order to calculate these independent measures d' and β, the rating data were reclassified as 'low' (ratings between 1 and 5), or 'high' (ratings between 6 and 10), before re-analysis and the outcome subjected to analysis of variance, as before. The main results, on perceptual sensitivity, are given in Table 13.2.

The first finding here is that young males were perceptually insensitive to the differences in potential cost between 'overt' and 'covert' offences, relative to the d' scores obtained from the other three subgroups. The second finding is that the group given no

Table 13.2   *Index of sensitivity (d′) to the difference in seriousness between 'overt' and 'covert' offences as a function of the age and sex of drivers, and their instructed judgemental standpoint.*

| Instructed standpoint | Age/sex subgroup | | | | All age and sex subgroups combined |
| | Younger | | Older | | |
	Male	Female	Male	Female	
No specific instructions (NI)	0.97	1.15	0.83	1.52	1.12
Personally involved in consequences (PI)	1.49	1.17	1.35	1.77	1.45
Personally responsible for offence (PR)	1.07	1.12	1.57	1.66	1.35
Social Consequence (SC)	1.14	1.78	1.64	1.79	1.59
All instructed standpoint groups combined.	1.17	1.31	1.35	1.68	1.38

Significant differences (independent orthogonal contrasts)
Younger v. Older, $p < 0.01$: Male v. Female, $p < 0.025$: Younger males v. Others, $p < 0.025$ NI v. PI, PR and SC, $p < 0.01$.

specific judgemental instructions were perceptually insensitive to the 'overt'–'covert' distinction. The results of the analysis of β scores showed no reliable effect of any of the main variables.

The main implication of these results is that most of the young male drivers' tendency to undervalue the seriousness of 'covert' offending can be attributed, not to the fact that they adopt a different decision criterion from that of other drivers, but to their relative inability to perceive that offending driving behaviour carries information which knowledgeable adjacent road users can employ in setting their margins of safety. In other words, it is not that they treat danger lightly, but rather that they do not assess the dangers accurately. It follows that attempts to alter the young male offender's value system by simple moralising will be relatively ineffective and may, indeed, be counter-productive. It appears that this group of offenders would benefit more from better instruction in hazard perception on the road, especially the subtler aspects of hazard associated with certain potentially dangerous road-user behaviour. The implication of this interpretation for the design of penalties against traffic offences, is that the penalties for less experienced drivers should comprise educational rather than simply punitive measures. In this respect it is encouraging that the scores of perceptual sensitivity, shown in Table 13.2, revealed improvements when subjects were given specific judgemental instructions. This suggests that an educational component of traffic penalties would be effective, even for the deviant group of young male drivers. (cf. McBride and Peck, 1970; Peck, 1976; Schuster, 1969, 1978; Tallquist, 1971). In the longer term, this approach should produce more appropriate costing of the seriousness of traffic offences and thus reduce the tendency for relatively inexperienced offenders to regard penalties as unduly harsh or lenient, simply because of their own perceptual insensitivity to the hazards associated with some offensive behaviours.

SUMMARY AND CONCLUSIONS

There is evidence that young drivers and male drivers are over-represented in statistics on offences against road traffic legislation. By treating the traffic offence as a rational decision, it has been possible to elucidate certain problems, of both a general and a specific nature, which would not be identifiable if offending were regarded simply as moral deviance.

The general problem arises from the fact that the *costs* of offending are largely *intrinsic* to the traffic environment, whereas the *payoffs* for offending behaviour are mainly derived from *extrinsic* factors. This may cause difficulty for many drivers when costs and payoffs have to be valued in order to maximise the expected gain of alternative actions. The solution appears to lie in the provision of more accurate and more immediate information on both costs and payoffs, using factors intrinsic to the traffic system. Some examples of this approach are given.

A questionnaire study of the *values* attached to specified offences by motorists showed that there is general agreement on the relative seriousness of traffic offences. Thus a points system of penalties could be designed to operate with perceived equity between offences, acting as additional, although somewhat delayed, feedback on the cost of behaving in socially undesirable ways. However, the study identified young male drivers as a deviant group, in relation to the low absolute values of seriousness assigned to traffic offences. Thus there is a risk that penalties will be perceived as unduly harsh by this group of drivers and not operate effectively to alter their behaviour.

A second study showed that these deviant values attached to offences by the young male driver are not simply the result of his using different decision criteria or values. It appears that he is relatively insensitive to the hazards associated with certain road user behaviours, particularly 'covert' offending, which cannot be perceived and used in establishing safety margins.

It follows from this interpretation of the data that a moralising approach to the modification of offending driver behaviour will be ineffective, if used in isolation. Penalties must include an educational component, to highlight the peculiarly hazardous nature of certain offences and thus allow the inexperienced driver to value such behaviour more appropriately. This approach would also reduce the tendency for inexperienced drivers to regard heavy penalties as excessive, by clarifying the costs of certain offences to which they may be perceptually insensitive.

Both studies demonstrate that drivers are responsive to a more educational approach, which specified the standpoints from which the potential seriousness of offences is judged. This is encouraging for the design of penalties against traffic offences as a system of social feedback on undesirable behaviour.

NOTE

1. The APU research reported here formed part of a three-year project on 'Relative contributions of attitudes and skills to accident causation among younger drivers', which was sponsored by the Department of the Environment, Transport and Road Research Laboratory, 1972–5.

REFERENCES

I. D. Brown, 'Motorway crashes in fog – who's to blame?', *New Scientist*, *48* (1970) 544–5.

I. D. Brown and A. K. Copeman, 'Drivers' attitudes to the seriousness of traffic offences considered in relation to the design of sanctions', *Accident Analysis and Prevention*, *7* (1975) 15–26.

E. O'F. Campbell, 'Investigation of exposure to risk factors among young drivers (16–25 years) 1969–1971', *Canadian Journal of Public Health*, *63* (1972) 504–7.

C. J. Colbourn, 'The relative importance of attitudes and skills to accident causation among younger drivers', Unpublished Project Report to the Department of the Environment, Transport and Road Research Laboratory (1975).

R. M. Dawes, 'Formal models of dilemmas in social decision-making', in S. Schwartz and M. F. Kaplan (eds.), *Human Judgement and Decision Processes: Formal and Mathematical Approaches*, (New York: Academic Press, 1975).

R. M. Dawes, H. Shaklee and F. Talorowski, 'On getting people to cooperate when facing a social dilemma: Moralising helps', *Decision Research Report 76–8* (Oregon Research Institute, 1976).

Department of the Environment, *Drinking and Driving* (London: HMSO, 1976).

D. M. Harrington and R. S. McBride, 'Traffic violations by type, age, sex, and marital status', *Accident Analysis and Prevention*, *2* (1970) 67–79.

V. J. Konečni, E. B. Effeson and D. K. Konečni, 'Decision processes and risk taking in traffic: Driver response to the onset of yellow light', *Journal of Applied Psychology*, *61* (1976) 359–67.

R. S. McBride and R. C. Peck, 'Modifying negligent driving behaviour through warning letters' State of California Motor Vehicles Report (1969) Sacramento, California.

J. A. Michon, 'Traffic participation: Some ergonomic issues', *Institute for Perception TNO, Soesterberg, Report No. IZF* (1973) 14.

R. Näätänen and H. Summala, *Road-user Behaviour and Traffic Accidents* (Oxford: North-Holland Publishing Company, 1976).

L. R. Newsome, 'Risk taking as a decision process in driving', *UK Department of the Environment, TRRL Supplementary Report 81 UC*, (1974).

R. C. Peck, 'Towards a dynamic system of driver improvement program evaluation', *Human Factors*, *18* (1976) 493–506.

D. C. Pelz and S. H. Schuman, 'Are young drivers really more dangerous after controlling for exposure and experience?', *Journal of Safety Research*, *3* (1971) 68–79.

S. H. Schuman, 'A field trial of young drivers', *Archives of Environmental Health*, *21* (1970) 462–7.

D. H. Schuster, 'Follow-up evaluation of the performance of driver improvement classes for problem drivers', *Journal of Safety Research*, *1* (1969) 80–7.

D. H. Schuster, 'Cognitive accident-avoidance training for beginning drivers', *Journal of Applied Psychology*, *63* (1978) 377–9.

P. Slovic, B. Fischoff and S. Lichtenstein, 'Cognitive processes and societal risk-taking', in J. S. Carroll and J. W. Payne (eds.), *Cognition and Social Behaviour* (Potomac, Md.: Lawrence Erlbaum Associates, 1976).

G. M. Stephenson, 'Psychology, the law and socio-legal studies', Paper presented to the Social Sciences and the Law Committee of the SSRC, Oxford (1977).

O. Svenson, 'Changing the structure of intuitive estimates of time-savings', *Scandinavian Journal of Psychology*, *12* (1971) 131–4.

O. Svenson, 'Experience of mean speed related to speeds over parts of a trip', *Ergonomics*, *19* (1976) 11–20.

J. A. Swets, *Signal Detection and Recognition by Human Observers*, (New York: Wiley, 1964).

J. A. Swets, W. P. Tanner, & T. G. Birdsall, 'Decision processes in perception', *Psychological Review*, *68* (1961) 301–340.

A. Tallquist, 'Therapeutic measures and the traffic offender', in *The Human Factor in Road Traffic* (Stockholm: Statens Offentliga Utredningar, 1971).

D. H. Taylor, 'Drivers' galvanic skin response and the risk of accident', *Ergonomics*, *7* (1964) 439–51.

G. J. S. Wilde, 'Social interaction patterns in driver behaviour: An introductory review', *Human Factors*, *18* (1976) 477–92.

H. Woodrow, 'Time perception', in S. S. Stevens (ed.), *Handbook of Experimental Psychology* (New York: Wiley, 1951) 1224–36.

14: Some suggestions for Sex Law Reform

Donald J. West

Academics like to justify personal opinions on controversial legal topics by claiming to base their views on high-sounding general principles, such as Mill's pronouncements on liberty or Professor Hart's celebrated declaration of the independence of law and morals (Hart, 1962). Although guilty of this myself before now, the present discussion will be limited to simpler, pragmatic considerations, taking each case for reform on its separate merits. One needs to consider which groups of people fall foul of the law, why they do not or cannot conform, what is the nature of the harm they bring about, and whether the problems underlying their offending behaviour might be alleviated without resort to the criminal law. I am less concerned with whether the laws adhere to a consistent philosophy than whether, in their practical application, they contribute to the resolution of conflicts between citizens without generating worse troubles than the disturbances they are intended to settle.

Standards of sexual conduct, and related concepts of marital and family obligations, are of great importance because they affect patterns of child rearing, determine for life the style and character of our most intimate relationships, and constitute ideals against which individuals measure their own worth. Sex laws impinge upon our personal attitudes and way of life more closely than most other branches of criminal law. At the same time, sex laws remain peculiarly controversial. Laws condemning personal violence, robbery and abuse of authority receive support in all societies because they reflect values held by the mass of humanity everywhere. Sexual values are more varied, not only between cultures, but between the classes and generations within our own pluralistic society. The scope for conflict is enormous, and made worse by the historical linking of sexual attitudes with religious and tribal affiliations. Different groups attach great emotional and moral significance to deviations from their own particular sexual ideals, and tend to treat any detected lapse very harshly. To this day, in many parts of the world, an extra-marital pregnancy leads to rejection and destitution. In Hitler's Germany homosexuality was reason enough for incarceration in a concentration camp.

In my view some of our sex laws, instead of imposing a civilised rationality, continue to reflect outdated ideas and harsh punitive approaches. In a species of moral overkill the law attempts to deal with some relatively harmless forms of misconduct as if they posed a desperate threat to society. Especially in relation to young persons the law intrudes into private conduct that would be better controlled by more informal methods. Because of the impracticability of rigorous enforcement some sex laws tend to operate in an arbitrary and unjust manner according to the discretion of individual enforcement agencies.

The difficulty arises in part because many sex laws originated during periods of history when there was real justification for regarding as antisocial the pursuit of sex other than as a means of procreation within marriage. With the reduction in infant mortality, and with the pressure on limited resources caused by a vastly increased population, it no longer seems wasteful to expend sexual energy on pleasure without procreation. Efficient contraception enables those who cannot care for children to avoid producing them. Improved medical treatment has greatly reduced the likelihood of death or disablement from venereal infections. As the goal of economic and social equality between men and women comes closer, the woman is no longer obliged to demand the promise of permanent financial support from a husband before she dares consent to sex.

There are powerful psychological as well as social reasons for trying to modernise and rationalise sex laws. Even in this supposedly permissive age a great deal of personal unhappiness arises from lack of sex education, failure to acquire socio-sexual skills and a pervasive feeling of guilt and anxiety about sexual matters. Clinical experience with sexual offenders suggests that many individuals fall into deviant sexual practices through fears and inhibitions about ordinary sex, rather than through bold defiance of social norms. Repression, prudery, ignorance, guilt, lack of sexual outlet and unbearable loneliness are more typical of the case histories of sex offenders than are insatiable sexual appetite or lack of conscience. The criminalisation of relatively harmless examples of non-conformity, and the severe punishments, both legal and social, meted out to non-violent sex offenders, serve to increase irrational anxieties. Paradoxically, such measures are liable to provoke some of the very problems they are intended to solve.

Of course modern law has become less restrictive than traditional religious proscriptions. Masturbation, pre-marital and extra-marital sexual relations and even, in certain circumstances homo-sexual activities, are not crimes. There are, however, several areas in which further relaxations might prove beneficial. Four aspects of sex law will be considered: the control of homosexuality, the control of prostitution, the protection of minors from sexual contacts and the law on incest.

HOMOSEXUALITY

In England and Wales, but not in Scotland or Northern Ireland, an important change in the law on homosexuality came about in the Sexual Offences Act, 1967. This abolished the offences of gross indecency and buggery between males provided the acts took place between no more than two persons in private, with both parti-cipants consenting and over twenty-one, and not serving members of the armed forces or members of the crew of a merchant ship at sea. It seems unreasonable that parts of the United Kingdom should still maintain, at least in theory, that all homosexual acts are crimes. The application to men in the services or at sea of a criminal law different from that used for civilians seems both impertinent and an unnecessary injustice. There are already available internal discip-linary mechanisms adequate to suppress any behaviour endanger-ing good order. Other occupational groups, such as the police, teachers and the womens' services, where overt homosexual behaviour might be considered equally inconvenient, control themselves successfully without this additional law.

The most irritating anomaly of the Sexual Offences Act, 1967, in the eyes of the Campaign for Homosexual Equality, is the fixing of an age of consent at twenty-one. This is far higher than the age when girls can consent to intercourse and contract marriages (presently sixteen), higher than the age of majority when a man can vote and serve in the army (now eighteen) and higher than the age fixed by most other countries which permit adult homosexuality.

Given the decision to decriminalise male homosexuality, laws which deal differently with homosexual and heterosexual behaviour appear anomalous. The preservation of a higher age of consent for homosexuality than for heterosexuality is supported by those who believe that young men who have not yet acquired a stable sexual orientation may be influenced towards homosexuality if they can participate in heterosexual or homosexual behaviour with equal impunity. Most of the available evidence, however, suggests that the determinants of sexual orientation mostly occur much earlier in life and have little to do with seduction as the term is commonly understood. Even if homosexual experience in youth does contribute to the likelihood of acquiring persistent homosexual interests, it is doubtful how far society should try to interfere. Granted that the promotion of heterosexuality is a desirable aim (although even this has been challenged) young men with a vacillating sexual orientation may not make the best of heterosexual husbands. Using the criminal law to persuade them into conformity could make for problems later. In these days of equality between the sexes it is a wonder that no one has gone so far as to suggest employing the criminal law in a similar way to protect girls from lesbianism or to coerce them into heterosexuality.

The statutes make no discrimination, but supporters of the law against youthful homosexuality claim that it is primarily directed against older homosexuals who set out to lead younger, inexperienced males astray. Of course, in reality, it is often the younger partner who calls the tune in sexual matters, but some older men may exploit privileged positions as employers or authority figures, or may seek out vulnerable, homeless youngsters, in order to obtain sexual cooperation. This could have some effect upon a youth's sexual adjustment, although it is noteworthy how many young male prostitutes retain their heterosexual preference after years in the trade. Some countries make explicit provision in their criminal codes for the protection of youths and girls from sexual exploitation by persons in authority over them, but it is doubtful whether, under modern conditions, it is necessary or appropriate to extend such protection beyond childhood.

In my opinion all methods of control, including the age of consent, should be as far as possible the same for both heterosexual and homosexual behaviour. There is, however, an understandable reluctance to recognise homosexuality as a fully legal alternative to heterosexual living. Homosexuals may enjoy robust mental health and lead productive lives, but they are denied parenthood, their condition is often linked with promiscuous habits which others find obnoxious, and they are still at a practical disadvantage as members of a widely disapproved of minority group. At present, the homosexual minority poses no great threat, but if the numbers attracted to homosexual living were to increase substantially this would be potentially disruptive for the family unit system on which society depends. This fear of opening the floodgates to a new wave of homosexuality is probably unfounded. There are powerful biological factors favouring heterosexual development, and much evidence suggesting that an exclusively homosexual orientation is likely to occur only when peculiar upbringing or other environmental circumstances contrive to hamper heterosexual learning, or when early conditioning of an unusually powerful and persistent kind serves to link sexual gratification with homosexual rather than heterosexual expression (West, 1977).

There are a number of laws and practices relating to homosexuality that do not apply to heterosexuals and should be abolished. Homosexual behaviour, even in private, is an offence if a third person is present. Sexual contacts with boys carry higher maximum penalties than sexual contacts with under-age girls. The act of anal intercourse is singled out for severer penalties than oral sex, a matter, as Lady Wootton once quipped, of 'queer geography'. (Incidentally, in this regard heterosexuals fare worse, for anal intercourse between man and wife still carries a maximum penalty of life imprisonment.) Persons introducing homosexuals to each other, even though the ensuing behaviour may be perfectly legal, can be prosecuted for procuration. Printing advertisements for homosexual contacts can constitute the offence of conspiring to corrupt public morals. Homosexual acts in public places are punished more heavily than heterosexual indecency. Heterosexual propositioning is not prosecuted, but the offence of importuning, originally introduced to discourage touting on behalf of female prostitutes has been widely used, often by plain clothes police, to trap the unwary homosexual.

Since the Sexual Offences Act the incidence of offences of indecency between males recorded by the police has doubled, from 840 in 1967 to an average of 1660 over the four years 1973–6. Roy Walmsley (1978) of the Home Office Research Unit, who has made a study of this phenomenon, points out that there has been a simultaneous increase in the proportion of apprehended offenders actually prosecuted, and that some police areas contribute highly disproportionately to the total of recorded offences. One might wonder whether the increase reflects a spread of homosexual involvements among men under twenty-one, but Walmsley reports that the increase is largely due to homosexual acts between males over twenty-one who are apprehended in public conveniences. To account for the increase he favours the explanation that, since the 1967 Act introduced summary trial for these offences, some police forces have taken advantage of the greater ease with which such prosecutions can be brought and with which cases can be settled quickly without a protracted legal contest. If this is so, it provides an interesting example of a legal reform producing effects contrary to expectation. It also suggests the existence of a large reservoir of offences which can be made to yield a variable number of 'crimes' according to the level of police activity.

Few people would argue for the abolition of all penalties for the misuse of lavatories, but the nuisance might be reduced in other ways. It would be interesting to know whether countries in which the police tolerate saunas that are known to be primarily used by homosexuals experience less trouble in their public conveniences. If alternative facilities for meeting, such as gay bars, were encouraged and allowed to advertise openly, it may be that fewer men would resort to the perils of the urinal.

PROSTITUTION

Even if it were desirable to do so, no Western country has succeeded in abolishing the oldest profession. Few English women today are driven to prostitution by sheer necessity, but there will always be some who prefer the thrill of quick gains to the drudgery and discipline of conventional work. Without such an outlet we might well suffer from more female thieves and robbers. Many of the clients of prostitutes (Gibbens and Silberman, 1960) are men who cannot find sexual contacts even in a permissive age. They may be physically deformed or unattractive, social isolates, migrant workers separated from their womenfolk, men whose calling takes them away from home for long periods, men who cannot tolerate a close emotional relationship or men who need partners for deviant sexual practices. Apart from these special minorities there are enormous numbers of men who like sexual variety and find it simpler and less disruptive to their marriages to seek out prostitutes than to establish liaisons within their own social circle. The availability of prostitutes may well prevent the break-up of families and reduce the incidence of sexual assaults, but these plausible contentions are hard to verify scientifically.

English law does not ban acts of prostitution as such, but merely attempts to control undesirable side effects, such as soliciting in the streets, profiteering by third parties, brothel keeping and advertising (Sion, 1977). However, the laws have become so all-embracing that it is almost impossible for a prostitute to operate without herself or her associates breaking the law. Prostitutes and their clients have to find each other and to find somewhere to go, but practically every means open to them is illegal. Penalties for soliciting in public places (which includes doorways and windows as well as streets, parks, pubs and cafés) were increased by the Street Offences Act, 1959, which also abolished the need for the prosecution to prove annoyance. Advertisements in magazines and shop windows can involve the publishers or displayers in charges of 'living on the earnings of prostitution' or of 'conspiracy to corrupt public morals'. If a prostitute lives with a boy-friend or a husband, he is presumed to be living on the earnings of prostitution unless he can prove the contrary. The owners of night-clubs, massage parlours or escort agencies who permit female staff to prostitute themselves may be similarly charged, or else charged with procuration. Owners or occupiers of houses or other premises who allow them to be used for prostitution or as a brothel (which means two or more women working together) also risk prosecution. Publicans risk the loss of their licences if they allow their bars to be used by prostitutes. Persons who supply goods or services to prostitutes, such as taxi drivers, are also subject to prosecution. Not surprisingly, prostitutes experience difficulty in finding accommodation, because owners do not want legal complications and those willing to ignore the law demand exorbitant rents for doing so.

One result of this legal persecution is that prostitutes tend to congregate in red light districts where professional criminals will cater to their needs and provide some protection from the law, from the neighbours and from dangerous clients. In return they work under orders and hand over most of their gains. Some of them become extremely dependent upon the pimps, especially if they are being supplied with prohibited drugs. It is an unhappy outcome for the girls, and also for their clients, who must pay for and cope with the girls' criminal entourage. The neighbours have to put up with noise, brawling and public obscenity, but are fearful of retaliation if they complain (Harrison, 1975).

An official report on street offences (Home Office, 1976) was curiously complacent about this state of affairs. In contrast, a pressure group for one of the better known threatened areas, the Save Shepherd Market Campaign, claims that criminal organisers have taken over and developed prostitution rackets on a vast scale involving billions of pounds annually. Residents of the areas where such businesses have set up are discomfited and terrorised, and the clients receive services that are often dangerous and squalid and sometimes frankly bogus. These campaigners reject total suppression as impracticable, but they would like the law to circumvent the criminal element by permitting well-regulated introductory agencies to operate legally, thus providing the possibility of prostitution at a more modest and civilised level.

The distinguished legal academic, Professor Tony Honoré (1978), although he takes a less benign view of the sex trade than I have expressed, proposes some excellent reforms. Soliciting should not be an offence unless annoyance is established, but in sensitive residential areas the regulations might have to be stricter. The crime of living on immoral earnings should be strictly limited to the abuse it was originally intended to control, that is the use of threats or improper pressure to obtain a complete or substantial livelihood from a prostitute's earnings. Advertisements, provided they are not obscene, should be permitted, even if they refer to deviant sex, since one of the functions of the profession is to cater for this. Even though it might help to contain the spread of venereal disease, Professor Honoré rejects the idea of state licensing of prostitutes and brothels. He thinks the state should not promote a system that encourages men to break their civil duties to their wives. A more pragmatic consideration is that prostitutes and their clients do not necessarily want to use brothels, and they are unlikely to conform to regulations that prevent them from making their own arrangements. One might add that the regular use of houses or other premises for the business of prostitution could be controlled by the local authority rather than by the criminal law on sexual behaviour.

AGE OF CONSENT

Under the law as it is at present, any male who has sexual intercourse with a girl under sixteen commits a crime subject to two years' imprisonment if she is thirteen or over, or to life imprisonment if she is under thirteen. Similarly, any male who touches a girl under sixteen indecently commits a sexual assault punishable by two years' imprisonment if she is thirteen or over, or by five years' imprisonment if she is under thirteen. The law, as opposed to prosecution and sentencing practice, takes no account of the age of the male participant. A youth who indulges with a willing girl close to himself in age may be prosecuted on the same basis as an older sexual deviant who seeks out a child because he cannot obtain, or is not attracted by, adult women.

The apparent injustice of these arrangements is mitigated by the fact that youths are rarely prosecuted. Each year the number of girls under sixteen who have abortions or produce illegitimate births is some three times the number of males prosecuted for sexual intercourse with minors. This large amount of discretion creates the suspicion that some of the offenders selected for prosecution are chosen unfairly. In one case known to me, a mother had a quarrel with her young daughter, after which she denounced her daughter's boyfriend, although up till then she had tolerated, even encouraged, their relationship. A committee appointed by the Swedish government to consider the law on sex offences recently recommended lowering the age of consent to fourteen, giving as one reason the objectionable nature of the official interventions which do occasionally occur in connection with adolescent sexual relationships.

In England, the age of consent was raised from twelve to thirteen in 1875 and then to sixteen in 1885, in order to discourage parents from selling their children to the procurers of prostitutes (Stafford, 1964). That risk is now slight and would be better dealt with by a law directed against procuring minors. Abolition of the notional age of consent, perhaps with the substitution of a rebuttable presumption that girls under fourteen cannot give informed consent to sexual acts, would have several advantages. The control of childrens' developing sexual curiosity and desire to experiment would be taken out of the criminal law and placed firmly where it belongs, in the hands of parents and guardians. Doctors and counsellors wanting to give contraceptives to young girls at risk would be relieved of anxiety about encouraging crime.

Exceptional instances of defiant promiscuity, because of the harm done by girls producing babies they cannot look after, would still need restraint. This could be achieved, as at present, by juvenile court Care Orders, which are intended for the protection and control of children whose parents cannot or will not perform the task. It is a reflection of current social attitudes, not the fault of the law, that this provision is used for promiscuous runaway girls, but hardly ever for promiscuous runaway boys. Nothing is gained, however, by a law that allows prosecution of the boy, but not the girl, for behaviour for which they were equally responsible.

Proposals to abolish or lower the age of consent excite strong opposition on the grounds that this would promote premature sexual experimentation and weaken the powers of parents and teachers in their efforts to control such behaviour. One answer to this has just been cited, namely the Care Order. No one wants to encourage irresponsibility, but given proper contraceptive safe-guards, and some sophistication about emotional as well as physical relationships, the supposed harmfulness of youthful sexual experience is not universally accepted. Dr Alex Comfort once commented that we may eventually come to realise that chastity is no more a virtue than malnutrition. More serious, perhaps, is the objection that children would no longer be adequately protected from the predatory sexuality of adults. In point of fact, what parents are rightly concerned about is unwanted, intrusive sexual be-haviour by adults towards children. Since these incidents normally come to light when the child complains to others, there should be no difficulty in bringing prosecutions for sexual assault in the true sense of the word.

A problem might arise because some small girls deliberately behave enticingly, and others are easily persuaded to collaborate in the touching and fondling which is all that the typical child molester wants. Such conduct by a young girl does not imply a real appreciation of the significance of what is happening, or justify the offender in taking advantage. However, especially in the case of more mature girls, assailants could claim that the victim consented and knowingly cooperated in spite of her subsequent complaints. As in rape cases, there could then follow an unseemly court room battle with the young victim having to withstand counter-accusations from a desperate adult defendant threatened with the prospect of imprisonment under conditions in which solitary confinement may be the only way of escape from continual execration and repeated assaults. This complication would be avoided by the introduction of a system on the lines of that in force in Israel, where the child victims of sex offences do not have to undergo the ordeal of appearance at the trial, but are interrogated privately by an experienced social worker on behalf of the court, who can put to them any objections or arguments raised by the defence. Doubtful as this procedure may seem to the legal traditionalist it is probably a safer way of extracting reliable information from a child than the recital in open court of a previously rehearsed and edited version of events. It also avoids what is the worst feature of these cases, namely the stress to which the child is subjected, both by the trial process and by the adult reactions, which are likely to be far more damaging than the sexual incident itself (Gibbens and Prince, 1963).

To conclude, my proposals are that sexual contacts with girls over fourteen should be prosecuted only if they can be dealt with as ordinary sexual assaults, that contacts with girls under fourteen should continue to be dealt with as assaults unless the defendant can prove otherwise, and that child victims should be protected from exposure in court by an Israeli-type system of private examination.

INCEST

Sexual intercourse between father and daughter, usually a daughter in her early teens, is the commonest kind of incest. Such incidents frequently continue for years before finally coming to light through adventitious circumstances, such as an unexpected pregnancy, a father's attempts to restrict the daughter's contacts with boys of her own age, or jealousies arising when a father turns his attentions from one daughter to another. Marital relationships in incestuous families are often fraught, with wives content to turn a blind eye to what is happening because they are relieved by the decrease in their husbands' demands upon them. The whole family may collude with the incestuous relationship to avoid a break-up of the household. Indeed, incest offenders may be regarded as good fathers apart from their sexual quirk, which in some cases emerges only after drinking. There are decidedly worse ways that parents can abuse their children than by sexual intimacy. Surprisingly, many of the victims appear relatively undisturbed by the sexual incidents, although upset by the conflicts which follow upon discovery. On the other hand, if the children are feeling worried and guilty they cannot take the problem to the parents, who are the source of the trouble, and may be at a loss to know whom to turn to for help.

For the family as a whole, and especially for the child victim, prosecution of the father is catastrophic. He is liable to a substantial period of imprisonment, and if his wife opts to take him back on release the social services have the power to remove all the children. The families that allow incest to come to the attention of the authorities are typically poor, socially inadequate, overcrowded and not well-endowed intellectually, and they are already labouring under complex emotional problems without the added burden of the criminal process. It is desirable that such families should be helped informally by social workers and psychiatrists without having to be processed through the courts, but so long as these affairs count as serious crime, people feel an obligation to report to the police, even though they can no longer be prosecuted for failing to do so.

The specific crime of incest was first introduced to English statute law in 1908. As Hall Williams (1974) has pointed out, the great majority of cases presently prosecuted as incest could be dealt with by laws against sexual assault or sexual interference with minors. Even if, as suggested earlier, the age of consent were abolished, all the more serious cases of incest, that is all those involving an unhappy, complaining child or young person, could be dealt with as sexual assaults. A difficulty might arise in cases in which the participants are content with their relationship, but someone else, perhaps the mother, complains. Under these circumstances a juvenile court could decide that the child is in need of protection and could order her removal from the home. This might be considered problematic if the behaviour in question did not amount to crime, but no more so than the decision to remove uncontrollably promiscuous girls. One social reason for protecting young girls from incest is the above-average risk of genetic defects in the event of pregnancy.

It may be argued that the incest law should be retained in order to counteract the primitive attitude of some fathers who consider they have a right to enjoy their own daughters without interference. However, so long as the juvenile courts continue to regard their function as one of ensuring that children receive socially acceptable standards of care, not merely an absence of criminal assault, this argument has little force. If a special law is required to protect children from parents, it would be better to have a wider statute directed against any adult who, as parent, guardian, teacher, medical attendant, etc., exploits a situation of dependency by making sexual contact with a person under eighteen who is under his care.

In all the four problem areas I have touched upon my suggestions have been in the direction of relaxing rather than tightening the law. My reasons are, as indicated at the outset of the paper, both social and psychological. The law continues to reflect outdated ideas and punitive attitudes; is often unenforceable or enforced unfairly; and gives rise to further social problems by driving the illegal activity underground. But one of the considerations which impels me in this direction is the irrational guilt and anxiety and ignorance that for many people still surround the pursuit of sex. Attempting to deal with fairly harmless acts of non-conformity with harsh criminal laws creates a great deal of further distress, and indicates a misunderstanding both of the causes of such behaviour and of the likely impact of such measures on the individuals concerned.

REFERENCES

T. C. N. Gibbens and J. Prince, *Child Victims of Sex Offences* (London: ISTD, 1963).

T. C. N. Gibbens and M. Silberman, 'The clients of prostitutes', *British Journal of Venereal Diseases, 36* (1960) 113–17.

J. E. Hall Williams, 'The neglect of incest: A criminologist's view', *Medicine, Science and the Law, 14* (1974) 64–7.

P. Harrison, 'The new red light districts', *New Society, 33* (666) (1975) 69–72.

H. L. A. Hart, *Law, Liberty and Morality* (Oxford: Oxford University Press, 1962).

Home Office, *Report of the Working Party on Vagrancy and Street Offences* (London: HMSO, 1976).

A. M. Honoré, *Sex Law* (London: Duckworth, 1978).

A. Sion, *Prostitution and the Law* (London: Faber, 1977).

Ann Stafford, *The Age of Consent* (London: Hodder and Stoughton, 1964).

R. Walmsley, 'Indecency between males and the Sexual Offences Act 1967', *Criminal Law Review*, (1978) 385–452.

D. J. West, *Homosexuality Re-examined* (London: Duckworth, 1977).

Table of Cases and Statutes

Subject Index

Author Index